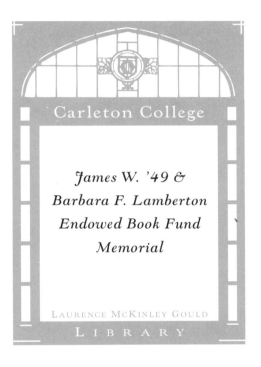

Hobbes and His Poetic Contemporaries

Hobbes and His Poetic Contemporaries

Cultural Transmission in Early Modern England

Richard Hillyer

HOBBES AND HIS POETIC CONTEMPORARIES
© Richard Hillyer, 2007.

First published in 2007 by
PALGRAVE MACMILLAN™
175 Fifth Avenue, New York, N.Y. 10010 and
Houndmills, Basingstoke, Hampshire, England RG21 6XS
Companies and representatives throughout the world.

PALGRAVE MACMILLAN is the global academic imprint of the Palgrave Macmillan division of St. Martin's Press, LLC and of Palgrave Macmillan Ltd. Macmillan® is a registered trademark in the United States, United Kingdom and other countries. Palgrave is a registered trademark in the European Union and other countries.

ISBN-13: 978–1–4039–7617–8
ISBN-10: 1–4039–7617–1

Library of Congress Cataloging-in-Publication Data

Hillyer, Richard.
    Hobbes and his poetic contemporaries : cultural transmission in early modern England / by Richard Hillyer.
        p. cm.
    Includes bibliographical references and index.
    ISBN 1–4039–7617–1 (alk. paper)
        1. Hobbes, Thomas, 1588–1679. I. Title.

B1247.H55 2007
192—dc22   2006051028

A catalogue record for this book is available from the British Library.

Design by Newgen Imaging Systems (P) Ltd., Chennai, India.

First edition: May 2007

10 9 8 7 6 5 4 3 2 1

Printed in the United States of America.

Contents

Preface

As a Methusaleh (1588–1679), Hobbes had many contemporaries. Because he spent two decades living abroad, his social and intellectual ties extended beyond his native England. I am not merely parochial, however, in focusing on his relations with just seven poetic contemporaries, compatriots all. Three such foils are those authors most frequently portrayed as incorporating some features of his work in their own: Sidney Godolphin (1610–43), Abraham Cowley (1618–67), and Rochester (1647–80). These poets are illegitimate heirs whose debt to Hobbes has been much overstated. A second trio of foils encompasses authors whose links with Hobbes have won insufficient recognition: Jonson (1572–1637), Edmund Waller (1606–87), and Sir William Davenant (1608–68). I augment these sometime neighbors of Hobbes with Sir John Suckling (1609–41). After a detailed introduction establishing the complex profile of Hobbes's own career as a published author, my discussion alternates between sometime neighbors and illegitimate heirs for a total of eight chapters.

Additional men of letters playing significant roles are John Collop (1625–post 1678), Charles Cotton (1630–87), Dryden (1631–1700), and John Sheffield, third earl of Mulgrave and duke of Buckinghamshire (1649–1721). Still one more John (Aubrey, 1626–97) features in a twofold capacity: Hobbes's first biographer with by far the longest of his "Brief Lives," he also offers valuable testimony about other figures I discuss. Too often dismissed as gossipy and unreliable, rarely but sometimes embraced uncritically, Aubrey's erratic records can be helpful in various ways if assessed carefully, on a case-by-case basis.

I make no attempt to animate my terms of convenience: Hobbes's sometime neighbors never ask to borrow his tools; his illegitimate heirs avoid all legal imbroglios. In contrast to Harold Bloom, whose paradigm of authorial anxiety has itself exerted a broad impact, I neither reconstruct a psychodrama nor posit any general theory of influence. Nor do I depict Hobbes's poetic contemporaries as belated ephebes, seven dwarves deferring to the snow white of his sagacious head. One of them on my account (Jonson) qualifies as an eminent precursor for

Hobbes himself. But in no cases have I simply assumed that any traffic between Hobbes and his contemporaries must have traveled exclusively along a one-way street. Because I am as much interested in the process of cultural transmission leading to Hobbes's ideas as in that imparting their legacy, I do not portray him autonomously as a climate of opinion, while recognizing that in common with his contemporaries he inhabited one. Moreover, my priority was not to establish the relative excellence of the parties concerned, but to meet the challenge of an interdisciplinary study by keeping them on the same plane. The fruitful misprision so central to Bloom's conception of cultural transmission also has no equivalent in my discussion, which cannot avoid giving attention to misunderstandings of Hobbes's thought, but mainly seeks profit in attempting to offer an accurate reading of his ideas and the extent to which they were grasped in his own day—or have been since.

Today, most readers know Hobbes as a philosopher. Though such a classification misrepresents neither his outlook nor his range of interests, this protean polymath also made independent contributions as a bible-scholar, classicist, historian, linguist, literary theorist, mathematician, poet, political analyst, scientist, and translator. Above all, however, he worked with words, not only when most self-consciously literary but also when most self-consciously scientific, reserving numbers and symbols for the mathematical demonstrations that remain the least valued portion of his output. Moreover, though geometry inspired the innovative methodology through which he sought to build an all-encompassing philosophical system that has secured him a permanent place in the history of ideas, he himself blurred the theoretically sharp division between this highly specialized form of discourse and every other mode of writing in which he engaged.

Though the excellence of Hobbes's best English prose has assured his high rank as a stylist, my intention has not been to reassert or strengthen his literary credentials, by pointing to the merits of his own writing or by linking him with poetic contemporaries. Whereas (conversely) I have not attempted to deny his ability to write superbly, I have been more concerned with understanding why he used the words that he did at any given point and whether his choices made sense. Though even Homer nods in this case too, I was not simply looking for inevitable signs of fatigue, carelessness, and lack of inspiration, but rather for more telling symptoms of strain or inconsistency in the very fabric of Hobbes's enterprise.

In thus foregrounding Hobbes the writer, however, I do not mean to neglect Hobbes the talker. On the contrary, I have attempted as much as possible to recover the most elusive of all his many words—those he expressed in conversation. Though only so much can be made of unrecorded speech, merely remembering that he enjoyed a social existence keeps him on a plane where he belongs, with poetic contemporaries who included friends of his (Jonson, Waller, Davenant, Godolphin), dispelling the widespread tendency to perceive him as an isolated thinker abstracted from any environment besides that of the history of ideas, his only company other disembodied Great Minds.

To place Hobbes among (mainly) lesser writers is thus not to cut him down to size but to gain a valuable point of comparison from their relatively more stable and commensurable identities. Precisely as fellow authors of a less unusual kind, they help throw into bold relief the scope of his own writing and the assumptions he made about his audience; they also furnish a useful index of his thought's originality and impact over its protracted development. As inhabitants of a culture he sought to transform by insistently linking his theoretical findings with current events unfolding as he wrote, they monitored or participated in the same theologico-political conflicts furnishing the simultane-ous backdrop for and primary focus of his life's work. Whereas they share more in common with each other than they do with him, even when contrasted as his sometime neighbors and illegitimate heirs, their individuality should not be slighted.

Nonetheless, I have generally adopted the same mode of interpre-tation when dealing with their words as I have with Hobbes's. But I would again stress that this procedure is not tantamount to redefining him as a literary figure. Though the close readings that I learned how to perform as an undergraduate took place during sessions of practical criticism invariably focusing on short poems, I no more believe that such texts can be profitably interpreted through that approach alone than that only those sorts of texts benefit from such an approach. I quote the evidence on which I rest my case and have at least attempted to be faithful to the words' context, not only on the page but as defined by other frameworks— biographical, historical, intellectual— as appropriate. But though I like to think that my combination of non-blinkered close reading and circumspect open-mindedness has broken fresh ground in every chapter, it is not entirely without precedent.

I have heeded Richard Strier's injunctions about the importance of paying attention to "particular, historically conditioned indeter-minacies" and of resisting "any sort of approach to texts that knows in advance what they must be doing or saying," but with this qualification: some preconceptions are inevitable and even helpful

when we encounter a familiar genre (such as satire, which plays by
its own rules, especially when dealing low blows), or form (such as
neoclassical distichs, my term for closed heroic couplets typically
featuring symmetrical phrasings based on likeness or difference).[1]
By contrast, the classification system whereby libraries divide books
by or about Hobbes between philosophy and political science barely
hints at the variety of his oeuvre and the variability of his method
within individual parts of it. Though he wrote no neoclassical distichs,
he won praise as if he had done so; if he did not in fact serve as one,
he would have made a very good satirist.

Jon Parkin has revised the usual "understanding of the relationship
between Parker, Marvell and Hobbes" (because Samuel Parker "was
not as Hobbesian as his opponents would have liked to imply," whereas
Marvell "deliberately adopted a *more* Hobbesian approach").[2] Whether
this argument is correct in itself I do not offer to judge, for it pertains
to contemporaries of Hobbes whom I have not attempted to address
in my own discussion. I freely concede that there may be many such
contemporaries whose writing I do not know well enough to assess
on this dimension and that warrants further or reexamination for
the degree of its "Hobbesian approach." But when working within the
limits of my own investigation I have received encouragement from
Parkin's example of how flexibility of judgment need not preclude the
drawing of distinctions worth preserving and might even sharpen them.

In this preface as elsewhere, I have arranged my endnotes in such
a way that each portion of my study can be read as an essentially self-
contained unit. As a consequence, readers primarily interested in
Davenant, say, can focus on one chapter. Though I have not presented
a single argument from end to end, however, my discussion accumu-
lates significance as it goes and will make most sense if read entire, in
the designated sequence. This holds especially true for my handling of
chronology.

Firm dates for works establish year of first publication (or sometimes
in the case of plays, of first performance). Approximate dates (ca.)
specify period of composition. Unless otherwise specified, dates given
for texts echo the edition followed in each case.

I have made these silent emendations: reversing italics presented as
the norm rather than the exception; re-transposing swapped u and v, i
and j; regularizing long s; dropping numbers preceding stanzas in
short poems; suppressing indentations marking the beginning of
verse-paragraphs; omitting deleted passages retained by the editor
of Hobbes's correspondence; lowercasing all but the initial capital at

the beginnings of poems; and modifying the capitalization of some titles. I only specify the provenance of square-bracketed content and italics in cases where I saw some room for doubt.

For their invaluable help in the preparation of this manuscript, I should like to thank my editor, Farideh Koohi-Kamali, and her assistant, Julia Cohen.

Chapter One

"How He Did Grow": Hobbes, Hobbes, and Hobbes

I: "last . . . first"

As A. P. Martinich clarifies, Hobbes wrote "two trilogies."[1] One houses increasingly long versions of his political philosophy, with each time a greater emphasis on religion: *The Elements of Law* (manuscript circulation 1640), *De Cive* (1642, revised edition 1647), and *Leviathan* (1651). The other presents Hobbes's complete philosophical system in Latin: *De Cive* again *(Elementorum Philosophiae Sectio Tertia De Cive)*, *De Corpore* (1655), and *De Homine* (1658). Such doubling reveals conflicting priorities: to be as comprehensive and as topical as possible. For Tom Sorell, the British Civil Wars constituted one of "two great upheavals" that shaped Hobbes's thought: it "was local, political, dangerous, and as Hobbes believed, deeply irrational," whereas

> The other was largely Continental, benefited people in obvious ways, showed what reason could accomplish when properly guided and applied. This was the upheaval in scientific ideas that Hobbes thought had been started by Galileo. Mainly on the strength of writings occasioned by the first upheaval Hobbes claimed to have contributed something important to the second.[2]

But the completion of *Elementorum* had to await the Interregnum, a relatively quiet period for Hobbes. By contrast, the Short Parliament's convening motivated the circulation of *Elements*, and the appearance of the intended third section of *Elementorum* preceded that of the first and second by more than a decade on grounds explained in *De Cive* itself as Hobbes reviews his entire system's arrangement:

> While I was filling it out, and putting it in order, writing slowly and painfully (for I was thinking it through not composing a rhetorical exercise), it happened that my country, some years before the civil war broke out, was already seething with questions of the right of

Government and of the due obedience of citizens, forerunners of the
approaching war. That was the reason why I put the rest aside and
hurried on the completion of this third part.

Here, too, Hobbes even sheds doubt on the integrity of the whole:
"And so it has come about that the part which was last in order has
come out first; especially as I saw that it did not need the preceding
parts, since it rests upon its own principles known by reason."[3]
    As if taking a hint, most specialists in Hobbes pay little attention
to *De Corpore* and *De Homine*; but the issue of whether and how
the three sections are linked remains controversial, like much else in
his work. Martinich suggests that "one must separate logical relatedness from epistemological relatedness. Logically, the principles in
De Corpore entail, according to Hobbes, the doctrines of *De Homine*,
and those entail the doctrines of *De Cive*. Epistemologically, the principles of *De Cive* can be known 'by experience,' as Hobbes says" (89–90).
Sorell acknowledges that Hobbes sometimes seems to be offering his
political commentary in the context of "a science for the initiated" (15),
but sees

> no tension . . . between Hobbes's placing his civil philosophy last in
> the order of demonstrating the sciences, and his saying that civil
> philosophy can be understood perfectly well independently of the prior
> sciences. Civil philosophy *can* be acquired with no preliminaries, but if
> it is being approached out of a wish to know as much as one can, then it
> is best approached last, by way of prior sciences that make it more
> intelligible. (26)

In further respects, too, Hobbes's desire to influence the political culture
of his age had an impact on the sort of philosopher he would be, often
to paradoxical effect.

II: "nothing else to do"

According to Hobbes's *Considerations upon [His Own] Reputation,
Loyalty, Manners, and Religion* (1662), where he counters personal
attacks mounted by the rival mathematician and former parliamentarian John Wallis, *Elements* succeeded only too well: "Of this treatise,
though not printed, many gentlemen had copies, which occasioned
much talk of the author; and had not his Majesty dissolved the [Short]
Parliament, it had brought him into danger of his life." Six months
later, the Long Parliament's convening put Hobbes at graver risk: this

time there would be no such dissolution, so he left England in November 1640 for ultimately more than a decade of self-imposed exile, chiefly in Paris, becoming in *Considerations*' boast "the first of all that fled."[4] Hobbes's flight under these circumstances has puzzled commentators, who speculate that he exaggerated his prominence and peril. "Hobbes's decision to seek sanctuary abroad" Quentin Skinner partly attributes "to the fact that he had become so closely associated with the Cavendishes," his chief employers, "who had in turn become associated with the hated policies of the court."[5] Moreover, the topicality that perhaps recommended *Elements* to "many gentlemen" besides its dedicatee (William Cavendish, duke of Newcastle) would have limited their ability to give that text its due: they had little time to absorb the unfamiliar language of this most self-consciously scientific expression of Hobbes's political philosophy. For Skinner, "Hobbes's resolute refusal to engage with the rhetorical techniques so central to classical and Renaissance civil science must have occasioned a considerable shock of surprise to his original readers" (308).

In France, Hobbes did not forget his compatriots' travails, as *De Cive* attests. But its first edition reached a predominantly non-English audience on a very small scale. As Richard Tuck and Michael Silverthorne note in their introduction, "It should not be supposed that because the book was in print, it was significantly more widely known than the manuscript *Elements*" (xiii). As issued by "a mass-market publishing house," according to Tuck, the revised *De Cive* reached a larger audience, but only greater numbers of English readers because so many compatriots had now joined Hobbes in exile.[6] If Hobbes had died from the grave illness he contracted in the fall of 1647, when he received his last rites, he might have remained a prophet without honor in his own land, while still ranking from a Continental perspective as a major figure in the history of ideas.[7] Disrupting his life, his exile also fostered continuity, giving him a fourth and final stay on the Continent reprising at greater length the highlights of the third (1634–36). According to the prose form of the two Latin memoirs he composed in advanced old age, he again "became involved in scientific inquiry with Mersenne, Gassendi, and with other men who were all well known for their learning, and their vigour in reasoning."[8] Whereas Pierre Gassendi was one of Hobbes's closest friends, Marin Mersenne was that and more: as Noel Malcolm notes, this Minim friar represented "the center of a huge network of scientific and philosophical correspondents."[9] Because Mersenne was away from Paris or hampered by ill health during the four years preceding his death in September 1648, Hobbes's involvement with him probably diminished after the middle of the decade. By then, however, Hobbes held a secure place in that "huge network" and would probably have retained it if not snared in other, less congenial webs.

Though his vehement anti-Catholicism never weakened his friendships with persons whose faith he thus vilified, it annoyed leading figures in his home away from home, where in any case he fell on the wrong side of one of the many wrangles afflicting the faction-ridden Stuart court-in-exile. He thus "fled" once more across the Channel, but in the opposite direction, returning to England.[10] The conclusion of his final stay abroad had nonetheless coincided with the composition of *Leviathan*, guaranteeing his immortality in his native land. In the short run, this masterpiece also meant that Hobbes could continue the topical commentary begun with *Elements* and extended in *De Cive*: it had direct relevance to the Engagement newly required of every adult male, to "declare and promise" to be "true and faithful to the Commonwealth of England, as it is now established, without a king or House of Lords."[11] An embarrassment of riches now confronted Hobbes's English readers, with *Elements* repackaged as *Humane Nature* and *De Corpore Politico* (both 1650), and *De Cive* translated as *Philosophical Rudiments Concerning Government and Society* (1651); Malcolm confidently attributes this version's long-uncertain authorship to Cotton (*Aspects*, 234–58). The firestorm of controversy ignited by Hobbes's ideas nonetheless focused overwhelmingly on *Leviathan*, as primarily a post-Restoration phenomenon not diminishing when he prepared a somewhat more conciliatory Latin translation (1668). At least indirectly, he had now reached a wide audience in his native land for the first time, but with consequences he could not have wished.

For David Johnston, the decade between the circulation of *Elements* and *Leviathan*'s publication marked a profound shift in Hobbes's approach: he came to believe that his thought would make a greater impression if presented in a more overtly persuasive manner.[12] Corroborated by Skinner (6 n.28), this argument explains the sharp contrast between the self-consciously scientific *Elements* and the highly literary *Leviathan*, as well as the transitional character of *De Cive*, especially in its revised edition. Though the most fully realized expression of Hobbes's desire to influence the political culture of his age made a huge impression on his compatriots, however, it became such a byword for all forms of immorality that the sort of philosopher he would now be was almost wholly determined by his concomitant reputation as the supposedly atheistical Beast of Malmesbury.

This notoriety meant that he could only continue practicing the obedience he preached by ceasing to preach it: even though he had regained much of the favor with Charles II that he had forfeited under circumstances necessitating his abrupt departure from Paris in 1652, the restored monarch "refused Hobbes's request to publish any works on politics," as Martinich notes (*Dictionary*, 17). One notable casualty of this ban was *Behemoth*, Hobbes's history of the Civil Wars, which he composed during the 1660s. Excluded from the Royal Society, Hobbes still managed to engage in disputes with some of its leading members; but these often rancorous exchanges did nothing to enhance his reputation: his mathematics had become outdated.[13] Moreover, even these long-running battles proved insufficient for his prodigious intellectual stamina, which continued unabated to the very end of his life. At an age when most men would rest content if they could only find their spectacles, he translated both of Homer's epics because, according to his preface "To the Reader, Concerning the Virtues of an Heroic Poem" (1677), "I had nothing else to do"; he also supposed that such work "might take off my adversaries from showing their folly upon my more serious writings, and set them upon my verses to show their wisdom."[14] Following the Great Plague and the Fire of London, widely interpreted as signs of God's displeasure with His English subjects, Hobbes found himself at risk of being prosecuted for heresy. According to Tuck, such charges were mooted not only in 1666 but also in 1667, 1674, 1675, and even 1680 (33–34). Hobbes thus felt obliged to become an expert on heresy (see Martinich, *Dictionary*, 136–39); but at least this Damoclean sword created an outlet for his stupendous energy.

As with *Elements*, he had succeeded only too well: *Leviathan* "occasioned much talk" that sometimes "brought him into danger of his life"; but in this case, the responses he aroused have survived in a form more tangible than that of his possibly self-flattering recollection. They recast his whale of a book as an inadvertent Trojan horse containing much deemed thrillingly or reprehensibly shocking, including affronts to conventional thinking that he himself would not have recognized. His fate was thus not exile but alienation from his own words and the enforced termination of his work.

III: "some ill opinions"

Not every post-Restoration response to Hobbes's ideas flew to extremes of censure or acclaim. In his will (1679), Thomas Shadwell stipulated: "I give to my sonne John five pounds for mourning and my Latine and philosophicall bookes with Mr. Hobbes his workes warning him to have a care of some ill opinions of his concerning government but hee may make excellent use of what is good in him."[15] If he thought they promoted the conduct depicted in his play *The Libertine* (1675), Shadwell would not have recommended such "workes" with so muted a caution. "Following Hobbes's arguments, Don John argues a mechanical theory of the will ruled by the strongest desires," Maximilian Novak nonetheless judges of the play's main character, adding that "Shadwell clearly did his homework for presenting a philosophic basis." Whereas Novak also stresses of "Don John and his libertines" that "their indiscriminate rampage of murder and rape is mainly silly," and that "Shadwell's thuggish Don John is as far as anyone might imagine from wits such as Rochester and [Sir George] Etherege," all perceived or self-professed practitioners of libertinism travesty Hobbes's thinking.[16]

Though any such distinction can never be airtight, attempts have been made to draw a line between representations of Hobbes's ideas that are more pure (Hobbesian) or less so (Hobbist).[17] As James Turner shows, the broad category of libertinism encompasses different kinds of self-consciously free thinking; the term Hobbist must itself remain elastic.[18] A useful rule, however, is that Hobbists espouse Hobbes's doctrines in a form so distorted and extreme as to mirror or inspire that found in vilifications of his work. Eager to shock, post-Restoration libertines embraced the atheistical Beast of Malmesbury relentlessly pilloried and caricatured by the ecclesiastical establishment; he in turn fathered sins committed by sons of doubtful legitimacy. In effect, as Earl Miner remarks, "Hobbes has been unfairly criticized for views that [Samuel] Butler held. What Hobbes believed true of man in a state of nature, Butler held evident for civilized man."[19]

Warren Chernaik rightly complains that "studies of Restoration drama tend to assume, rather than analyse or substantiate, the influence of Hobbes," instancing how Harold Weber "attempts to distinguish between 'the Hobbesian libertine of [William] Wycherly and the philosophical libertine of [William] Congreve', without defining either term of this simple binary opposition."[20] But Chernaik's own dichotomies offer little improvement:

> Within the libertine tradition in the Restoration period, we find, along with the pessimistic view of human nature . . . a far more optimistic view, which can be described as Epicurean rather than Hobbesian. It is not generally recognised that there are two quite different kinds of libertine heroes in Restoration comedy, rakes and rovers, one aggressive and exploitative and the other happy-go-lucky, accepting whatever pleasures the moment may bring. (42–43)

When Chernaik notes of late-seventeenth-century English drama that "Latitudinarian influence on the plays, like that of Locke, is probably indirect rather than direct, and indeed . . . the two lines of influence are not entirely separate" (44), he writes with a circumspection absent from his treatment of Hobbes's impact on contemporary literature, one he does "tend to assume," albeit not at the expense of any impulse to "analyse or substantiate."

Chernaik pinpoints more accurately than he realizes Hobbes's contribution to Hobbism by explaining how

> Libertines . . . reinterpreted Hobbes, choosing to emphasise certain aspects of his philosophical system and ignore others as it suited them, and in the process—quoting or paraphrasing Hobbes out of context as unscrupulously as his opponents did—transformed arguments intended to prove beyond doubt the absolute necessity for submission to authority into a manifesto of the "natural liberty of Man." (24)

So total a transformation retains nothing from its putative source. Chernaik nonetheless phrases contrasts to forge connections: "Where Hobbes and Lucretius challenged false, illegitimate authority, the libertines assumed that *all* authority was illegitimate"; "a young man's philosophy, a rebellion of the sons against the fathers," thus retains an intellectual dimension it would otherwise lack (25). Possibly, however, "the sons" took every one of their cues from "the fathers," resembling Hobbes's "opponents" in method and content because such opposition taught them the inverted terms of their own. When Hobbes's enemies reproached him for sponsoring Hobbism, they did him and themselves a disservice; parodying his work, they produced cribs for would-be libertines. Such latent Hobbists no longer faced the laborious task of misreading Hobbes to reach the same false impression of his work generated by his adversaries; they could just reverse the polarity of diatribes against his thought, discerning that father knew best what would most displease him in his own progeny.

Whereas Hobbes's ideas' perceived embodiment in the Hobbist era has received too much attention, too little has been paid to impacts of and on his thinking during an earlier period, when his views could be neither represented nor misrepresented in others' words or deeds because they had not yet been fully formulated, or at any rate recorded in writing. Though Hobbes as a political philosopher ended up gagged, he did not begin finding his voice in that role until he was already fifty-two, older than Rochester, Suckling, and Godolphin would ever be, though more years still lay ahead of him than they attained in their life-spans. Even so, his younger days were probably as formative in his own case as the equivalent period is in anyone's existence; and he possibly shared his opinions in conversation at a stage when he was already too old to learn many new tricks, but still too young to have found the most appropriate outlets for his gifts.

Such unusually late blooming virtually invites Jean Hampton's error when she illustrates how "Hobbes's work was particularly respon-sive to the political turmoil of his day" by observing that "The Thirty Years' War ravaged Europe during all of his early adult years, from 1618 to 1648."[21] Though Hobbes when that conflict began had lived as long as it would last and was twice as old when it ended, authors should be young when their careers are too. Martinich likewise distorts chronology in making James I preside over Hobbes's "adolescence and early childhood."[22] This blunder seems to conflate two influences on Hobbes's thinking that Martinich in the same source plausibly identifies and treats as related: a general indebtedness to "views prevailing when James I assumed the throne in England" (308), when Hobbes was fifteen, and a more specific debt to that monarch's thinking about politics and religion (335).

Tuck registers one advantage gained by *Elements* as a tardy debut: "Hobbes's whole philosophical enterprise, coming as it did so late in his life, has the character of mature reflection on an entire culture with which he was already completely conversant."[23] Given the loss of every conversation feeding into or out of that developing conver-sancy, however, scholars tracing the evolution of Hobbes's ideas can only study the surviving paper trail, but must somehow illuminate the hefty portion of his intellectual life falling into the category of prehistory—his "dark years," as Miriam Reik calls them (20). Most efforts to reconstruct Hobbes's thinking prior to 1640 minimize the scientific interests occupying him during the 1630s, stressing the signif-icance of underlying connections between the terminus ad quem of his major original works and two sorts of terminus a quo: his formative experiences and earliest productions of any kind.

IV: "Twins at once"

Malcolm speculates that Hobbes's membership of the Virginia Company influenced his subsequent writings about natural law and natural right; diligently attending its meetings from 1622 to 1624, he also became a shareholder in its Bermudan offshoot (*Aspects*, 53–76). Tuck remarks of a statement Hobbes made in April 1639 as a routine part of his service to the Cavendishes that one of its points—"every man may lawfully seeke to secure himself upon his owne suspitions, whether they be well or ill grounded"—"is in effect the fundamental proposition of Hobbes's political thought!" ("Moral Philosophy," 206 n.33). This identification possibly means only that *Elements* was then sufficiently advanced (at least in mind) for Hobbes to apply its gist in one limited context where it seemed relevant. On the other hand, his political philosophy's development from an earlier stage had possibly gained much from many prior instances when his humdrum existence as a savant-servant to the Cavendishes generated insights having an enduring significance no longer tied to their immediate occasion.

Hobbes traced his most formative experience to a trauma so early that it caused his premature birth. In the verse form of his Latin memoirs, he explained how the approach of the Spanish Armada created such a mood of apprehension that "my Mother Dear / Did bring forth Twins at once, both Me, and Fear" (254). Typifying his approach to his subject, Martinich takes these words at face value (*Hobbes*, 1–2). But Hobbes here wrote in a medium often linked by his contemporaries with the cultivation of an arch wit whose nearest equivalent in his native tongue can be found in the poetry of John Cleveland. As Sir Leslie Stephen notes, Hobbes "Characteristically . . . speaks of his timidity with a certain complacency."[24] Smug about being "first of all that fled," he took no less satisfaction in being coeval with fear. Because fear's prominence as a motive in Hobbes's account of human nature struck many of his contemporaries as an affront to their dignity, they often retorted that his maxims on this score applied only to himself. Aubrey records that "His work was attended with envy, which threw severall aspersions and false reports on him. For instance, one (common) was that he was afrayd to lye alone at night in his chamber."[25] Hobbes turned into a source of defiant pride the ridicule he received for his views about fear.

V: "a Foolish Thing"

The far from commonplace nature of Hobbes's perspective on fear emerges indirectly from his translation *Eight Books of the Peloponnesian War, Written by Thucydides* (1629); published when he was already forty, it has been much scanned by scholars seeking clues as to the evolution of his own thought. Esteemed a classic, this rendering nonetheless includes a passage that Martinich terms "tendentious," but significantly: "Given that Hobbes is reading a conceptual relation between fear and courage into Thucydides' text, it is plausible that he was already thinking about such relationships on his own rather than being guided by Thucydides" (*Dictionary*, 83). Other scholars stress how little creative wrenching Hobbes needed to do to make *Eight Books* his own: its modern editor judges that it "apparently crystallized for Hobbes many of the ideas fundamental in his later political philosophy"; Leo Strauss sees it as "heralding" its translator's "philosophic life-work."[26]

In both forms of his Latin memoirs, Hobbes explains his rationale for putting Thucydides's history into English: it shows how "Democracy's a Foolish Thing, / Than a Republick Wiser is one King" (256); through its analysis, "the weaknesses and eventual failures of the Athenian democrats, together with those of their city state, were made clear" (246). If these retrospective statements mean that Hobbes thought his translation had topical relevance for his contemporaries at the time of its publication, he was benefiting from hindsight (claiming after the Civil Wars to have predicted some such disaster) or acknowledging that his perspective during the early years of Charles I's reign had been exceptionally pessimistic. In his preface to *Eight Books*, Hobbes noted that he had delayed publication, having finished this work "long" beforehand, whatever he meant by that (8). The earlier the completion, the less reason he had to see a political crisis impending in Britain: "democrats" or proponents of "a Republick" were as thin on the ground in the 1620s as for some time to come, except as products of intemperate rhetoric.

David Norbrook nonetheless disputes that "republicanism was largely a response to, rather than the cause of, the execution of Charles I," dating "the emergence of republican literary culture" to a prior period and judging the impact of Lucan's *Pharsalia*, especially as translated by Thomas May (1627), "a classic example of a phenomenon repeatedly denounced by Thomas Hobbes": the corrupting influence of a university education centering on texts from classical antiquity that might be understood as fostering sedition.[27] A letter by William Rand (August 1651) convinces Norbrook that Hobbes was not alone among his contemporaries in grasping this potential: its author professes having "long bin with Mr Hobbs, that ye reading of such bookes as Livy's History has bin a rub in the way of ye advancement of ye Interest of his Leviathanlike Monarchs" (282–83). Even if "Leviathanlike" does not disqualify Rand's claim to "long" likemindedness, Norbrook undermines its validity from another direction: "in 1651 a member of the [Samuel] Hartlib circle lamented that not enough use was being made of the printing press," because "more books should be translated into English and Livy's *History* should be made available in a cheap, compact edition to instill a cult of liberty" (282). Had Rand's "long" agreement with Hobbes been at all widely shared, such an emergent "cult" as a process of cultural transmission should have been more decisively advanced or thwarted by the beginning of the Interregnum.

Moreover, Mark Curtis argues that

> The effect of university education on Stuart politics operated in more subtle but nonetheless significant ways than those that Hobbes condemned. The universities were dangerous—though not the "core of rebellion"—because they were, paradoxical as it may seem, too successful in carrying out their primary task of training men for service to Church and State. As vigorous, effective institutions of higher education they unwittingly worked against the peace and tranquillity of the realm not because they instilled subversive doctrines but because they prepared too many men for too few places.[28]

Hobbes was an exception to this rule in his ultimately secure position with the Cavendishes and would have had less to worry about if more of his fellow graduates had attained a comparable tenure.

Arguably, too, "a rub in the way of . . . Leviathanlike Monarchs" and "a cult of liberty" are not the same, though Norbrook's analysis depends on their rough equivalence—hence the weight he attaches to Hobbres's testimony as an opponent of republicanism. On the assumption that Hobbes would have been familiar with "the rising temperature of political debate in the drama, which was engaging with sensitive political issues," as in the case of Jonson, "who was fighting a rearguard action against the fashion for news and subversive politics in works like *The Staple of News*" (1626), Norbrook concludes that Hobbes's "aim in the translation, clearly signalled in his editorial comments, was to contain the excesses of the current cult of classical liberty by presenting a sceptical, conservative perspective on democracy" (59). Thus, Hobbes's retrospective view of *Eight Books* neither exaggerates his foresight nor expresses his own alarmism, but rather confirms the early emergence of republicanism: "the translation can be seen as his considered response to the whole troubled decade of the 1620s" (58). To compensate for a paucity of other evidence, Norbrook takes at face value Hobbes's later hints about the topical contribution made by his version of Thucydides's history: "If we use the term 'republican' " to denote someone who would "desire a state without any kind of monarchy," Norbrook acknowledges, then

> we can say that there were very few republican readers of Lucan in
> pre-Civil-War England. But [his] poem did become identified with a
> particular kind of political grouping that, while not specifically anti-
> monarchical, had distinct hankerings after a severely limited monarchy
> which, as far as some absolutist theorists were concerned, would be in
> practice little better than a republic. (40)

This argument makes Red Scaremongers reliable on American
communists during the 1950s, except that Hobbes stood apart from
other "absolutist theorists" in the sheer extent to which he conflated
republicans and advocates of mixed monarchy—groups typically not
interchangeable in their own eyes or anyone else's. In addition, most
histories of Britain do not treat the 1620s as uniformly "troubled";
rather, they stress the swift deterioration of crown–parliament relations after the standard honeymoon phase accompanying Charles I's
accession.

As a topical commentary, *Eight Books* would have been notably
bleak, even if shaped by the fierce and protracted debate over the
Petition of Right (1628); the murder in the same year of George
Villiers, first duke of Buckingham (August); and the unconstitutional
events of March 2, 1629, when (in the words of J. P. Kenyon) "the
Commons, in hysteria, forcibly postponed their own dissolution by
locking Black Rod out and holding the Speaker down in his chair."[29]
But the political context in which Hobbes's translation first reached
print cannot supply his motives for writing it. He had certainly
completed it before witnessing the incarceration of Sir John Eliot, one
of the more outspoken members of parliament in the later 1620s and
a figure regarded by Charles I as an irresponsible demagogue guilty of
fostering the climate of hostility toward Buckingham; here was an
apparent instance of the mob oratory repudiated in *Eight Books'*
introduction, which deplores "desperate actions undertaken upon the
flattering advice of such as desired to attain, or to hold what they had
attained, of authority and sway amongst the common people" (13).[30]

Whether Hobbes was benefiting from hindsight when explaining
Thucydides's role in his own intellectual development, those later
commentators are who agree with the substance if not the letter of his
retrospective claims; and understandable efforts to illuminate his
"dark years" risk projecting a false light. Even so, the sheer number
and variety of parallels different readers have discovered between

Hobbes's original work and his version of Thucydides's history make a collectively forceful case.

Aubrey's account of Hobbes's voluntary exile has a bearing on when the author of *Eight Books* became so convinced that "Democracy's a Foolish Thing": "he told me that bp. Manwaring (of St. David's) preach'd *his doctrine*; for which, among others, he was sent prisoner to the Tower. Then thought Mr. Hobbes, 'tis time now for me to shift for my selfe, and so withdrew into France, and resided at Paris" (1: 334). At some point after the Restoration, therefore, Hobbes identified *"his doctrine"* as indistinguishable from that of the royal chaplain Roger Maynwaring, who in 1628 had been fined £1,000 and forever disabled from holding any office for preaching in support of Charles I's forced loan of the previous two years, which Hobbes helped collect, under circumstances described by Johann Sommerville (9). Made bishop of St. David's in 1636, when belatedly rewarded by the same king who eight years earlier had been pressured into condemning his sermons, Maynwaring suffered a further reversal when imprisoned by the Long Parliament. With *Elements*, Hobbes made a contribution sufficiently similar to Maynwaring's to render him liable in his own opinion to the same ultimate fate.

As Martinich notes, however, "The context in Aubrey's biography suggests that Hobbes was claiming to have influenced Manwaring" (*Dictionary*, 9)—an assertion hard to square with Hobbes's oeuvre in 1628 unless the completed but unpublished *Eight Books* qualifies as a topical commentary already shaping others' opinions. Hobbes's contemporaries nonetheless took seriously his claim to recognize Maynwaring's *"doctrine"* as in some sense his own; modern scholars have generally followed suit. In summarizing the royal chaplain's views, Sommerville comments that another cleric (Robert Sibthorp) argued along similar lines (9–10); he also points out that "Locke traced the origins of absolutist thinking in England to the sermons of Sibthorp and Maynwaring," and that John Whitehall, Algernon Sidney, and Edward Hyde, earl of Clarendon, all concurred in linking Hobbes with those clerics because of their political views (80). Though the apparent brazenness with which Hobbes appropriated Maynwaring's position and denied that sermoneer's primacy in occupying it possibly reflected only his own anxiety to establish himself as first in the field, it could mean that he felt confident his retrospective claim would be regarded as just because, even before he had finished translating Thucydides's history, he had long been expounding *"his doctrine"* in person to anyone giving him a hearing.

VI: "the worst thing"

Eight Books' own primacy (as Hobbes's first publication) has been challenged by Noel Reynolds and Arlene Saxonhouse, who argue that Hobbes wrote three discourses published anonymously in 1620: *Upon the Beginning of Tacitus, Of Rome*, and *Of Laws*. The first of these builds on an analysis of the origins of government written by a historian whom Reynolds and Saxonhouse plausibly style "the Roman Thucydides."[31] Annotating Tacitus's account of Augustus Caesar's establishing himself as sole ruler of Rome after a long spell of republicanism, *Upon the Beginning* often makes points directly relevant to constitutional issues arising in England during the 1650s, and does so in terms characteristic of Hobbes's political philosophy:

> when a mighty and free people, is subdued to the tyranny of one man, it is for the most part after some long and bloody Civil War. For civil war is the worst thing that can happen to a State: wherein the height of their best hopes can come but to this, to venture and hazard their own, to overthrow their friends' and kindred's fortunes. And they that are at the worst, have reason to be content with, and wish for any change whatsoever. (37)

This discourse also explains how Augustus "would not presently take unto him the Title belonging to Monarchy, especially not the name of King," but initially "affected the Title of Tribune . . . because he thought it best to make his faction sure with the Commons, who at that time were the strongest part of the State, by having the Title and Authority of their Protector" (37, 43–44). If Reynolds and Saxonhouse are correct in their attribution, Hobbes had not needed the emergence of Oliver Cromwell as Lord Protector to envisage a political context where the chaos of civil war yielded to the imposed authority of an individual embodying sovereign power as a king in all but name, having published his thoughts on the subject at about the same age at which Rochester, Godolphin, and Suckling all died. If Hobbes did not pen *Upon the Beginning*, some other political analyst active in Jacobean England, almost a decade before the appearance of *Eight Books*, had anticipated two of his most singular traits: dispassionate evaluation of even "the tyranny of one man" as a constitutional development not automatically to be deplored; and, conversely, a readiness to suppose that when "Rome utterly lost her liberty" she made a vital gain—freedom from anarchy (36).

Upon the Beginning also foreshadows one of many ways in which responses to the Exclusion Crisis (1679–81) and ensuing Glorious

Revolution (1688) would be colored by complex associations to the conflicts of 1640–60: its analysis resembles that offered in Dryden's *Dedication of the "Æneis"* (1697). Suggesting that "we are to consider" the original author "as writing his Poem in a time when the Old Form of Government was subverted, and a new one just Established by *Octavius Caesar*: In effect by force of Arms, but seemingly by the Consent of the *Roman* People," Dryden explains how

> *Virgil* having maturely weigh'd the Condition of the Times in which he liv'd: that an entire Liberty was not to be retriev'd: that the present Settlement had the prospect of a long continuance in the same Family, or those adopted into it: that he held his Paternal Estate from the Bounty of the Conqueror, by whom he was likewise enrich'd, esteem'd and cherish'd: that this Conquerour, though of a bad kind, was the very best of it: that the Arts of Peace flourish'd under him: that all Men might be happy if they would be quiet . . . he concluded it to be the Interest of his Country to be so Govern'd: To infuse an awful Respect into the People, towards such a Prince: By that respect to confirm their Obedience to him, and by that Obedience to make them Happy. This was the Moral of his Divine Poem.[32]

Dating from either end of the seventeenth century, *Upon the Beginning* and Dryden's preface in their shared language illustrate one continuity in an Augustanism already shaping English culture well before 1660.

VII: "in love with geometry"

Before translating Thucydides's history and possibly annotating its Roman counterpart, Hobbes rendered Euripides's *Medea* in Latin iambics (ca. 1602); but Aubrey records how this piece of juvenilia had gone missing when its author sought it out "to have seen how he did grow" (1: 329). "The play seems to have deeply affected Hobbes," notes Martinich: "He refers to *Medea* four times in his writings, more than to any other non-Homeric literary work" (*Hobbes*, 7). Reik attempts to pinpoint this profound effect: "the tragedy unraveled in the play resembles the terrible vision of society's dissolution in his own works" (27). Moreover, Skinner stresses that "Euripides was more interested than any of the other ancient dramatists in the rhetorical arts, and above all in the art of presenting moral dilemmas in the form of 'statements and replies,' " characterizing *Medea* itself as "a play in which the power of eloquence to excuse evil is scrutinised in a way that gave the story a special standing among English humanists of the Renaissance" (174). In addition, Daniel Mendelsohn senses a kinship between *Medea*, first performed at the outbreak of the Peloponnesian War, and Thucydides's history of that conflict.[33]

The possible value to Hobbes of all his early translations emerges indirectly from Ruth Wallerstein's insightful remarks about the formation of the neoclassical distich, for she speculates that an overall trend in seventeenth-century poetry "toward the didactic and the generalized reflection" occurred as a byproduct of the following phenomenon:

> A translator has before him a concentrated expression which exhibits as a whole an organic reality and scope of meaning larger than the sum of its parts. Thus it is natural that as a translator, in his endeavor to get this whole, he should, in seizing the concept or expression which he is to translate, state it to himself in more explicit and logically complete terms than the original. The original gathers much in one creative flash; any other statement seems tenuous beside that flash and accordingly tends to explain itself in order to gain completeness. This fact produces in translations a tendency to paraphrase and to sententious generalization.[34]

These observations convey how writing or reading verse translations possibly influenced the structure and content of English poetry, but also how Hobbes in translating Thucydides's words might have been predisposed to extract from or read into them his own equivalent of the neoclassical distichs' "didactic and . . . generalized reflection." Whether or not his, *Upon the Beginning* reveals how much generalizing could occur in connection with a handful of sentences, with "a tendency," in this case self-conscious, "to paraphrase and to sententious generalization."

On the other hand, *Eight Books* has been regarded as not only the debut of his political philosophy but also the culmination and conclusion of his career as a Renaissance humanist. Hugh Trevor-Roper judges that Hobbes was loyal to " 'civil history', history as an empirical science, containing its own rules, which could be deduced from it and applied in practice," but only "till he was seduced by the apparent certainties of mathematics."[35] Hobbes's preoccupations shifted considerably when he underwent the Eureka experience described by Aubrey, which transpired "in a gentleman's library," apparently in Geneva (ca. 1630):

> Euclid's Elements lay open, and 'twas the 47 El. libri I. He read the proposition. "By G——," sayd he, "this is impossible!" So he reads the

demonstration of it, which referred him back to such a proposition; which proposition he read. That referred him back to another, which he also read. Et sic deinceps, that at last he was demonstratively convinced of that trueth. This made him in love with geometry. (1: 332)

Acknowledging the objection that "Hobbes probably did have some prior interest in and knowledge of geometry," Martinich stresses that "there is a difference between learning something and being struck by its power and importance" (*Hobbes*, 84, 85). But there is also a difference between being convinced in one's own mind of certain perceived truths and being capable of convincing others to share the same perception. The essential continuity of Hobbes's career and the revolutionary impact of his discovery of geometry can be reconciled if he is seen as a thinker whose core convictions had settled in early adulthood, when most people achieve a fixed outlook, but who did not find an opportunity to air his views in his own words, in their most enduring form, until he was satisfied that after much searching he had developed a methodology whose "certainties" were not specious and could win converts because of their secure foundations.

Nonetheless, the Elizabethan, Jacobean, and early-Caroline Hobbes must remain shadowy figures because the inarguable paper trail he left as a political philosopher did not commence until 1640 or become widely familiar for another two decades, which in turn explains why a thinker born in the wake of the Spanish Armada routinely perplexes students of English literature embarking on surveys of the long eighteenth century, as no living fossil embedded in the syllabus (albeit only to be remembered as the front end of a chimera whose hindquarters are and Locke).

Chapter two focuses on the arresting case of Davenant as a sometime neighbor of Hobbes standing so close at one juncture as to blur a helpful distinction possibly drawn by Hobbes himself: "the nature of a comparison, implies but a similitude, and affinity of one thing to another, and not a total and absolute agreement" (*Of Laws*, 117).[36]

Chapter Two

"To Governe the Reader": Hobbes and Davenant

I: "benefit and gratitude"

Hurrying to complete *Leviathan*, Hobbes had no time to read Davenant's heroic poem *Gondibert* (incomplete when published in 1651) or its lengthy preface (first printed the previous year). As Richard Tuck notes, Hobbes produced "the last ten chapters of *Leviathan* (about 90,000 words) in considerably less than a year," under intense pressure: he "sent instalments of his manuscript for setting in type each week from Paris to London, with proofs being sent back each week in return—an astonishing method of publishing."[1] Nonetheless, *Gondibert*'s preface credits Hobbes for giving the poem "a daylie examination as it was writing"; and his familiarity with both the verse and prose of this intended magnum opus informs *The Answer of Mr. Hobbes to Sir Will. D'Avenant's Preface before "Gondibert"* (1650).[2]

Moreover, as Hobbes clarified in *De Cive*, "we are not looking for friends" as such "but for honour or advantage from them," in that "*benefit* and *gratitude* go together."[3] He did not disqualify his *Answer* as the testimony of one "bribed by the honor you have done me, by attributing in your Preface somewhat to my Judgment," but stressed mutual "advantage" instead: "I have used your Judgment no lesse in many thinges of mine, which comming to light will thereby appeare the better. And so you have your bribe againe" (54). Usually, Hobbes downplayed his debts to others; but if slow to acknowledge assistance, he was little given to flattery either.

In the jeering volume *Certain Verses Written by Severall of the Authors Friends: To Be Re-Printed with the Second Edition of "Gondibert"* (1653), Davenant's credentials as a figure commanding Hobbes's respect receive at least backhanded endorsement. Whereas "Upon the *PREFACE*" merely supposes that Davenant represents "the best of Poets heroick" for anyone prepared to "believe" such authorities as an unnamed "Stoick," "The Author upon Himself" acknowledges that even "old *Hobbs*" cannot "Defend me from dry bobbs," and "To *DAPHNE* on His Incomparable Incomprehensible Poem *GONDIBERT*" mocks Davenant's name and the inclusiveness of his work:

> So have I heard the great *Leviathan*,
> Let me speak true, and not bely-a-man,
> Raign in the Deep, and with tyrannick Power
> Both Costick *Codd*, and squallid *Sprats* devour. (273, 277, 283)

Whereas Hobbes here suffered with Davenant, the reverse process has not operated in the poet's favor: Clarence DeWitt Thorpe's valuable guide to Hobbes's aesthetics ranks Davenant as merely one of "Two Disciples" (with Walter Charleton).[4]

By contrast, James Winn counters the trend toward belittling Davenant for producing in *Gondibert* a foreshortened work trailing an inflated preface, suggesting ways in which both mountain moved and emergent mouse contributed to Dryden's apprenticeship.[5] Moreover, Keith Thomas considers Davenant "one of the few individuals from whom Hobbes seems to have been prepared to learn," seeing this as evidence that Hobbes shared the aristocratic outlook maintained by many figures in his life.[6] Though I find this larger claim unconvincing, Thomas's more limited point raises the question of why Hobbes's interchanges with Davenant were not fraught with the tensions so swiftly ruining his relationship with Descartes.[7] However little realized, Davenant's soaring literary ambitions still marked him as a rival. Remarking that *Gondibert*'s preface "virtually, like Shelley, makes the poet an 'unacknowledged legislator,' " David Gladish stresses that "Davenant took this obligation to heart": the title-piece from his debut collection, *"Madagascar," with Other Poems* (1638), seeks "to coax Prince Rupert into invading the island of that name" (xv). Comprehending Davenant's later collaboration with Hobbes therefore involves assessing where the two beforehand had begun thinking along similar or complementary lines.

II: "in hope to git"

Though Davenant as poet laureate had the responsibility of articulating Charles I's vision of government, he is usually viewed as closer to the queen. During the Civil Wars, he served as Lieutenant General of

Ordnance under *Elements*' dedicatee, Newcastle (November 1642 to August 1643), apparently at Henrietta Maria's behest, but then went to sea, supplying royalists with munitions acquired through her connections on the Continent. He thus proved "the great pirott" identified by an adversary also conceding that "No man hath don . . . more hurt, and . . . been a greater enemy to the parliament."[8] When finally captured, he was en route to fulfilling the future Charles II's commission to replace the existing governor of Maryland, named after the queen. Slated for execution, Davenant gained a reprieve through the aid of intercessors (Milton possibly included). By contrast, Hobbes avoided criticizing Henrietta Maria, but scarcely extolled her when *Behemoth* rebuts objections raised against her "for all the favours that had been shown to the Catholics," accusing her critics of meaning "to force her to hypocrisy, being hypocrites themselves."[9]

Hobbes proved no more partial to Sir Thomas Wentworth, earl of Strafford, though *Behemoth* did ridicule how Charles I's then right-hand man had been executed in May 1641 because "he had traitorously endeavoured to subvert the fundamental laws and government of the realm," treating such logic as absurd: "I understand not how one law can be more fundamental than another, except only that law of nature that binds us all to obey him, whosoever he be, whom lawfully and for own safety, we have promised to obey" (67, 67–68). But *Behemoth* still held against Strafford his apparent apostasy as a former champion of the Petition of Right: "it is very likely" he "came over to the King's party for his own ends, having been so much against the King in former Parliaments" (72). By contrast, Davenant took part in the Army Plot of April 1641—an abortive attempt to rescue Strafford by force.[10] Unlike his fellow plotters, Davenant did not escape arraignment; but his "Humble Remonstrance" sufficiently mollified members of the Commons to secure his release on bail of £4,000, after which he slipped across the Channel to return under Newcastle's command. But Davenant the Army Plotter had changed his mind or placed his loyalty ahead of his feelings: his ode "To the King on New-Yeares Day 1630" wishes him members of parliament "Who not rebell, in hope to git / Some office to reclaime their wit"—unmistakably a gibe at Strafford, though too common a form of cynicism to represent any particular link with Hobbes.[11]

Insofar as Davenant rebukes Strafford amid wholesale condemnation of unruly members of parliament, however, his attitude closely resembles Hobbes's. "To the King" wishes Charles I "A Session . . . of such who can obey, / As they were gather'd to consult, not sway" (17–18). Though the magnetic attraction of rhyme perhaps helped generate a couplet conflating two options ("consult" and "obey") as the sole alternative to "sway," the crudeness of Davenant's political vision seems to drive the clumsiness of his phrasing. His rhetoric proved equally heavy-handed in a song, "So musicall as to all Eares," from his masque *Salmacida Spolia* (1640), assuring the king and queen how

> All that are harsh, all that are rude,
> Are by your harmony subdu'd;
> Yet so into obedience wrought,
> As if not forc'd to it, but taught. (5–8)

Martin Butler remarks "The devastating concessions in Davenant's syntax" here (centering on "As if"), revealing "the confusions in his vocabulary, as he hesitates between rival languages of educational harmony, and discipline, suppression and control."[12] Davenant did not always strike so confused or monitory a note: his song "Whilst by a mixture thus made one," from his masque *The Temple of Love* (1635), pays tribute "To CHARLES the mightiest and the best, / And to the Darling of his breast, / Who rule b'example as by power" (13–15); and his verse-epistle "To the Queen" (ca. 1640–41) insists that "Accurst are those *Court-Sophisters* who say / When princes yield, Subjects no more obey" (41–42). But these sentiments constitute exceptions to the rule, as A. M. Gibbs acknowledges in his notes (412). Confirming the consistency of Davenant's political vision during the decade spanned by "To the King" and *Salmacida Spolia*, the ode also anticipates the masque in a chorus acclaiming Charles I "th' example and the Law, / By whom the good are taught, not kept in awe" (7–8, 15–16, 23–24, 31–32). Possibly reflecting Davenant's imperfect command of neoclassical distichs, these lines nonetheless typify the half-heartedness with which he drapes velvet glove over iron fist: "Law" here is a redundant feature of Charles I's dual identity, unless some subjects need to be "kept in awe," belying the pacific effectiveness of his "example."[13]

Though Hobbes's formulations seldom take so maladroit a form, his refusal to countenance any constructive role for parliaments ensures that he, too, can only approve members who "consult" if this means "obey." Hobbes's fundamentally crude view of parliaments anticipated Whiggism: he likewise refused to distinguish among sessions or members, but saw ubiquitous knavery and folly rather than an overall disposition toward constitutional reform as making the Civil Wars inevitable from an early stage. Notwithstanding the Long Parliament's unprecedented tenure, *Behemoth* denies it any special character: "I can make no other judgment, but that they who were then elected, were just such as had been elected for former Parliaments, and as likely to be elected for Parliaments to come" (39). *De Cive* explains "why a large group is ill suited to deliberation": "each member has to make a long, continuous speech to express his opinion; and deploy his eloquence to make it as ornate and attractive as possible to the audience, in order to win a reputation" (123). Though Hobbes often invokes classical parallels when documenting contemporary abuses of rhetoric, he generally offers clarifying appeals to familiar history or myth; here, however, he makes the implausible claim that every member of parliament brought the houses' proceedings to a halt as an aspirant Demosthenes or Cicero. Davenant also wrote as if parliaments overflowed with would-be orators: his ode wishes Charles I a better future including "*Prætors,* who will the publique cause defend, / With timely gifts, not Speeches finely pend" (25–26). Though members acting rightly rather than wrongly would still be "*Prætors,*" Davenant's terminology presumably punctures the self-importance of the latter group alone, while damning them as praters.

Other pretentious praters obnoxious to Davenant and Hobbes alike included ecclesiastical controversialists and practitioners of scholasticism. Hobbes's *Answer* stresses the danger posed by "Unskillful divines" professing inspiration: "when they call unseasonably for *Zeale* there appears a spirit of *Cruelty*; and by the like error instead of *Truth* they rayse *Discord*; instead of *Wisedome, Fraud*; instead of *Reformation, Tumult*; and *Controversie* instead of *Religion*" (48). Davenant similarly saw theological disputation as destructive: according to his verse-epistle "To the Lord Cary of Lepington, upon His Translation of Malvezzi" (1638),

> Knowledge, ere it did practise to controle,
> No Weapon was, but Diet of the Soule;
> Which, as her nourishment, she might enjoy,
> Not like Controverts, others to destroy. (21–24)

As Hobbes pinned high hopes on human reason, provided it could avoid what he considered the self-evident absurdities of scholasticism, so Davenant assumed a comparable position in his verse-epistle "To Henry Jarmin" (1638), explaining how "The Studious" perversely "Admit not Reason to be naturall" (making it "now their Art"), obscure everything "With dark Schoole-Clouds," produce merely "sophistick, uselesse science," and all because of "Their pride; who

rule as chiefe on Earth, because / They only can expound their owne
hard Lawes" (37, 39, 44, 42, 45, 49–50). Again stressing the will to
power, Davenant would surely have approved how Hobbes's *Leviathan*
drew on Job not only for its title but also for the image of a "power"
sufficiently "great" to be an over-awing "King of the Proud."[14]

In these occasional poems to Henry Jermyn, earl of St. Albans, and
Henry Carey, second earl of Monmouth, Davenant shows his general
inclination to question the motives of any "legislator." Because not
even the "unacknowledged" kind was exempt from such scrutiny, his
verse-epistle "To Edward Earl of Dorset" (ca. 1644?) addresses self-
important praters from another but characteristic angle:

> Ah, What are Poets? Why is that great Law
> Conceal'd, by which their numbers seek to awe
> The Soules of Men? Poets! whom love of Praise,
> A Mistress smile, or a small Twigg of Bayes,
> Can lift to such a pride as strait they dreame
> The Worlds chiefe care is to consider them. (1–6)

Himself prone to such hubris, Davenant informs his patron how
encouraging one "Of this fond race" will only cause delays if Dorset is
summoned to serve the state with feats of arms or political advice:
"you should stay to tread the Lists, or sit / In Councill, till you read
what I have writ" (7, 13–14). Gibbs suggests that Davenant alludes to
Dorset's "appointment to the position of President of the Privy Seal in
1644"; otherwise, the epistle can only be dated as from before 1652,
when its addressee died (423). Davenant's poem grows more pointed
if coinciding with Dorset's assumption of so important an office. Thus,
the blame for any disruption here is entirely Dorset's ("To this presumptuous glory am I grown, / Since you adorn'd my Muse and
made her known")—hence the folly of "planting still new Nurseries of
Bay" (15–16, 18).

Davenant develops his theme of public service by contrasting it
with rural retirement: "happy he that can securely please / His courser
Soul with ignorance and ease," who "knowes no more of Nature
then what yields / Growth to his Heards, and Summer to his
Fields," who "Studies Art but for his wooing Cloathes," and "Whose
Country-Courage is his hunting Oathes" (19–24). This ironic portrait
of bumpkin bliss concludes with one clear advantage denied courtiers:
the happy rustic "shall rest untroubled with the feare / Least *Orpheus*
useless Sons should vex his Eare" (25–26). Therefore Davenant's
patron "must suffer still," though "ceaselesse Courtships from afflicting

Wit" do at least promise immortality: "when Time should rest his Feet, / The Windes shall cease to breathe and Flouds to meet," Dorset's "great Name / Shall make the last discourse of Dying Fame" (27–32). As Isabel Rivers observes, "donating eternity through verse . . . is the supreme compliment, but . . . suggests the superiority of the poet to his subject."[15] Ridiculing pretentious poets and conceding his own vanity, Davenant refrains from probing Dorset's motives for enduring and even encouraging so tenacious a burr. But then again, "*Orpheus* useless Sons" can generate purple patches of the sort with which Davenant's poem concludes. Such eloquent lines must sound like singing for supper, however, when their author has so banteringly established the bartering relationship between poet and patron, with a tone epitomized by "all you get" (27).

Whereas many contemporaries deemed Strafford a loyalist for hire, Davenant thus approached Hobbes in so broadly establishing self-interest as a motive, even erecting it as a "great Law" for poets. From this perspective, Strafford's alleged conduct begins to look normative rather than blameworthy. According to Roger Lockyer,

> both King and Commons acted on the assumption that supply and redress of grievances were intimately linked and that some sort of bargaining was inevitable if the demands of both parties were to be satisfied. But this was predicated upon an even more basic assumption, that it was the duty of subjects to relieve the King's necessities and the moral obligation of the King to remedy abuses in his government. Bargaining was a secondary stage, and if it became too pronounced it distorted the relationship between the King and the representatives of his people and led to the sort of merchantlike dealing that James abhorred.[16]

That this "secondary stage" had already begun being "too pronounced" by the start of the next king's reign readily emerges from the same historian's explanation of how an "auction of the prerogative" continued under Charles I in such a way that "the element of bargaining was explicit, for the Commons deliberately held up their vote of supply until the King had accepted the Petition of Right which they had framed" (135). David Smith blurs an important point when generalizing about the Short Parliament that whereas "a majority of the Lords accepted that supply should precede redress, in the Commons . . . most members preferred, as in 1614, 1626 and 1628, to engage in direct redress-supply bargaining."[17] If this process had been "direct" (rather than obvious in retrospect), less confusion would have accompanied an "element of bargaining" that could become "explicit" without being thinkable in those terms. Though the extent to which Hobbes's economic vocabulary establishes him as a theorist of market values remains disputed, he stood out from his contemporaries in his twofold insistence that sociability involves seeking "honour or advantage" and that "*benefit* and *gratitude* go together."[18] Davenant's epistle to Dorset suggests that he had similarly come to see mutual back-scratching as a feature of life, even before his own relationship with Hobbes had assumed that form—unless a later dating for the poem moves it into that period of reciprocity, with the poet's quest for "that great Law" and his specific formulation of it a legacy of the two men's interchanges.

III: "not by common Mapps"

Davenant's impulse to demystify "Conceal'd" motives reflects his early penchant for Baconian empiricism: according to Aubrey,

> He was preferred to the first dutches of Richmond to wayte on her as a page. I remember he told me, she sent him to a famous apothecary for some Unicornes-horne, which he was resolved to try with a spider which he incircled in it, but without the expected successe; the spider would goe over, and thorough and thorough, unconcerned.[19]

Arthur Nethercot makes too much of this story when he supposes that Davenant's efforts entitled him to membership in the Royal Society and could have spared its fellows the trouble of repeating his experiment some three decades later.[20] Gladish nonetheless draws attention to Bacon's profound significance for *Gondibert* (ix–xi, xv–xvii), most readily apparent in Astragon, the founder of a scientific academy (and thus a considerably updated version of the romance-wizard, especially given the poem's eighth-century setting). On the other hand, the poem's preface hails Hobbes rather than Bacon as a beacon of enlightenment: "you move not by common Mapps, but have painfully made your owne Prospect; and travaile now like the Sun, not to informe your selfe, but enlighten the World" (24). There is no reason to suppose, however, that Bacon and Hobbes were anything but complementary figures for Davenant.

Aubrey reports of Hobbes that "The Lord Chancellour Bacon loved to converse with him. He assisted his lordship in translating severall of his Essayes into Latin, one, I well remember, is that *Of the Greatnes of Cities:* the rest I have forgott." According to Aubrey, too,

> His lordship was a very contemplative person, and was wont to contemplate in his delicious walkes at Gorambery, and dictate to Mr. Thomas Bushell, or some other of his gentlemen, that attended him with inke and paper ready to sett downe presently his thoughts. His lordship would often say that he better liked Mr. Hobbes's taking his thoughts, then any of the other, because he understood what he wrote, which the others not understanding, my Lord would many times have a hard taske to make sense of what they writt. (1: 331)

Notwithstanding Hobbes's superior aptitude for bringing home the Bacon, splitters have stressed his increasingly retrograde contempt for empirical research. But at least some of his misgivings probably stemmed from his frustration over being excluded from the Royal Society on some combination of prudential, political, and personal grounds. Moreover, the ultimately sharp contrast between Hobbes's approach to science and Bacon's had scarcely begun to be apparent until late in Hobbes's life, long after Bacon's death had ended the close working relationship depicted by Aubrey. Above all, both thinkers promoted the concept that "Knowledge is power"; though Sir Leslie Stephen concedes that these words, "a running title in the *Advancement of Learning*" (1605), might not have been supplied by the author himself, he also stresses that "they clearly represent Bacon's meaning."[21] Davenant himself gives reasons for supposing that lumpers have a better case than splitters: his own approach to knowledge ranged widely enough to encompass both Bacon and Hobbes, as well as to include literary criticism promoting the poet as "virtually . . . an 'unacknowledged legislator,' " and, at the other extreme, verses subjecting poets themselves to scrutiny, not to propound any "great Law," but to uncover one.[22]

Baconian piths stud *Gondibert*'s preface: "Story, where ever it seemes most likely, growes most pleasant" (3); "Nature . . . is the only visible power, and operation of God" (7); "worthinesse and unworthinesse . . . are defin'd by Opinion" (8); "*Learning* . . . is not Knowledge, but a continu'd Sayling by fantastick and uncertaine windes towards it" (8); "humor is the Drunckenesse of a Nation which no sleep can cure" (11); "Injustice . . . is the naturall scandall cast upon authority, and great force" (12); "the people . . . are never willing either to buy their peace or to pay for Warre" (12); "life" is that "for which the world was only made" (14); "Nature" is "the Vicegerent of God" (14); "Reason" is "the most profitable Talent God hath given us" (14); "Mony is the life blood of the People" (34); "Experience . . . is the best Art" (34); "intestine Quarrell is held more barbarous then forraign Warr" (35); "obedience . . . is the uttermost designe of governing" (35); "love of popularity . . . shewes the Minde, as meanly borne as bred" (36); "contriving the lastingnesse of Goverment . . . is the principall worke of Art" (40); "Religion . . . is our Art towards God" (42). These Bacon bits can nonetheless be viewed as more specifically Hobbesian. Remarking that "Davenant has a genial way of tossing out some of his most important precepts and definitions in parenthetical phrases," Winn observes how, "Rhetorically," this procedure creates the effect that the author "is merely reminding his reader of principles everyone accepts," though "in fact these are challenging assertions" (74). Similarly, Quentin Skinner notes of Hobbes's seemingly proverbial expressions that "The rhetorical approach to commonplaces is reversed in every case: rather than asking us to accept his arguments because they can be 'accommodated' to accepted beliefs, Hobbes asks us to endorse those beliefs because they can be shown to follow from his own arguments."[23] Ralph Ross conveys another dimension of this frequent recourse to apparent "commonplaces": "A rhetorical device that Hobbes often employs is a use of the language of a tradition, sometimes weighed down by scholarship about Greek and Latin words and roots, or ancient history, and then a sudden switch to what it all means in his own more hardheaded terms."[24]

But whereas Davenant's "challenging assertions" disguised as universal "principles" resemble Hobbes's "commonplaces . . . reversed," they often figure in a text so diffuse as to illustrate his point in *Leviathan* that

> without Steddinesse, and Direction to some End, a great Fancy is one kind of Madnesse; such as they have, that entring into any discourse, are snatched from their purpose, by every thing that comes in their thought, into so many, and so long digressions, and Parentheses, that they utterly lose themselves: Which kind of folly, I know no particular name for. (136)

Not always "long," Davenant's many "digressions" make "Parentheses" ubiquitous in both poem and preface: one *Gondibert*-parody consists mainly of bracketed content (281–83). There is nonetheless much else in Davenant's intended magnum opus, especially its prose, to show that he and Hobbes thought alike on many points during their collaboration.

IV: "huge Empire"

Gondibert's title-character pursues the same paradoxical mission as his dead sire—"To join all sever'd Pow'rs (which is to end / The cause of War) my Father onward fought"—because

> One Family the world was first design'd;
> And though some fighting Kings so sever'd are,
> That they must meet by help of Seas and winde,
> Yet when they fight 'tis but a civil warre. (II.viii, 40, 37)

In contrast, Hobbes aspired not "to end / The cause of War" but to banish internecine conflict by promoting a sovereign power capable of matching King Aribert, whose "Subjects" have become "safe from each other" because of his "Laws," according to Gondibert himself (III.iv, 21). Hating internecine conflict, Hobbes deemed wars among nations unavoidable: "Concerning the Offices of one Soveraign to another," *Leviathan* stipulates that "the Law of Nations, and the Law of Nature, is the same thing" (394). But whereas for Hobbes the anarchy prevailing in the state of nature could only be pointlessly violent, he supposed that individual nations' potential to engage in hostilities brought benefits. *Leviathan* thus explains how

> in all times, Kings, and Persons of Soveraigne authority, because of their Independency, are in continuall jealousies, and in the state and posture of Gladiators; having their weapons pointing, and their eyes fixed on one another; that is, their Forts, Garrisons, and Guns upon the Frontiers of their Kingdomes; and continuall Spyes upon their neighbours; which is a posture of War. But because they uphold thereby, the Industry of their Subjects; there does not follow from it, that misery, which accompanies the Liberty of particular men. (187–88)

As David Gauthier comments, "Hobbes would have approved our phrase *cold war*; it expresses well what he took to be the permanent relationship of nations."[25] Cold wars heating to the boiling point also had merit in Hobbes's eyes, as regulated by rough justice: greater powers would dominate lesser ones, by conquest or coerced alliance, but always to mutual advantage. *Leviathan* thus cites one notable instance where victors on the battlefield augmented their own triumph by ensuring that the losers did not come away empty-handed:

> the Romans when they had subdued many Nations, to make their Government digestible, were wont to take away that grievance, as much

as they thought necessary, by giving sometimes to whole Nations, and sometimes to Principall men of every Nation they conquered, not onely the Privileges, but also the name of Romans; and took many of them into the Senate, and Offices of charge, even in the Roman city.   .

Leviathan maintains that such an arrangement was what "our most wise King, King *James*, aymed at, in endeavouring the Union of his two Realms of *England* and *Scotland*. Which if he could have obtained, had in all likelihood prevented the Civill warres, which make both these Kingdomes at this present, miserable" (251). Though Gondibert's idealistic vision of a world-uniting war to end all wars looks wildly impractical from any standpoint, it therefore exceeds the scope of Hobbes's thinking about international relations only insofar as Hobbes restricted his optimism about what imperial power could accomplish, drawing examples from ancient history and "present" troubles, and otherwise proved too intent on establishing his case for guaranteeing peace within commonwealths to parse foreign-policy issues with any thoroughness.

Less idealistic than Gondibert and more focused than Hobbes on the merits of imperial expansion, Davenant not only advocated Prince Rupert's colonization of Madagascar but also created through his preface's remarks on land-grabbing a Leviathan of his own: "the largnesse is likewise as needfull, as the vastnesse of the Sea; For God ordain'd not huge Empire as proportionable to the Bodies, but to the Mindes of Men; and the Mindes of Men are more monstrous, and require more space for agitation and the hunting of others, then the Bodies of Whales" (31). Whether it reflects his acquaintance with *Leviathan*, fostered Hobbes's own imagination, or occurred as an independent development, Davenant's cetacean imagery also figures in his preface's observation of *"Leaders* of *Armys"* that "Sometimes with the Eye of Envy (which inlarges objects like a multiplying-glasse) they behold . . . *Statesmen*, and think them immense as *Whales*; the motion of whose vast bodys can in a peacefull calme trouble the Ocean till it boyle" (34, 35).

Likewise common to both authors as a possible case of reciprocal influence, and in this instance one where their thinking overlapped not only at the figurative level, is their bold but ill-informed perspective on the inhabitants of the New World. Davenant's preface justifies imperial expansion by noting how

he that beleevs men such moderate Sheep as that many are peacefully contain'd in a narrow Folde, may be better inform'd in *America*; where little Kings never injoy a harmlesse neighborhood, unlesse protected defensively amongst them selves, by an Emperour that hath wide possessions, and priority over them (as in some few places) but when restrained in narrow dominion, where no body commands and hinders their nature, they quarrell like Cocks in a Pitt; and the Sun in a days travaile there, sees more battailes (but not of consequence, because their Kings though many, are little) then in *Europe* in a Yeare. (31)

The parallel passage in *Leviathan* attempts to flesh out Hobbes's theoretical reconstruction of the universal anarchy prevailing in the state of nature: he acknowledges that

It may peradventure be thought, there was never such a time, nor condition of warre as this; and I believe it was never generally so, over all the world: but there are many places, where they live so now. For the savage people in many places of *America*, except the government of small Families, the concord whereof dependeth on naturall lust, have no government at all; and live at this day in that brutish manner, as I said before. (187)

A. P. Martinich censures Hobbes for showing no better understanding of Native Americans, especially given that his involvement with the Virginia Company placed him in good stead to know more about such matters than most of his contemporaries (*Hobbes*, 64). But Hobbes's complacent certitude also represents a loss of nerve, for his theory required no example beyond this extrapolation: "Howsoever, it may be perceived what manner of life there would be, where there were no common Power to feare; by the manner of life, which men that have formerly lived under a peacefull government, use to degenerate into, in a civill Warre" (187). In its repetition of "many places," too, Hobbes's writing is slack or devious: the multiple examples offer one illustration.

Though Davenant's views about *"America"* are equally unenlightened by today's standards, they also complement Hobbes's by bridging two concerns of his that never meet in his own work, at least so explicitly: the state of nature and the benefits of imperial expansion. Whereas Davenant's patronizing view of "little Kings" involves trivializing their "battailes" as "not of consequence," he stresses, too, how such figures suffer because they "never injoy a harmlesse neighborhood." Moreover, the inconsequential character of their conflicts matches Hobbes's emphasis that wars can be productive or not, with universal anarchy never entailing any benefits. If one of the "little Kings" could sufficiently dominate the others, his subjects would thereby leave the state of nature in acquiring "an Emperour" not arriving from abroad. Davenant's Native Americans thus occupy an intermediate stage between the state of nature and a truly "protected" community: "little Kings" have imposed a degree of rule, but within such "narrow dominion" that they need subjugation by "an Emperour that hath wide possessions" to move further away from an anarchy still highly prevalent, though no longer total.

In contrast, Davenant's preface merely echoes or agrees with Hobbes when disparaging "The passion of Historians . . . who in dispraise of evil Princes are often as unjust and excessive as the common People: for there was never any Monarch so cruell but he had living subjects, nor so avaritious but that his subjects were richer then himself" (8). Similarly, Davenant's preface explains how

> Obedience proceeds from ample consideration, of which knowledge consists; and knowledge will soone put into one Scale the weight of oppression, and in the other, the heavy burden which Disobedience lays on us in the effects of civill Warr: and then even Tyranny will seem much lighter, when the hand of supreme Power bindes up our Load, and lays it artfully on us, then Disobedience (the Parent of Confusion) when wee all load one an other; in which every one irregularly increases his fellows burden, to lessen his owne. (39)

In these instances, Davenant ponders much the same matters as Hobbes in much the same words; both authors failed to see how tenaciously their contemporaries would persist in regarding "Tyranny" as intolerable under any circumstances. The preface Hobbes added to the revised *De Cive* rejects category-muddling not regarded as his own: "How many Kings, themselves good men, have been killed because of the one error that a Tyrant King may be rightfully put to death by his subject?" (8).

V: "ranging of the mind"

As Davenant and Hobbes when collaborating thought alike about the superiority of "Obedience" to "Disobedience," and of "the hand of supreme Power" to "Confusion," regardless of whether it belongs to "a Tyrant King," so they thought alike about thinking itself. "*Witte,*" according to Davenant's preface, "is a Webb consisting of the subtlest threds, and like that of the *Spider* is considerately woven out of our selves; for a *Spider* may be said to consider, not only respecting his solemnesse, and tacite posture (like a grave Scowte in ambush for his Enemy) but because all things done, are either from consideration, or chance" (18). Davenant had no need to complicate his "Webb" metaphor and associated *"Spider"* simile with a more distant level of association ("grave Scowte") that adds little to an already evocative and self-explanatory image of a creature embodying "consideration" through its "solemnesse, and tacite posture." Perhaps he felt that "woven out of our selves" lacked force without the corollary point that arachnid activities resemble those of humans too. Equivalent to "knowledge" when "ample," according to Davenant's claims about "Obedience," the "consideration" practiced by his *"Spider"* parallels a trait *Leviathan* defines by false etymology as "a putting an end to the *Liberty* we had" and entailing this process:

> When in the mind of man, Appetites, and Aversions, Hopes, and Feares, concerning one and the same thing, arise alternately; and divers good and evill consequences of the doing, or omitting the thing propounded, come successively into our thoughts; so that sometimes we have an Appetite to it; sometimes an Aversion from it; sometimes Hope to be able to do it; sometimes Despaire, or Feare to attempt it; the whole summe of Desires, Aversions, Hopes and Fears, continued till the thing be either done, or thought impossible, is that we call DELIBERATION. (127, 126–27)

According to Hobbes, too, this trait "is no lesse in other living Creatures then in Man," though he offers no examples of how "Beasts also Deliberate," even in the absence of reason (127). Perhaps Hobbes had spent less time than Davenant in viewing creatures not only unfazed by powdered "Unicornes-horne" but also capable of a protracted "consideration."

Another of Davenant's definitions of *"Witte"* involves neither "Webb" nor *"Spider"* but assumes a highly "woven" texture including instead of "a grave Scowte" a more complex image drawn from a military context. According to his *Poem to the Earl of Orrery* (ca. 1650–57),

> Reason grown bold, because her strength she knows;
> Which, when with growth enlarg'd, more active grows;
> Which like a Ship of War, well ballasted,
> Does with her Ballasts weight augment her speed;
> Which does such quickness in her strength comprise,
> That she to action does together rise
> A standing Army and a running Force,
> As apt to move with Canon as with Horse;

Then in small strengths divides and marches far,
Where Northern Ignorance makes Winter-war;
Yet her Retreat bravely at last secures:
Reason, like this, is Wit; and such is yours. (341–52)

Gibbs parallels this passage with "Davenant's flexible definition of Wit in the Preface to *Gondibert*" (399), not as expressed in terms of "consideration," but as worded thus: "It is in Divines Humility, Exemplarinesse and Moderation; in Statesmen Gravity, Vigilance, Benigne Complaisancy, Secrecy, Patience, and Dispatch. In Leaders of Armys Valor, Painfulnesse, Temperance, Bounty, Dexterity in Punishing, and rewarding, and a sacred Certitude of promise" (18–19). The flexibility of Davenant's conception of "Wit" in *Poem* occurs within a narrower span, however, as focusing on the military role performed in Ireland by Roger Boyle, Baron Broghill and first earl of Orrery, and depends on the poet's own ingenuity for its cunning disposition of "threds," as fusing medium and message. Davenant himself resembles "a Ship of War, well ballasted": his metaphysical conceit derives "quickness" from the same cumbrous object to which he also imparts a paradoxical "speed" increased by "weight." Though the vessel in question is all the heavier as laden with troops, who are stationary only with respect to its deck, Davenant again turns lead into quicksilver with the further paradox of "A standing Army and a running Force." But the passage's rapidity also reflects the freedom of Davenant's associations (most obvious in three lines each beginning "Which"), offering an equivalent to *Leviathan*'s example of how even "wild ranging of the mind" can be readily followed:

> a man may oft-times perceive the way of it, and the dependance of one thought upon another. For in a Discourse of our present civill warre, what could seem more impertinent, than to ask (as one did) what was the value of a Roman Penny? Yet the Cohærence to me was manifest enough. For the Thought of the warre, introduced the Thought of the delivering up the King to his Enemies; The Thought of that, brought up the Thought of the delivering up of Christ; and that again the Thought of the 30 pence, which was the price of that treason: and thence easily followed that malicious question; and all this in a moment of time; for Thought is quick. (95)

Unable to resist a gibe at the Scots' virtual sale of Charles I (January 1647), albeit distanced as stemming from a "malicious question," and though he ruins a joke to explain it, Hobbes, too, shows how "Reason" when "enlarg'd" not less but "more active grows."

VI: "Arts delib'rate strength"

Davenant's *Poem* does not refer to the widely detested concept his contemporaries usually associated with the phrase "A standing Army"; but other passages in his work suggest he would have favored such an institution. Indeed, the same text praises Orrery for embodying a superior trait becoming seemingly more redundant as Davenant warms to his theme in explaining how

> Civility does those with softness gain
> Whom Armies else by rigour must restrain:
> Armies, whose civil strength prevents the wrongs
> Attempted by unarm'd uncivil Throngs:
> And thus as Pow'r does scatter'd strength collect
> And Arm, that it from Throngs may Pow'r protect,
> So should the People that form'd Force esteem,
> Since from their own fierce rage it rescues them. (257–64)

These words offer advance justification of the Peterloo massacre: the "Throngs" who "should" show gratitude to the "Armies" policing them are "uncivil" but also "unarm'd," thus requiring altogether less "rigour" to "restrain" them. The pro-military bias apparent here and often informing Davenant's work marks a major difference between his thinking and Hobbes's.

This contrast becomes most notable when *Gondibert* rules that "To conquer Tumult, Nature's sodain force, / War, Arts delib'rate strength, was first devis'd" (I.i, 4). Davenant's partiality to "A standing Army" with full policing capacity proves so strong that his creation myth omits to explain whose artistry curbed "Nature's sodain force" and by what authority such "Tumult" became illicit. Because he seeks to explain the origins of civil society, as Hobbes did, but does so in such a different manner, the two of them diverge more sharply on this topic than on any other. Though this comparison might seem rather unfair to Davenant, as linking the bedrock of Hobbes's entire political philosophy with a pair of lines incidental to the extant plot of an unfinished narrative, *Gondibert*'s preface assigns heroic poetry a scope equivalent to that of Hobbes's doctrine. Neither Davenant's conception of the military nor his ambitions as a poet brought him into overt conflict with Hobbes during their collaboration. But whereas Davenant and Hobbes tacitly agreed to differ over the source of "Arts delib'rate strength" and its relationship to "Nature's sodain force," they could only avoid competing in their respective fields of expertise by dancing around how substantially their aims overlapped.

VII: "Poet . . . Philosopher"

Hoping to produce a richer harvest than the "pleasant little volume of verse" that Gladish supposes "could be put together out of excerpts from *Gondibert*" (ix), Davenant in his preface credits Hobbes with having

> perform'd the just degrees of proceeding with Poets; who during the gayety and wantonnesse of the Muse, are but as children to Philosophers (though of some Giant race) whose first thoughts (wilde, and roaming farre off) must be brought home, watch'd, and interrogated, and after they are made more regular, be encourag'd and prais'd for doing well, that they may delight in ayming at perfection. By such a Method the Muse is taught to become Mistress of her owne, and others strength. (24)

Also humbly, Davenant rejected his own past efforts, taking "occasion to accuse, and condemne, as papers unworthy of light, all those hasty digestions of thought which were publish'd in my Youth; a sentence not pronounc'd out of melancholy rigour, but from a cheerfull obedience to the just authority of experience" (20–21). Older and wiser, Davenant was also now more ambitious for his work—a trait derided as pretentious in the doggerel of *Gondibert*'s detractors. But even as he thus made bold claims for a poet's potential scope, Davenant belittled himself too: as Gibbs notes, he cultivated throughout his career two competing personae, "the grave father and the facetious son" (xlvii). The epistle to Dorset could not be so "facetious" about "*Orpheus* useless Sons" if it did not adopt the characteristically "grave father" perspective that such trivia as contemporary poetry should never hamper a mature man's appropriate preoccupation with affairs of state. Insofar as the resourceful and incoherent Davenant had long been accustomed to working both ends of the spectrum, tensions were bound to inform any tidy recapitulation of his poetic career as a clear-cut victory where he renounces his "facetious" tendencies and denies having embodied "grave father" values other than those imported through his submission to Hobbes. Even in the predominantly self-mortifying scenario sending poets back to the classroom for remedial discipline and encouragement, Davenant cannot help adding the frame-jarring detail that they belong to "some Giant race"; moreover, their ultimate triumph will see "the Muse" established as "Mistress of" not only "her owne" but also "others strength" (a conspicuous relapse into "presumptuous glory").

With respect to Hobbes, however, Davenant was deferring to the authority of a "grave father" and usurping it too. Socially and intellectually close, they were standing on each other's turf, without apparently perceiving the risk of stepping on each other's toes. Whereas Sidney's *Defence of Poesy* (1595) rejects arguments promoting history or philosophy as superior to poetry and asserts the opposite view, Davenant's preface stakes the similar claim that "Poets are of all Moralists the most usefull" (41), but only addresses the potential for rivalry among different modes of discourse when digressively maintaining that Plato's exclusion of virtually all forms of literature from his ideal republic has been misunderstood (43). Davenant's chief concern is not poetry's standing among the arts but its role in running the state. Summarizing his main argument, Davenant claims that

> wee have first observ'd the Foure cheef aides of Goverment, (*Religion, Armes, Policy,* and *Law*) defectively apply'd, and then wee have found them weake by an emulous warr amongst themselves: it follows next, wee should introduce to strengthen those principall aides (still making the People our direct object) some collateral help; which I will safely presume to consist in Poesy. (37)

In short, *Gondibert* is Davenant's *Leviathan*.

Convesely, *The Answer* is Hobbes's preface to *Gondibert:* having the last word on all things literary, he also keeps Davenant's name more current than it otherwise would be, though there is no disentangling from either work of literary criticism which views authentically belong to which author. In brevity and clarity, *The Answer* reads as a tacit rebuke of Davenant's garrulousness; but it also sounds typical of its author. Moreover, the two texts only diverge explicitly when Hobbes objects to Davenant's remarks about old men's vanity and bitterness (19–20). In the last of his *Answer*'s rebuttals on this score, Hobbes admonishes Davenant, "you will be forced to change your opinion, hereafter when you are old; and in the meane time you discredit all I have sayd before in your commendation, because I am old already" (55). Hobbes furthermore stresses that the commonplace "old Age is a returne to childhood" had originally referred to "weaknesse of body" alone, but "was wrested to the weaknesse of minde, by froward children, weary of the controulment of their parents, masters, and other admonitors" (54). The remarks eliciting this response had been merely digressive, however; and Davenant had already made amends for his blunder before committing it, with his apposite humbling of all poets as giddy "children" eager to accept "controulment" from no "admonitors" but graybeard philosophers, they alone having the combined carrots and sticks necessary in leading their charges towards "perfection." This momentary disjuncture between *Gondobert*'s preface and Hobbes's *Answer* is thus amusingly irrelevant, especially because both texts concur on all important topics, including this one: "He therefore that undertakes an Heroique Poeme (which is to exhibit a venerable and amiable Image of Heroique vertue) must not onely be the Poet, to place and connect, but also the Philosopher, to furnish and square his matter" (50). These words (Hobbes's) betray no awareness of the fundamental oddity of a philosopher's taking over a poet's perspective, agreeing with him by dictating what he should do, and then congratulating him on having done it, thereby recommending a poem whose ambition extended to the adoption of political aims encompassed by his own life's work.

Stipulating what the author of a heroic poem must be and do, Hobbes reconciles poet and philosopher as coworkers in an architectural project. But in the non-figurative medium shared by poets and philosophers, division of labor typically corresponds to different or even rival approaches to language. Abjuring metaphor as a vehicle for philosophical writing, however, Hobbes often resorted to it, sometimes in the same breath: according to *Leviathan*, "The Light of humane minds is Perspicuous Words, but by exact definitions first snuffed, and purged from ambiguity," whereas "Metaphors, and senslesse and ambiguous words, are like *ignes fatui*" (116).[26] Whether Hobbes's well-known self-contradictions on this point reflect his own inconsistency or the inherently figurative character of language, they nonetheless pale in comparison with another and more all-encompassing aspect of his thinking about language that has attracted much less attention: his fundamentally incoherent conception of eloquence. He spent his entire career as a published author exposing abuses of rhetoric, but gave no clear idea of artful language's legitimate ends.[27]

VIII: "Reasons Ensignes"

The hostility toward speechmakers that Davenant expressed in his ode "To the King" remained a constant throughout his oeuvre. *Gondibert* comments that "Orators . . . sway / Assemblies, which since wilde, wilde Musick like," noting how "soon lov'd Eloquence does Throngs subdue; / The common Mistress to each private Minde; / Painted and dress'd to all, to no Man true" (III.v, 75; II.iv, 52). In his *Poem upon His Sacred Majestie's Most Happy Return to His Dominions* (1660),

Davenant similarly opines that "*Orators* (the Peoples *Witches*) may / Raise higher Tempests then their skill can lay," as in "Making a civil and staid *Senate* rude, / And stopless as a running multitude" (183–86). The role of such "skill" proves critical when his *Poem* addressed to Orrery attempts to distinguish between use and abuse of rhetoric: "What is judicious Eloquence to those / Whose Speech not up to others reason grows, / But climbs aloft to their own passions height," he ponders, marveling how "yet they think their Eloquence like that / By which you sodainly end long debate" (265–67, 279–80). To convey the supremacy of Orrery's speeches, Davenant draws on one of his own areas of expertise:

> Yours can all Turnes and Counter-turnings find
> To catch Opinion, as a Ship the winde;
> Which blowing cross, the Pilot backward steers,
> And shifting Sayles, makes way when he Laveers.
> As this is Eloquence so is it yours;
> Which in the Tongues fierce war, fled Truth secures;
> And when the Few would to the Many yeild
> Lifts Reasons Ensignes higher in the Field. (283–90)

Hobbes likewise inveighed against abuses of rhetoric, associated demagoguery with mob rule, and deemed "judicious Eloquence" better than any other kind; but on this last point, he also fell into "Turnes and Counter-turnings" where his navigational abilities to a surprising extent deserted him.

According to *Leviathan*, "Eloquence is power; because it is seeming Prudence" (151). The second half of this dictum restricts eloquence to that of political figures whose artful language permits them to deceive themselves and others by appearing wiser than they truly are. *Leviathan* clarifies the implications of Hobbes's succinct definition by distinguishing prudence from sapience (117); by noting that "A plain husband-man is more Prudent in affaires of his own house, then a Privy Counsellor in the affaires of another man" (138); and by explaining how

> Men that have a strong opinion of their own wisdome in matter of government, are disposed to Ambition. Because without publique Employment in counsell or magistracy, the honour of their wisdome is lost. And therefore Eloquent speakers are enclined to Ambition; for Eloquence seemeth wisedome, both to themselves and others. (164)

Convinced that eloquence "is seeming Prudence," Hobbes assumes that persons with "a strong opinion of their own wisdome," another kind of "seeming Prudence," are also "Eloquent speakers," which does not follow. He creates the vicious circle traced: politics disastrously attracts "Eloquent speakers"; but his own formulations offer no alternative outlet for eloquence itself.

Here Hobbes presents the obverse of his sweeping view of all members of parliament as self-conscious orators: a diminished sense of eloquence as the primary means of persons "enclined to Ambition" in no creditable way, but purely out of vanity. The second of these distortions in the scope of his statements nonetheless plays a more prominent role in his work because he equated political rhetoric with eloquence but also distinguished between them, an equivocation having major ramifications for his own approach to language. "Eloquence is power" haunts his entire political philosophy: he never wavered in his hostility toward those he judged abusers of rhetoric nor ceased aspiring to be eloquent himself. Fittingly, in *Leviathan*'s "Review, and Conclusion," he perplexingly admits that "There is nothing I distrust more than my Elocution; which neverthelesse I am confident (excepting the Mischances of the Presse) is not obscure" (726).

De Cive defines *"Eloquence"* as a faculty "whose end (as all the masters of Rhetoric point out) is not truth (except by accident) but victory," because "its task is not to teach but to persuade" (123). The same work later comments how "No one was more made for sedition than *Catiline*; he is portrayed in *Sallust* as having *adequate eloquence but little wisdom.*" In Hobbes's interpretation, such a verdict "separates *wisdom* from *eloquence*, attributing the latter to him as essential to a born rabble-rouser, denying him wisdom because wisdom dictates peace." The passage quoted at the beginning of this paragraph suggests Hobbes would approve Sallust's separation of powers. Instead, he now corrects him on this very point, because

> There are two kinds of *Eloquence*: one is a lucid and elegant exponent of thought and conceptions, which arises partly from observation of things and partly from an understanding of words taken in their proper meanings as defined. The other *eloquence* is an agitator of the passions (e.g. *hope, fear, anger, pity*), and arises out of a metaphorical use of words, adapted to the passions. The former fashions speech from true principles, the latter from received opinions of whatever kind. The art of the one is Logic, of the other Rhetoric. The end of one is truth, of the other victory. Both have their uses, the one in deliberation, the other in exhortation. For one is never separated from *wisdom*; the other almost always is. (139)

Thus, eloquence initially does not encompass "two kinds" and has but one "end"—"victory" (though "truth" might arise incidentally). In the correction of Sallust, however, "victory" and "truth" are the opposed goals of different forms of eloquence, "Both" of which "have their uses."

IX: "Civil Philosophy"

Including a pair of standard dichotomies, Hobbes's contrast between two sorts of eloquence looks familiar. His earliest readers would most likely have first encountered logic and rhetoric taught as separate subjects. Such readers would also have known that Plato had affirmed the superiority of the Socratic method as a vehicle for establishing truth and denounced sophists for their neglect of philosophy in merely teaching rhetorical stratagems capable of securing under certain circumstances an essentially empty victory. Leo Strauss maintains that Hobbes's indebtedness to Aristotle has been obscured by the vehemence of his hostility toward Aristotelianism but that he came to favor Plato most among the philosophers of classical antiquity. Strauss himself thinks that Hobbes was wrong in supposing Plato's philosophy superior to Aristotle's because of its reduced dependence on words (139–51). But if the nominalist Hobbes had already reached such a conclusion when writing *De Cive*, he might have interpreted Plato's own eloquence as based on "an understanding of words taken in their proper meanings as defined." Otherwise, the better of Hobbes's two sorts of eloquence in its entirety fits only his own philosophy; all else falls into the category of rhetoric.

But perhaps Hobbes was referring to eloquence in a political context alone; that his remarks had been prompted by Sallust's characterization of Catiline favors this unstated specification. Moreover, Hobbes in his "Epistle Dedicatory" for the English *De Corpore* (1656) would claim to have been an innovator, classifying "Civil Philosophy" as "no older (I say it provoked, and that my detractors may know how little they have wrought upon me) than my own book *De Cive*."[28] For Hobbes, "Civil Philosophy" encompassed the study of politics from a scientific perspective reflecting the methodology outlined in his description of the better of his two kinds of eloquence, which thus houses *De Cive* itself in microcosm. Though Hobbes on this reading again monopolizes the right sort of eloquence, he now classifies not all other discourse as rhetoric, but only rival approaches to an understanding of politics. He still adopts an extreme position, though not one more so than his sweeping claim that all members of parliament seek "to win a reputation" with "a long, continuous speech" rendered "as ornate and attractive as possible."

Whatever resemblance Hobbes might have discovered between Plato's philosophy and his own "words taken in their proper meanings as defined," the two thinkers obviously differ in other respects. For the purposes of this chapter, the most significant contrast involves a similarity. Whereas the poetic Plato banished virtually all poetry from his ideal state, the classicist Hobbes rued the legacy of antiquity as fomenting sedition: of the influence exerted by Aristotle, Cicero, and unnamed others, *Leviathan* maintains that

> by reading of these Greek, and Latine Authors, men from their child-hood have gotten a habit (under a false shew of Liberty,) of favouring tumults, and of licentious controlling the actions of their Soveraigns; and again of controlling those controllers, with the effusion of so much blood; as I think I may truly say, there was never any thing so deerly bought, as these Western parts have bought the learning of the Greek and Latine tongues. (267–68)

But if Hobbes could forget classical literature's considerable merit (and its role in inspiring the Ovidian turn "controlling those controllers"), his *Answer* sharpened his case against "Unskillful divines" with this contrast: "in the Heathen Poets, at least in those whose workes have lasted to the time wee are in, there are none of those indiscretions to be found, that tended to subversion, or disturbance of the Commonwealthes wherein they lived" (48–49). As for contemporary literature, Hobbes permitted poetry its own validity: he did not fear that it would promote "a false shew of Liberty." The only restrictions that his *Answer* imposes reflect his own principles as a literary critic (partly commonplace, partly idiosyncratic) and how his theoretical prescriptions chiefly concern heroic poems such as *Gondibert*. Beyond the realm of political discourse, he could countenance forms of eloquence given more to rhetoric than to logic, provided they met modest stipulations. But Davenant's preface forcefully brings *Gondibert* into that realm; and when Hobbes generously counters the poet's deference to philosophers' "controulment" by portraying both kinds of authors as coworkers in an architectural project, he weakly addresses an issue left open to question by his incoherent conception of eloquence—why philosophers' language rather than poets' best combats the "controlling" of those who should be "controllers."

X: "establishing, and destroying"

Franker than Hobbes in making "controulment" as central to their collaboration as to their shared political focus, Davenant was perhaps being simply more indiscreet. In an analogy distilling the complexity of his intellectual engagement with Hobbes, Davenant's preface assures him that

> when by the strict survay and Goverment that hath been had over this Poem, I shall think to governe the Reader (who though he be noble, may perhaps judge of supreme power like a very Commoner, and rather approve authority, when it is in many, then in one) I must acquaint him, that you had not alone the trouble of establishing, and destroying; but injoy'd your intervals and ease by Two Colleagues; Two that are worthy to follow you into the Closets of Princes. (24)

Davenant's parenthesis reveals how fully he shared Hobbes's animus against mixed monarchy and other forms of divided sovereignty. The context portrays Hobbes as a figuratively absolute ruler for his editorial influence on *Gondibert* (this blue-penciling implicitly likened to the "establishing" and "destroying" of states), but only to clarify the text's supervision by a triumvirate after all. Though Davenant did not "think to governe the Reader" until he had submitted to Hobbes's "Goverment," he aspired to rule his audience more than metaphorically, ousting his ostensible mentor as the self-authorizing authorizer of all authority.

As John Dewey notes, "Hobbes is in the somewhat paradoxical opinion of holding that while all order proceeds from the unquestioned authority of the sovereign, the permanent and settled institution of sovereignty itself depends upon a recognition of the scientific truths of morals and politics as set forth by him."[29] Similarly, Joseph Cropsey grasps that Hobbes

> did not solve perfectly the problem of who is to indoctrinate the indoctrinators, for at one and the same time he nominated the clergy to be the indoctrinators of the many and himself to be the indoctrinator of the clergy, while he instantly and violently alienated that order of men in ways and to a degree that the world knows well.[30]

As Martinich also observes, "Hobbes did not see the benefits of analytic geometry, and denigrated the advantage of symbolizing mathematical problems," for "he thinks of all geometrical entities as physical objects, and all except for a point are generated by motion."[31] Aside from ensuring that Hobbes's conception of mathematics had become outmoded during his lifetime, these limitations in his thinking about geometry would relate little to his methodology as a civil philosopher if his ideas here did not depend on the manipulation of "physical objects" as opposed to symbols, and thus require some pragmatic basis for their implementation: like Archimedes, he needed a place to stand before moving the world. *Gondibert* and its preface compound these problems of scope with the added complexity of Davenant's equivocal stance toward Hobbes's authority.[32]

XI: "Conquest . . . of Minds"

Whereas Hobbes in his philosophy of motion established God as the first mover, but scarcely addressed how his political philosophy might be positioned to sway a mass audience, Davenant repeatedly confronted pragmatic issues of staging and production, not least when circumventing the closing of the theaters to introduce the earliest English opera, *The Siege of Rhodes* (1656). As Edward Dent observes, "The play is divided into five acts, called 'entries' in order to avoid any word which suggested the theatre."[33] Though the two authors could not have been further apart on this dimension, Richard Kroll claims that Davenant's keen awareness of drama as a medium permitted him to continue his engagement with Hobbes once their collaboration on the *Gondibert* project had ended.

For Kroll, Davenant's work as a playwright "makes us aware of how all knowledge involves the kinds of perspectives that only the stage can, in materializing them, render uniquely three-dimensional."[34] In Kroll's view (318), a concern with "perspectives" lies at the heart of Davenant's collaboration with Hobbes, inasmuch as his preface to *Gondibert* "proceeds by constant allusions to an architectural image, which . . . connoted for him the three-dimensional nature of the dramatic stage, of which his own critical text is implicitly a model," and inasmuch as *The Answer* features "an extended deliberation . . . on perspectival machinery" in its conclusion:

> I beleeve (Sir) you have seene a curious kind of perspective, where, he that lookes through a short hollow pipe, upon a picture conteyning diverse figures, sees none of those that are there paynted, but some one person made up of their partes, conveighed to the eye by the artificiall cutting of a glasse. I find in my imagination an effect not unlike it from

your Poeme. The vertues you distribute there amongst so many noble Persons, represent (in the reading) the image but of one mans vertue to my fancy, which is your owne. (55)

Leviathan's engraved title-page would offer another example of "one person" likewise "made up of . . . partes"; and Dent points out that Davenant's *Siege* "was not called a play or even an opera, but 'A Representation by the Art of Prospective in Scenes and the Story sung in Recitative Musick' " (57). Kroll himself nonetheless cautions, "Although Hobbes . . . reconciles the competing perspectives of different characters in *Gondibert*, his selection of the perspectival image renders his scepticism patent" (318). But one lampoon in *Certain Verses* bears the title "An Essay in Explanation of Mr. *Hobbs*, where He Tels the Author, *The Vertues You Distribute*," suggesting that Hobbes (again mocked with Davenant) was not nearly "patent" enough in his "scepticism" on this score, at least from a jaundiced viewpoint (284). I have also urged that the chief significance of "an architectural image" in Hobbes's eyes lay in the opportunity it afforded him of evading the seemingly inevitable clash encouraged by the traditional tension between poets and philosophers and by the immediate circumstances of his collaboration with Davenant.

Moreover, Davenant's "constant allusions" engage in self-parody by recurring in an ill-proportioned framework defying all expectations of orderly design, even as it ceaselessly invokes them: his preface begins by describing itself as "this new Building," but then embarks on a circumnavigation of Homer as "the eminent Sea-marke, by which [poets] have in former ages steer'd," asserting that "he hath rather prov'd a Guide for those, whose satisfy'd witt will not venture beyond the track of others, then to them, who affect a new and remote way of thinking; who esteem it a deficiency and meanesse of minde, to stay and depend upon the authority of example" (3, square brackets added). Sharing Hobbes's contempt for "authority" tamely followed, Davenant might also have known that *Elements* defines "A MARK" as "a sensible object which a man erecteth voluntarily to himself, to the end to remember thereby somewhat past, when the same is objected to his sense again. As men that have passed by a rock at sea, set up some mark, whereby to remember their former danger, and avoid it."[35] But whether he invokes buildings or markers at sea, Davenant in his preface writes as one essentially hostile to stable structures and signs. Even so, his inability in this context to keep his own house in order does not mean that his stagecraft was likewise ramshackle; rather, his ill-disciplined prose hints what he gained as a dramatist, working within the physical constraints of a theater and for the finite patience of a live audience.

Kroll does not deny Davenant's "tendency to arrest narrative movement," though he might have styled it a compulsion; moreover, he restricts its contribution to "our modern difficulties with the episodic and emblematic tendencies of heroic drama" and with much of *Gondibert* itself ("so difficult to read," as a partial consequence). But Kroll also assigns merit to the instances of such clogging that he cites: "the activity of self-scrutiny . . . imports its own form of political allegory, not least because under that aegis, literature deliberates on its own exemplary force." In this portion of his argument, however, Kroll cannot create an intellectual pedigree for such "political allegory" without resorting to this loose connection: "It is no accident that Davenant and Hobbes were *personal* friends" (315, italics added). The suspicion remains that "imports" is the operative concept, with Hobbes herded into place, logically and syntactically. Having established Davenant's career-long preoccupation with "the relationship between the art of virtuous rule and the rhetorical devices that make it viable in an epistemologically and morally compromised world," Kroll credits him with

> the assumption that the theatre provided a particularly sensitive climate within which to discuss the question, since drama—more than any other genre, and like the polity imagined in Hobbes's *Leviathan*—forges a compromise among many competing points of view, a compromise that, in Hobbes, becomes the institution of the state, but in drama can range from the conventions of stage setting itself, to the second-order languages that characters use about their circumstances, to the resolutions demanded by the five-act structure of English plays. (311)

Kroll's argument invites much the same suspicion when he turns from Davenant's plays to *Gondibert*'s preface, claiming that "In preferring poetic indirection to force as a means of rule—Hobbes also defends the necessity of metaphor as a vehicle of knowledge—both Davenant and Hobbes comment on the substance of their arguments at a second-order level" (318).

I find Kroll no more persuasive when he awkwardly maintains that "Dryden's greatest plays . . . owe a fundamental debt to Davenant's theatrical politics, yet with a seriousness and coherence that only a great writer could have achieved," for those "politics" are attributed to Hobbes as well (322). Kroll furthermore attests that "theatrical history contributes substantially to seventeenth-century political theory, since, like Hobbes, what Davenant and Dryden brought as playwrights to their political commitments forced them—at a theoretical level—to treat all human institutions as conventional" (324). Again, the "like" component seems forced. Even if "political theory" and "theatrical history" achieved a productive cross-fertilization in early modern England, I doubt that Hobbes's doctrines made much of a contribution, because he did not write "as playwrights" do and Kroll himself almost spells out the folly of supposing otherwise: "Dryden's royalism, like Davenant's, his predecessor as poet laureate, is shot through with the recognition that monarchy must respect the epistemological compromises epitomized in the proscenium stage" (322). Insofar as this holds true, it underscores the gulf dividing both poet-dramatists from Hobbes, a theorist of absolute sovereign power who acknowledged no such "compromises" and never gave much thought to the issue of whether his own scope as a writer was restricted by some equivalently circumscribed space.

Both the best and worst evidence for Kroll's position is Davenant's *Poem to the Kings Most Sacred Majesty* (1663):

> Conquest of Realms compar'd to that of Minds,
> Shews but like mischief of outragious Winds;
> Making no use of force but to deface,
> Or tear the rooted from their native place.
> Who by distress at last are valiant made,
> And take their turn Invaders to invade.
> From Woods they march victorious back agen
> To Cities, the Wall'd-Parks of Hearded-men.
> Victors by conqu'ring Realms are not secure,
> Nor seem of any thing, but hatred, sure:
> A King who conquers Minds does so improve
> The Conquer'd that they still the Victor love. (81–92)

Here, Davenant diverges from Hobbes and from his own vision of imperial expansion by denying that "Conquest of Realms" can achieve "secure" results. As in his conception of "War" as "Arts delib'rate strength," Davenant disagrees with Hobbes by adopting some elements that went into Hobbes's account of the origins of civil society, but adapting them to another and less coherent scenario. What looks like a parallel explanation of how people escape the universal anarchy prevailing in the state of nature proves a biased interpretation of the Civil Wars as a rejection of "Invaders" by those whose temporary retreat into "Woods" terminates in an odd kind of triumph: their re-occupation of "Cities, the Wall'd-Parks of Hearded-men." These newly "valiant" heroes are thus tamed, as if savage rather than merely keen to protect "their native place"; and this domestication stems from their armed resistance to an oppressive yoke imposed from abroad.

Davenant struggles here because he wishes to do more than acclaim the Restoration as a benign form of "Conquest," a regime-change achieved with little bloodshed and characterized by clemency toward all but a handful of scapegoats from the prior administration: he seeks to give those "at last . . . valiant made" a more active role than they performed and to portray Charles II's return as a new phase of civilization, two impulses that collide in producing tardily courageous figures whose efforts are rewarded when they themselves become sheep. The striking paradox that they "march victorious" into the domain of "Hearded-men" gives no more insight into the details of how political order can be achieved than Davenant offers in explaining what "To conquer Tumult . . . / . . . was first devis'd." The only coherence in the passage as a whole is Davenant's tacit encouragement that Charles II maintain his throne on the same bloodless terms on which it was restored to him, with a rule based on "love" rather than "force." Though this theme implies a need for "compromises" from the King, "love" also requires a populace disposed toward affection. On this point, Davenant's post-Restoration attitude differs little from that expressed in his masques from before the Civil Wars, except that he now clearly separates "forc'd to it" and "taught" as means of commanding "obedience"—as perhaps he only could do because the new regime was still young enough to be enjoying a honeymoon phase.

That Davenant should make his masque-like claim in a poem both does and does not invalidate Kroll's argument. The nuts and bolts of stagecraft have no place in Davenant's chosen medium; but he also addresses "the art of virtuous rule" without any recourse to some equivalent of "the proscenium stage." Moreover, his *Poem* only involves plays in a separate and apparently unconnected passage where he hails "The *Theatre*" as "the Poets Magick-Glass" (371); patriotically enthuses that "the *Dramatick* Plots of *Greece*, and *Rome*, / Compar'd to ours, do from their height decline" (376–77); refers in some detail to such technicalities as "*thorow lights*" and "plain contrivance" when advancing this claim about the "refin'd" state of English stagecraft (383, 387, 389); but makes an essentially muted point about the relationship between the restored monarchy and drama:

> If to reform the publick Mirrour (where
> The Dead, to teach their living Race, appear)
> May to the People useful prove, even this

(Which but the object of your leisure is
To respite Care, and which successivlie
Three of our last wise Monarchs wish'd to see,
And in a Century could not be wrought)
You, in three years, have to perfection brought. (401–08)

Though Davenant manages to install the theater as a central concern for "Three" generations of rulers, he also reduces it to "but the object of" Charles II's "leisure" and founds its triumphant march toward contemporary "perfection" on a hypothetical scenario: a "reform" that "May to the People useful prove" has no certain value in itself or any necessary role in promoting "the art of virtuous rule," whether by "Conquest . . . of Minds" or through some other means.

XII: "Dreyden himselfe"

In rejecting Kroll's particular case for affinities between Hobbes's thinking and that of plays Davenant and Dryden wrote independently or jointly, I do not deny that the two poet-dramatists were sufficiently likeminded to collaborate or that Dryden in other ways found Hobbes a stimulating figure. On this last point, however, Anne Barbeau has to my mind ruled definitively:

> Although a number of critics have noted that Dryden echoes some of Hobbes' ideas in his plays, they have often taken absolute positions, arguing either that Dryden followed Hobbes or that he condemned him outright by placing his doctrine in the mouth of "villains." What is fairly certain is that Dryden admired Hobbes enough to consider his philosophy an important basis of argumentation in his plays. Without referring to Hobbes by name, he places recognizably Hobbesian ideas in the mouths of his characters, chiefly tyrants and rebels. These are not simply "villains" but brilliant politicians and lawbreakers who justify their behavior by a complicated *Weltanschauung*.[36]

These judicious words persuade by making Hobbes the rule rather than the exception in Dryden's intellectual life as one who rapidly absorbed and selectively adopted a wide range of theoretical and ideological stances, too independent to fall for long under the sway of any single creed and too responsive to neglect potential stimuli of many different kinds. Nonetheless, "absolute positions" have continued to flourish since Barbeau passed judgment. Robert Hume offers this pithy but simplistic formulation: "Dryden does use Hobbesian ideas extensively—to characterize his *villains*."[37] But an impulse to exaggerate in this way responds to equally "absolute positions" that have tended most commonly to overstate the opposite case, by assuming that "use" automatically entails endorsement, even though Aubrey gave no warrant for such an inference when recording "from Mr. Dreyden himselfe" that this "great admirer" of Hobbes's "oftentimes makes use of his doctrine in his playes" (1: 372). Complaining that Hobbes's "influence on . . . drama has repeatedly been discussed, yet discussed in very limited terms," Derek Hughes offers counter-examples, involving Dryden, confirming that limits and precision go together; I quote two in chapter five.[38] Beforehand, I discuss authors whose encomiums for *Gondibert* establish them as most likely Hobbes's blue-penciling "Colleagues."

Chapter Three

"Plain Magick": Hobbes and Cowley

I: "exorbitancy"

Hobbes's *Answer* to Davenant judges that "The languages of the *Greekes* and *Romanes* (by their Colonies and Conquests) have put off flesh and bloud, and are become immutable, which none of the moderne tongues are like to be."[1] Soon celebrating the arrival of English literature's golden age, his compatriots then accumulated "Colonies and Conquests" at a rate shaming "*Greekes* and *Romanes*." On another important dimension, however, Hobbes could see how Davenant's *Gondibert* had outmoded classical literature. In "dissenting onely from those that thinke the Beauty of a Poeme consisteth in the exorbitancy of the fiction," disparaging "impenetrable Armors, Inchanted Castles, invulnerable bodies, Iron men, flying Horses, and a thousand other such thinges, which are easily fayned by them that dare," Hobbes's *Answer* rules that

> as truth is the bound of Historicall, so the Resemblance of truth is the utmost limit of Poeticall Liberty. In old time amongst the Heathen such strange fictions, and Metamorphoses, were not so remote from the Articles of their faith, as they are now from ours, and therefore were not so unpleasant. Beyond the actual workes of nature a Poet may now go; but beyond the conceaved possibility of nature never.

Though Hobbes's position spares him from "assenting to those that condemne either *Homer* or *Virgil*," it rests on the conviction that "old time" is as "remote" as the ancients' "Articles of faith"; the present therefore has little use for "strange fictions" (51).

Hobbes ignores the Christian Middle Ages, which by his logic should not have been so besotted with such supernatural properties as "Inchanted Castles." Perhaps this apparent loophole in his reasoning sees him finding the gentlest way possible to register how a profound and quite recent shift in cultural sensibilities had rendered "strange fictions" absurd. Less tactfully, he could have maintained that the denizens of a more rational age scorned such fanciful effusions in a manner impossible for medieval authors, whose perspective was about as credulous as the ancients' appeared to be. Leaving the Middle Ages out of account, Hobbes could avoid ranking the era of classical antiquity below one likewise prone to "exorbitancy," but at least free of pagan superstition. From this standpoint, his faith-based argument rationalizes a straightforward aesthetic response ("unpleasant") whose implications disturbed him, because it seemingly allied him with "those that condemne either *Homer* or *Virgil*." In any case, his professed Christianity did not make him so hostile to "strange fictions"; his attitude reflected his more advanced understanding of "the actuall workes of nature," and hence his more restricted appraisal of "conceaved possibility," based on scientific knowledge that neither antiquity nor the Middle Ages had possessed so amply. But this conclusion does not mean that Hobbes alone appraised *Gondibert*'s value in these terms; when Davenant's fellow poets found merit in his heroic poem, they concurred about its diminished "exorbitancy."

II: "some worthy *Knight*"

In writing "To Sir William Davenant, upon His Two First Books of 'Gondibert' " (1650), Waller claims that this unfinished work houses

> Such truth in love as the antique world did know,
> In such a style as courts may boast of now;
> Which no bold tales of gods or monsters swell,
> But human passions, such as with us dwell.[2]

In writing "To Sir *William Davenant*, upon his Two First Books of *Gondibert*, Finished Before His Voyage to *America*" (1650), Cowley similarly opines that

> Methinks *Heroick Poesie* till now
> Like some fantastick *Fairy Land* did show,
> *Gods, Devils, Nymphs, Witches* and *Gyants race*,
> And all but *Man* in *Mans chief work* had place.
> Thou like some worthy *Knight* with sacred Arms
> Dost drive the *Monsters* thence, and end the *Charms*.
> Instead of those dost *Men* and *Manners* plant,
> The things with that rich *Soil* did chiefly want.[3]

Though Henry Vaughan did not join Waller and Cowley by publishing his encomium with the object of its praise, he, too, extolled diminished "exorbitancy" when writing "To Sir William Davenant, upon his *Gondibert*" (1651):

> where before *heroic poems* were
> Made up of *spirits, prodigies*, and fear,
> And showed (through all the *melancholy flight*,)
> Like some dark region overcast with night,
> As if the poet had been quite dismayed,
> While only *giants* and *enchantments* swayed,
> Thou like the *Sun*, whose eye brooks no disguise
> Hast chased them hence.[4]

Whereas Waller's rhetoric sweeps out the old to usher in the new and Vaughan's toasts an enlightenment freeing "the poet" from being "dismayed" by his own subject matter, Cowley's so regretfully lingers over the very *"Charms"* whose banishment he reports that he attributes the anti-Spenserian accomplishment of purging *"Fairy Land"* to the quintessentially Spenserian figure of "some worthy *Knight* with sacred Arms."

Even as he developed connections with authors whose theory or practice prohibited *"Charms"* and the rhetoric traditionally accompanying them, or whose own mode of discourse allowed no room for *"Fairy Land"* except as a term of abuse, Cowley habitually reverted to "fantastick" language. The same tendency briefly emerges in Davenant's case when his preface to *Gondibert* cannot help adding the frame-jarring parenthesis "(though of some Giant race)" to his observation that "Poets . . . are but as children to Philosophers" (24); but Cowley cannot eliminate such creatures as *"Gyants race"* without re-importing them at the same time. As Davenant repeatedly swung between poles identified by A. M. Gibbs ("the grave father and the facetious son"), so Cowley acknowledged the benefits of sobriety without ever mastering his addiction to "exorbitancy."[5]

III: *"Gigantique Sence"*

David Trotter sees only one side of this Spenserian anti-Spenserianism when he claims of an "intellectual revolution" in seventeenth-century England (whereby "propositional truth" displaced "locutionary truth") that "this historical process left its mark more plainly on the poetry of Abraham Cowley than on the work of any other contemporary writer."[6] In Trotter's definitions, based on *Leviathan*, "propositional truth" involves "arguments taken from 'the thing itself, or from the principles of natural reason,' " whereas "locutionary truth" involves "arguments taken from 'the authority, and good opinion we have, of him that hath said it' " (4).[7] At one point, Trotter attributes the "revolution" in question to a meeting of minds: "During the 1640s Cowley, Hobbes and Davenant came to agree that myth ought no longer to be considered suitable subject-matter for poetry," in "a resolution which coincided with the emergence in the work of Hobbes of the alternative criterion of propositional truth" (57). More frequently, however, Trotter ignores Davenant in focusing on Cowley and links between his thinking and Hobbes's. Trotter does not make the mistake of simply repeating Arthur Nethercot's absurd claim that "Hobbes's general philosophical position . . . seems to have accorded with what young Cowley had been working out gradually by himself."[8] But at least part of Trotter's greater circumspection stems from phrasing his way around chronological difficulties, paucity of evidence, and obvious objections. Cowley's encomium for *Gondibert* dates from just after rather than "During the 1640s" and expresses a state of mind not so decisive as to purge his poetry of "exorbitancy" even then. Moreover, Cowley's poem responds to a collaboration between Davenant and Hobbes, not one between Hobbes and himself. As the phrases "coincided with" and "accorded with" equally concede, no record survives of any interchanges between Cowley and Hobbes before, during, or after their period of common exile (1644–52), though Aubrey placed them together "At Paris" as if they were then acquainted, without supplying any corroborating detail.[9]

A standing temptation to exaggerate the extent of Cowley's affinities with Hobbes nonetheless exists because Cowley included among his *Pindaric Odes* (1656) one addressed "To Mr. *Hobs*." But this poem only affords evidence of itself. Aside from acclaiming Hobbes for having dealt Aristotelianism a mortal blow (second strophe), it merely specifies that his achievement was novel and of colossal import—such that he seems to belong to *"Gyants race."* The advance marked by his thought thus displaced "Vast *Bodies*" of now outmoded wisdom, just as he, the "great *Columbus* of the *Golden Lands* of *new Philosophies*," exploring "the vast *Ocean*," required a "vast . . . *store*" of *"Eloquence"* for the expression of his *"Gigantique Sence"* (188, 189). John Laird queries the accuracy of such boundless "exorbitancy," commenting that Cowley

compared Hobbes to Columbus, but would have written more aptly had he said: "Thou great *Magellan* of the golden lands of new philosophies." The Columbus of the science of motion (if there was only one) was Galileo, not Hobbes; but Hobbes, in a greater degree than even

Descartes, should be called the first philosophical *circumnavigator* of the "new" intellectual globe.[10]

Laird also takes issue with these lines Cowley addressed to Hobbes:

The *Baltique, Euxin,* and the *Caspian,*
And slender-limb'ed *Mediterrean,*
Seem narrow *Creeks* to *Thee,* and only fit
For the poor wretched *Fisher-boats* of *Wit.* (189)

According to Laird, Cowley "was wrong" because "Hobbes saw all these seas (all except the Caspian) not simply as narrow creeks but essentially as parts of the unity of the oceans, and as the more intelligible because the oceans themselves had been explored" (v–vi). In Cowley's defense, such objections might be regarded as pedantic; but they do underscore the degree to which his response to Hobbes amounts to little more than riffing on *Leviathan*'s title, one thing he does seem to have had clearly in mind.

Doubling the significance of Cowley's ode to Hobbes, Trotter classifies its Pindarism as Hobbesian in its own right. Regarding Cowley's Pindaric ode "The Muse," Trotter observes that its author "had previously conceived the function of poetry in terms of the ceremonial role played by the poet," but "now wants to establish what kind of proposition a poem is, and ends up virtually identifying poetry with 'propositional truth' ": therefore it is no "coincidence" that "The next ode in the collection . . . offers an account of the intellectual achievement of Thomas Hobbes" (127). Trotter does not hesitate to associate freely here: this type of thinking plays a key role in his argument that Cowley's "Pindarism . . . made it possible to meet Hobbes on his own ground" (133). The paradigm is not now coincidence or non-coincidence but parity: Trotter maintains that "Cowley's interest in Pindar's inconstancy of argument is . . . equivalent to Hobbes's interest in discursion," his "theory of the association of ideas" (117, 116). Trotter thus derives an entire aesthetic, based on "difficulty and lack of connection," from "the equivalence between Cowley's version of the Pindaric ode and the radical psychology developed by Thomas Hobbes" (115). But Hobbes's *Answer* had eschewed such "difficulty," taking exception to

the ambitious obscurity of expressing more then is perfectly conceaved; or perfect conception in fewer words then it requires. Which Expressions, though they have had the honor to be called strong lines, are in deed no better then Riddles, and not onely to the Reader, but also (after a little time) to the Writer himselfe darke and troublesome. (52)

Moreover, *Leviathan*'s example of free association (quoted in chapter two) stresses the ease with which interpreters can deduce an underlying logic.

Trotter nonetheless makes a valid point in emphasizing how "Cowley was virtually alone among his contemporaries in celebrating, without qualification, the scope of Hobbes's achievement" (128). But Norberto Bobbio exaggerates when observing that "Hobbes had many enemies: at least in public, he had only enemies."[11] Moreover, not Cowley in his ode but Davenant in his preface to *Gondibert* managed "celebrating, without qualification," in the rather more specific form of acclaiming Hobbes as a *"circumnavigator"* of sorts: "you move not by common Mapps, but have painfully made your owne Prospect; and travaile now like the Sun, not to informe your selfe, but enlighten the World" (24). These words are as *"Gigantique"* in conception as Cowley's, as well as incoherent (if not self-consciously witty) for lauding a beacon of enlightenment with imagery drawn from pre-Copernican cosmology; but they strike me as more suggestive in a smaller span than "To Mr. *Hobs*" in its entirety. With additional room at his disposal, Cowley would have improved his ode by introducing some measure of "qualification"; making Hobbes's accomplishments less timeless and more finite would have reduced them, but from entirely mythic proportions to a chastened and not so vague "exorbitancy." Cowley's ahistorical Hobbes demonstrates how "To things *Immortal Time* can do no wrong" (190): his work floats free of any context.

IV: "Even to the *enemies* sight"

" 'Tis onely *God* can know / Whether the fair *Idea* thou dost show / Agree intirely with his *own* or no," Cowley's ode assures Hobbes, adding that "This I dare boldly tell, / 'Tis so *like Truth* 'twill serve our turn as well" (188). As a response to those accusing Hobbes of atheism, these lines would have a droll wit, and their estimate of his philosophy as a necessary fiction would possess great interest; but as comments engaging with no contemporary disputes, they merely shrug off controversy, thus failing to declare anything "boldly."

Cowley does not wholly ignore Hobbes's legion detractors; they experience his "solid *Reason*" as "A *shield* that gives delight / Even to the *enemies* sight, / Then when they're sure to *lose* the *Combat by't*" (190). This imagery derives from the arming of Aeneas in advance of his triumph over Turnus—a foregone conclusion, but not so easy a victory as to lack drama. Cowley explains and justifies his allusion in a note citing and commenting on several passages from Virgil's *Aeneid*, but only identifies Hobbes's *"enemies"* and their response to his novel and colossal contributions insofar as he here invokes "the case of mens arguing against *Solid*, and that is, *Divine Reason*; for when their argumentation is broken, they are forced to save themselves by flight, that is, by *evasions*, and seeking still new ground" (191). Moreover, meaningful *"Combat"* cannot occur when Hobbes meets no adversaries save inadvertent devotees flinging themselves under his unstoppable Juggernaut. Samuel Mintz makes a point different from and superior to Cowley's in commenting that "Hobbes's impact was subtle: he provoked intense hostility, but he also obliged his critics to employ his own method of rational argument. Their absorption of his method while they resisted his ideas is an extremely interesting feature of seventeenth-century rationalism."[12]

Quentin Skinner glosses Cowley's allusion to Virgil with "The shield of Hobbes's reasoning not only protects his philosophy against its enemies; like the armour of Demoleos in the *Aeneid*, it shines with so much brilliance as to be *decus et tutamen*, a thing of beauty as well as a means of defence."[13] For Skinner, this interpretation of the conclusion of Cowley's fifth strophe warrants the generalization that the whole poem "is striking not merely for its tone of extreme veneration, but for the emphasis it places on Hobbes's specifically literary talents and achievements" (234). Aside from ransacking his thesaurus for expressions of bigness, however, Cowley has little to say about Hobbes's "talents and achievements," "literary" or otherwise, especially in comparison with the verdict rendered by Mulgrave.

V: "huge extremes"

According to Mulgrave's poem "On Mr. Hobbes, and His Writings" (ca. 1680),

> In other authors, though the thought be good,
> 'Tis not sometimes so easily understood;
> That jewel oft' unpolish'd has remain'd;
> Some words should be left out, and some explain'd;
> So that in search of sense, we either stray,
> Or else grow weary in so rough a way.
> But here sweet eloquence does always smile,
> In such a choice, yet unaffected style,
> As must both knowledge, and delight impart,

> The force of reason, with the flowers of art;
> Clear as a beautiful transparent skin,
> Which never hides the blood, yet holds it in:
> Like a delicious stream it ever ran,
> As smooth as woman, but as strong as man.[14]

Mulgrave's words prove too specific in producing a sausage-like "skin" filled with "blood"; and "holds it in" is merely the worst example of his prosaic turn of phrase. But "On Mr. Hobbes" remains significant for linking its subject's "sweet eloquence" with the stylistic values upheld by English neoclassicism, likewise devoted to an ideal synthesis of such dichotomous concepts as "force" and "flowers," "smooth" and "strong." Pope's *Essay on Criticism* (ca. 1709) would show and tell how neoclassical distichs should be written, generating "the *Easie Vigour* of a Line, / Where *Denham*'s Strength, and *Waller*'s Sweetness join."[15]

Waller himself had nonetheless pioneered the aesthetic in question, even if Pope subsequently judged insufficient the example set by this author's poem "Of His Majesty's Receiving the News of the Duke of Buckingham's Death" (ca. 1628), which praises Charles I because "Such huge extremes inhabit thy great mind, / Godlike, unmoved, and yet, like woman, kind!" (1: 33–34). Moreover, Waller's eventual complementer Sir John Denham had depicted the perfecting of English poetry as a gradual process culminating in the work of the figure mourned by his elegy "On Mr. Abraham Cowley His Death and Burial amongst the Ancient Poets" (ca. 1667). Here, too, Denham finds reconciled "huge extremes" when lauding Cowley's writing in a language other than his native tongue:

> His English stream so pure did flow,
> As all that saw, and tasted, know.
> But for his Latin vein, so clear,
> Strong, full, and high it doth appear,
> That were immortal *Virgil* here,
> Him, for his judge, he would not fear.[16]

Though Denham does not dwell on these ramifications, his narrative of progress concludes by returning to square one and must reflect a pessimism much like Hobbes's about "moderne tongues" and their inability to "become immutable." Other accounts of England's literary history as a progressive refinement toward a neoclassical ideal celebrated how English poets could write like those of Augustan Rome without having to adopt their language, except indirectly.

Mulgrave's verses about Hobbes's "sweet eloquence" counter any pessimism about "moderne tongues" by extending the secure accomplishment of English neoclassicism to encompass his prose as well.

VI: "too *Poetical*"

For Denham a Virgilian author of Latin, Cowley himself aspired to be the English Pindar, but worried that such a departure from the trend toward "*Easie Vigour*" would be held against him. He attempted to forestall criticism by scrupulously explaining in appended notes every swerve occasioned by his seemingly erratic course. Such annotation further undermines his capacity to "dare boldly tell," concerning Hobbes's achievements or any other subject. Wishing to dazzle his audience with such sublime effects as the dizzyingly abrupt transitions characteristic of his Pindarism, he fatally compromised their audacity by making their logic fully apparent so that he would not appear mad. In lieu of chastened "exorbitancy," he anchored his flights of fancy with feet of clay. Laden with such baggage, "Dírcë's / Swan" himself could never have left the ground.[17]

Cowley's ambivalence about the scope of his own rhetoric emerges clearly from one of the notes for his ode to Hobbes. Referring to a passage in the poem's final strophe, its author explains that "The Description of the Neighbourhood of *Fire* and *Snow* upon *Ætna* (but not the application of it) is imitated out of *Claud. L. I. De Raptu Pros.*" (191). Cowley raises the possibility that Claudian in his poem about the rape of Proserpina proves guilty "somewhat of that which *Seneca* objects to *Ovid, Nescivit quod benè cessit relinquere*. When he met with a *Phansie* that pleased him, he could not find it in his heart to quit, or ever to have done with it" (192). These words, in turn, suggest that Cowley's "application" exhibits a similar lack of restraint. Proof that it does not comes from a passage comparable to Claudian's, but more obviously guilty of poor taste: "*Tacitus* has the like expression of *Mount Libanus, Præcipuum montium Libanum, mirum dictu, tantos inter ardores opacum, fidúmq; nivibus.* Shady among such great heats, and *faithful* to the *Snow*; which is too *Poetical* for the Prose even of a *Romance*, much more of an *Historian*" (192). Cowley thus raises but leaves unresolved the issue of what constitutes excess: phrasing too florid "even" for "a *Romance*" finds a place in his own ode (see below). Neither naming Cowley not acknowledging any resemblance between his own remarks and Seneca's objection to Ovid, Dryden in his preface to *Fables Ancient and Modern* (1700) instances a literary figure "sunk in his Reputation, because he cou'd never forgive any Conceit which came in his way; but swept like a Drag-net, great and small"; this verdict obviously applies to a recent predecessor who "could not find it in his heart to quit" what he fitfully knew how to resist.[18]

Alluding to how "*Contraries* on *Ætna*'s top conspire, / Here hoary *Frosts*, and by them breaks out *Fire*," Cowley contrasts Hobbes's "cold *Age*," apparent in the *"Snow"* covering his "reverend Head," with how he "fully still dost . . . / Enjoy the *Manhood*, and the *Bloom* of *Wit*" (190). Julia Griffin annotates these lines in part by remarking that "Hobbes had protested with spirit against despising the old at the end of his exchange with Davenant."[19] By implication, Cowley resists Davenant's error. But Cowley made a mistake of his own when presenting the continuing intellectual vigor of an old man as a miracle of nature rather than the mundane phenomenon that Hobbes himself took it to be in supposing that clever people could keep or even improve their wits with age.

Moreover, Cowley so disregards the terms on which Hobbes claimed to be an innovator (in pioneering civil philosophy) that he here passes up his easiest opportunity to relate Hobbes's work to its topical context. Britain's recent conflicts remain hovering in the wings when Cowley develops his Etna-based "huge extremes" by observing (via the "too *Poetical*" Tacitus) that "A secure *peace* the *faithful Neighbors* keep," because "Th'emboldned *Snow* next to the *Flame* does *sleep*" (190). A. B. Chambers notes that "*Contraries* . . . conspire" must invoke the Latin *conspiro*, meaning " 'breathe with' and hence 'join together,' " but questions whether Cowley "can succeed in blocking the unfavorable English sense of 'conspiracy' despite the seeming impropriety."[20] For Cowley's earliest readers, however, the Latin root would have been at least as salient as "the unfavorable English sense," which aside from its "seeming impropriety" receives no corroboration elsewhere in the ode. Indeed, the poem's notable shortage of political overtones undermines Nethercot's speculation that Cowley wrote it shortly before its publication, "while he was in prison and desirous of showing his admiration for and agreement with a great person who was also in high favour with Cromwell and his party" (150). Most discussions of Hobbes's standing during the Interregnum stress that he was left alone to pursue his studies and only embraced by the Protector in reports hostile to both of them. Furthermore, the ode's uncertain date of composition does not prohibit the view encouraged by all of its content: that it belongs to a period when Cowley's ambitions as a political poet had been disappointed and he was looking for different kinds of heroes to extol.

VII: "the late troubles"

As Davenant in *Gondibert* produced another *Leviathan*, so Cowley paralleled both *Gondibert* and *Behemoth* with his unfinished epic *The Civil War* (ca. 1643). But whereas Hobbes composed his own partisan history of that period with the benefit of hindsight, Cowley attempted a heroic narrative based on events unfolding as he wrote; and whereas Davenant's voyage to Maryland and subsequent imprisonment broke the momentum of a work possibly unsustainable in any case, *The Civil War* foundered because reality refused to conform to its expectations of a swift royalist victory, killing in the same instant Lucius Cary, second Viscount Falkland, and a plot assigning him a more triumphant role than martyr. Though Cowley's unfinished epic narrates a tragedy occasioned by the judicial murder of Strafford and in other respects also speaks the vocabulary of what Robert Ashton terms "Cavalierism red in tooth and claw," any resemblance to Hobbes's political philosophy is superficial; and such rhetoric probably reflects how the author was steeped in and consciously adding to propaganda issuing from the wartime royalist headquarters at Oxford.[21] Here and there, too, Cowley embraces the more moderate language of constitutional or mixed-monarchy royalism—anathema to Hobbes, but central to Falkland's own political vision.[22]

Whereas *The Civil War* continued the roundhead-bashing tradition begun by Cowley's play *The Guardian* (1642) and verse-satire *The Puritan and the Papist* (1643), subsequent years saw him transplanted to France and working as a royalist cryptographer and personal secretary to Jermyn. Because Cowley's removal from England had been voluntary, his return could be so too. But his movement in both directions seems to have been at Jermyn's behest. Apparently expected to serve as a spy on re-crossing the Channel, Cowley was a sufficiently high-profile royalist to be imprisoned almost immediately (1656). Inevitably shadowy because of the secrecy it often involved, his conduct at this juncture would now require cryptographical talents greater than his own for its decipherment. Raymond Anselment suggests that Cowley's "submission to divine will" during the Interregnum has been mistakenly interpreted as evidence of his "apostasy" and "support of Cromwell's rule."[23] The only certainties, however, are that Cowley's published works express ambivalence about Cromwell and his own political past, and that something he did before the Restoration—obviously not, *pace* Nethercot, the printing of an ode in Hobbes's praise—cost him the good opinion of Charles II, who was often swift to forgive, but in this matter never thawed. In the final years of his life, therefore, Cowley had few options besides "submission to divine will."

To conclude that the Civil Wars ended with the defeat of the royalist cause and Cowley's highest ambitions as a poet would be too simple. According to the preface he wrote for his collection *Poems* (1656), he by then had recognized the value of burying his hatchet: "I have cast away all such pieces as I wrote during the time of the late troubles, with any relation to the differences that caused them" (9). But he also frustrated his hopes of making a fresh start by the very terms in which he chose to explain the failure of his partisan political muse: "a warlike, various, and a tragical age is best to *write of*, but worst to *write in*" (7). By this logic, an age peaceful, uniform, and happy would have been as frustrating for any poet aspiring to accommodate milieu and métier. As Cowley understood, however, he was not obliged to write of the age in which he wrote. In a frugal exception to his self-imposed determination to "cast away" the likes of his *Civil War*, he cannibalized some of that poem's content for his biblical epic *Davideis* (1656).[24]

VIII: "a *Tyrant* is the *Thing*"

But this too would remain incomplete, a *Gondibert*-equivalent redux, as Cowley already knew when he published it, having composed just four of its projected twelve books. He acknowledged in his preface to *Poems*, "I have had neither *Leisure* hitherto, nor have *Appetite* at present to finish the work, or so much as to revise that part which is done with that care which I resolved to bestow upon it, and which the *Dignity* of the *Matter* well deserves" (12). Even though Cowley personally had failed, he insisted that biblical epic had great potential and now contented himself with passing the baton for that mission's fulfillment: "I shall be ambitious of no other fruit from this weak and imperfect attempt of mine, but the opening of a way to the courage and industry of some other persons, who may be better able to perform it throughly and successfully" (14). If Cowley invites ridicule for setting such store by a project that had defeated his own best efforts, he also anticipates a familiar modern type: poets who outlive their own creativity and turn to prescriptive criticism. Moreover, his instincts were sound: whereas Milton had no need of such prompting, his *Paradise Lost* (1667), appearing within months of Cowley's death, handsomely vindicated that predecessor's glimpse of what biblical epic might be. *Davideis* itself had realized some of that potential, at least insofar as its scope permitted Cowley to transcend the innate rhetorical disadvantages crippling his *Civil War*.

Though the revamped epic rehearsed historical events, these were not unfolding as Cowley wrote; they belonged to a completed sequence whose scriptural narration offered less room for embellishment than Milton would find in Genesis, but still furnished opportunities to expand considerably on details of description and characterization. In covering Old Testament history, too, Cowley could continue addressing the political issues that had so wholly preoccupied himself and his compatriots during the preceding decade and a half, without feeling any pressure to adopt a party line; he could reap all the advantages of writing at a distance, without sacrificing broad relevance. Here the comparison with Milton's finished epic is hard to make: commentators differ as to if and how *Paradise Lost* relates to the Civil Wars. More obviously than Genesis, the portion of scripture that Cowley took for his source lent itself to contemporary applicability, without forcing his hand in any one direction, as the debate over kingship in *Davideis'* Book 4 well illustrates by giving its author an opportunity to reference Hobbes's views on this score.

In Cowley's dramatic reconstruction of scripture, David narrates the whole topic of "the reasons of the *Change* of *Government* in *Israel*" and "how *Saul* came to the *Crown*" in "discourse with" and at the request of King Moab, his host (364). Though David thus recounts a very extensive period of history, Cowley cleverly makes Moab a patient but involved listener whose pertinent questions and comments vary and clarify the narrative without upstaging the main speaker. A good example of this dramatic approach occurs when David describes how Samuel, then the Israelites' sole ruler in his capacity as Judge, reluctantly accedes to their clamoring for a monarch. "You're sure the first . . . / Of *freeborn* men that begg'd for *Slavery*," Samuel mordantly observes, elaborating,

> I fear, my friends, with heav'enly *Manna* fed,
> (Our old forefathers crime) we lust for *Bread*.
> Long since by God from *Bondage* drawn, I fear,
> We build anew th' *Egyptian Brickiln* here.
> Cheat not your selves with *words*: for though a *King*
> Be the mild Name, a *Tyrant* is the *Thing*.
> Let his power loose, and you shall quickly see
> How mild a thing *unbounded Man* will be. (371)

Samuel's speech continues in this vein for another score of lines, at which point Moab "interrupts," as no longer able to hold back from remarking that

> The good old *Seer* 'gainst *Kings* was too severe.
> 'Tis *Jest* to tell a *People* that they're *Free*,
> *Who*, or *How many* shall their *Masters* be
> Is the sole doubt; *Laws guid*, but cannot *reign*;
> And though they *bind* not Kings, yet they *restrain*.
> I dare affirm (so much I trust their *Love*)
> That no one *Moabite* would his speech approve. (371–72)

Even as a king speaking up for kings, however, Moab recognizes that he should not blame the teller for his tale and politely bids him continue: "But, pray go on" (372). As tactful, David agrees (" 'Tis true, Sir, he replies"), while also excusing Samuel: "Yet men whom age and action renders wise, / So much great changes fear, that they believe / All evils *will*, which *may* from them arrive" (372). Thus summarized, Cowley's narrative presents a genuine debate featuring diverse opinions urged with equal vigor.

David's words about old men who "great changes fear" could be understood as pertaining to Hobbes, except that the politics would have to be reversed: his perhaps excessive anxiety that *"may"* would certainly prove *"will"* focused on "evils" permitted by the absence of a sufficiently sovereign power. In the second of his *Two Treatises of Government* (1690), Locke would rebuke Hobbes (though not by name) on precisely the grounds that he had exaggerated the perils of primal anarchy while minimizing the potential destructiveness of unchecked sovereign power: "This is to think that Men are so foolish that they take care to avoid what Mischiefs may be done them by *Pole-Cats*, or *Foxes*, but are content, nay think it Safety, to be devoured by *Lions*."[25] Conversely, Moab's sardonic response to Samuel's *"Jest"* about *"freeborn"* men" sounds like the sort of point Hobbes would have made in such a conversation. On the other hand, Samuel echoes Hobbes's nominalism, but draws opposite conclusions about the "Name" at issue in this context: Hobbes had always maintained that tyrants are no more than kings titled harshly. In Hobbes's politics, too, *"unbounded Man"* was a terrifying prospect as represented not by tyrannical power but by all humans in the state of nature.

If such reflections suggest that Cowley had a nuanced response to Hobbes's political philosophy, they mislead. Though he did not commit the mistake of forcing one of his biblical characters to serve as his mouthpiece, he made as big an error by obtruding his views in his notes. Whereas the material discussed thus far represents Cowley's imaginative response to portions of 1 Samuel 8, his annotations strictly limit his readers' own capacity for interpretation. Thus, the injunction "Cheat not your selves" receives this gloss: "It is a vile opinion of those men, and might be punished without *Tyranny*, if they teach it, who hold, that the *right* of *Kings* is set down by *Samuel* in this place" (396 n.16). Cowley's note adds more; but already his position is clear. That he attacks Hobbes is self-evident: *Leviathan* established its author as one who did both "hold" and "teach" the "vile opinion" in question—not least by interpreting the relevant scriptural passage as a lesson about the nature of "absolute power" (258); and the supposition that such a doctrine "might be punished without *Tyranny*" doses Hobbes with his own medicine (for being soft on tyrants). Though Cowley was free to differ from Hobbes, he does his poetry a disservice whenever he refuses to let it speak for itself. As he did not trust his readers to retain their seats in the Pegasean flights of his Pindaric odes, so he would not let them draw their own conclusions from his imaginative recasting of scripture. His failure of nerve in the later project was so total that he appended a note painting him into this absurd corner: "I would not have the Reader judge of my opinion by what I say" (272 n.24).[26]

IX: "Autoritie"

Nonetheless, and though Cowley himself never explicitly acknowledged as such, his ode in praise of Hobbes initiated one direction that he could pursue as commensurate with his great ambition: establishing himself as England's poet laureate of science by writing such further works as "Upon Dr. *Harvey*" (1663) and *To the Royal Society* (1667), extolling the physician who discovered how blood circulates through the body and a ground-breaking institution thus hailed by an inaugural member. If anything, "To Mr. *Hobs*" oversells its subject's scientific credentials as not just an exponent of the new philosophy but the "great *Columbus* of the *Golden Lands* of *new Philosophies*." Moreover, Cowley's *"Gigantique"* conception of Hobbes entails making no reference to such mundane specifics as Hobbes's early interest in optics, indebtedness to geometry, misplaced pride in his prowess as a mathematician, and veneration for his friend Harvey. In addition, though Charles Butler's close reading of one portion of Cowley's ode to the Royal Society strengthens the case for regarding "To Mr. *Hobs*" as a first draft for that longer and later Pindaric, Butler resists the logic of his own findings whenever they cast doubt on the personal significance of

Cowley's praise for Hobbes or suggest that the putatively new project of writing great poetry about great scientists involved contradictions.

Butler focuses on a single passage from Cowley's *To the Royal Society* to show that its hitherto obscure reference to Priapus makes sense as part of a cluster of associations whose richness and ambiguity he demonstrates at some length without giving those traits their full due.[27] Beginning with a tribute to Bacon for having banished "Autoritie" (448), Cowley's poem then applauds his iconoclasm in relation to another shibboleth, equipped with the disproportionately large penis of any Priapic statue (449). Butler gives reasons for thinking that this additional obstacle to the advance of science symbolizes the sterile logic-chopping of Aristotelian scholastics; these grounds include the point that *Leviathan*'s forty-sixth chapter mounts an attack on such figures and (together with a passage immediately preceding it) features words and phrases informing Cowley's literal and metaphorical content. For Butler, the same material had the most impact in shaping the view of Hobbes presented in Cowley's ode to him. Furthermore, Butler notes that this portion of *Leviathan* drew attacks from Seth Ward and John Wilkins, in terms that Thomas Sprat, bishop of Rochester, would echo when criticizing Hobbes (thought not by name) in his *History of the Royal Society* (1667), which Cowley probably read when preparing his ode addressed to that institution. Butler thus comments of the poet's overall disposition:

> That he should have framed his celebrated allegory of Francis Bacon using materials drawn from Sprat's negative account of Hobbes may seem strange, but it is a powerful illustration of the complexity of the relationship between the two philosophers, both in Cowley's own mind and in the attitude of the Society as a whole, which suffered a certain embarrassment at the personal connection between its spiritual founder and its most famous non-Fellow. (11)

Butler, however, does not rest his case here, adding a glib conclusion: "Cowley's ode casts Bacon's chivalric task in terms which make plain his continuing intellectual and imaginative debt to the author of *Leviathan*" (12).

Butler himself remarks the more than "strange" effect created by Cowley's presentation of Bacon "as one of Spenser's knights," noting how that poet's influence features in other ways, too, fostering Guy Laprevotte's "atmosphère de légende" (3). In addition, Butler recognizes a connection here with the Spenserianism of Cowley's Davenant as "some worthy *Knight*," though he finds a suitably indulgent way of glossing its incongruousness in both contexts: "There is a similarly paradoxical air to the ode 'To the Royal Society' " (4). Butler even introduces Cowley's remarkable confession in his essay "Of My Self" (1668) that the "Chance" discovery of a copy of Spenser's works in his "Mother's Parlour" when he was less than "twelve Years old" converted him into "a Poet as irremediably as a Child is made an Eunuch" (3).[28] Having opened the Pandora's box of an obsessively recurrent and emasculating Spenserianism, however, Butler makes haste to close it: "Only in the context of such ambivalence can we understand Sprat's observation . . . that Cowley 'had a firmness and strength of mind, that was of proof against the Art of Poetry it self' " (4).[29] But this verdict substitutes an admirer's posthumous rationalization for the vivid counter-impression created by the poet's own consciousness of the *"Poetical"* as a siren song he was seldom able to resist for long.

"Very little is said to indicate the positive content of Hobbes's work," as Butler himself acknowledges of Cowley's poem to the figure in question; "indeed, one might read the whole ode without learning more of Hobbes's ideas than that they are original and harmonious, and form a kind of rival system to the ancient learning." For Butler, this is just as well: it means that Cowley's "great emphasis on Hobbes's heroism in dismantling the existing structure of Aristotelian and post-Aristotelian philosophy" matches precisely the tenor of *Leviathan*'s forty-sixth chapter and its lead-in, the key texts informing *To the Royal Society*'s comparable stress on Bacon's achievement (8). This also means, however, that the chief accomplishment for which Cowley prized Hobbes he later attributed to Bacon, thus bringing into question his "continuing intellectual and imaginative debt to the author of *Leviathan*." Anti-Aristotelianism is by itself a "debt" of no great compass, especially as simultaneously or subsequently owed to Bacon as well. A legacy based on Cowley's (re-)acquaintance through Sprat with some of *Leviathan* is likewise no proof of any pervasive influence exerted by Hobbes. Butler nonetheless shows very little inclination toward skepticism in such matters, invoking of all things "Autoritie"— among other commentaries (including Trotter's), a study by Robert Hinman claiming that "Hobbes had a potent catalytic effect on all Cowley's thinking" (7); this purported chemistry remains as unsubstantiated as Nethercot's vision of Cowley and Hobbes moving independently into alignment.[30]

Miriam Reik thus misrepresents "To Mr. *Hobs*" when remarking that it "was written before the establishment of the Royal Society, but Cowley does not seem to have changed his mind about Hobbes subsequently, and by writing an ode to the Society as well, this poetic Fellow effected a harmony between them in his mind that did not exist in fact."[31] Bacon dominates *To the Royal Society* as "a mighty Man" no less colossal in mind and deed than Hobbes, and one who likewise vanquished Aristotelian scholastics, a "Learned Rout" over-awed by "the plain Magick of true Reasons Light" (449). In Cowley's imagery, "A Science so well bred and nurst," at least initially, had become an "old *Minor*," stultified during the course of an overly extended "Nonage" imposed by "Guardians, who were now Usurpers grown" (448). But this new "mighty Man" himself usurps the role for-merly occupied by Hobbes in Cowley's own account, occupies it with greater conviction because his title to it is established with much more detail, and thus sustains the official mythology of the Royal Society, which would not even accept Hobbes as a valid member, let alone as a worthy progenitor, but retroactively adopted Bacon as its Romulus and Remus. Thus, the same series of poems launching Cowley as the new philosophy's bard steadily writes Hobbes out of the picture, so that the only constants remain the poet's trenchant anti-Aristotelianism and his unresolved attempt to do justice to scientific heroes without waxing "too *Poetical*," engaging in anti-Spenserian Spenserianism or anti-Pindaric Pindarism, or by some other methods seeking to give equal weight to the twin halves of "plain Magick." Working like a Cowley evidently meant writing at cross-purposes.

Chapter Four

"Joynt Innterest": Hobbes and Waller

I: "as the story would have it"

Where Cowley found a symbolic parent of the Royal Society and Davenant a likely source of inspiration for the experiment involving "Unicornes-horne" described by Aubrey, Waller found a literary forebear.[1] Justifying his first collection of poems (1645), he explained in his preface how "I may defend the attempt I have made upon poetry, by the examples . . . of many wise and worthy persons of our own times; as Sir Philip Sidney, Sir Fra: Bacon, Cardinal Perron (the ablest of his countrymen), and the former Pope."[2] Aware that gentlemen, except when young, should not stoop to writing poetry, much less publishing it, Waller cites literary figures whose social eminence made their precedent unimpeachable.

Similarly, he strikes a cavalier pose to disavow any intention of printing his poems, placing them entirely at the disposal of Lady Sophia Bertie:

> if you publish them, they become your own; and therefore, as you apprehend the reproach of a wit and a poet, cast them into the fire; or, if they come where green boughs are in the chimney, with the help of your fair friends (for thus bound, it will be too stubborn a task for your hands alone), tear them in pieces, wherein you shall honour me with the fate of Orpheus; for so his poems, whereof we only hear the fame (not his limbs, as the story would have it), I suppose were scattered by the Thracian dames. (1: ix)

Orpheus only appears categorically different from such other literary forebears as Sidney: discarding the embellishments of "story" leaves probable truth intact, with a historical figure subject in ancient times to the same forces operating in Waller's day.

In his encomium "To Sir William Davenant," Waller gives that author's incomplete heroic poem *Gondibert* sole credit for developing an aesthetic whereby "human passions, such as with us dwell" oust "bold tales of gods or monsters" (2: 30, 29), though Hobbes's *Answer* to Davenant had no less firmly prized "actuall workes" over the "exorbitancy" of "strange fictions, and Metamorphoses."[3] But whereas Waller attempted no heroic poetry or literary theorizing of his own, he praised Davenant for what he himself had already begun accomplishing in advance of Hobbes's *Answer* as well, less by discarding "tales" than by rationalizing them in the same manner as his preface's treatment of the Orpheus legend.

II: "Story . . . Applied"

Waller's "To the Mutable Fair" (1645) invokes Hera's deception of Ixion, when "She, with her own resemblance, graced / A shining cloud, which he embraced," linking it to his own experience as "Thyrsis," who "lately, when he thought / He had his fleeting Celia caught," merely "filled his arms with yielding air" (1: 35–36, 39–40, 42). But Waller then characterizes this frustration as

> A fate for which he grieves the less,
> Because the gods had like success;
> For in their story, one, we see,
> Pursues a nymph, and takes a tree;
> A second, with a lover's haste,
> Soon overtakes whom he had chased,
> But she that did a virgin seem,
> Possessed, appears a wandering stream;
> For his supposèd love, a third
> Lays greedy hold upon a bird,
> And stands amazed to find his dear
> A wild inhabitant of the air.
> To these old tales such nymphs as you
> Give credit, and still make them new. (43–56)

Though Waller obviously alludes to Apollo chasing Daphne and Alpheus Arethusa, the third frustrated pursuit remains uncertain. Julia Griffin suggests Neptune and Coronis as the parties involved, Hugh Maclean Tereus and Procne.[4] On the one hand, Waller finds consolation that he shares his misfortune with "gods"; on the other, "old tales" prove relevant and credible as corresponding to current amatory conditions. Whereas Waller demystifies "strange fictions," akin to his own experience with Celia (mutability personified as everywoman), he does not attempt to explain how she eluded him: his phrasing equivocates between treating the object of his love as metaphorically or actually "A shining cloud," so that she is and is not removed from his grasp by a miraculous-seeming transformation.

Though Waller most explicitly reveals his way with "story" when he similarly explicates several examples at once, he names his approach in a more thorough rehearsal of the single legend wherein a god "Pursues a nymph, and takes a tree." According to "The Story of Phœbus and Daphne, Applied" (1645),

> Thyrsis, a youth of the inspirèd train,
> Fair Sacharissa loved, but loved in vain.
> Like Phœbus sung the no les amorous boy;
> Like Daphne she, as lovely, and as coy!
> With numbers he the flying nymph pursues,
> With numbers such as Phœbus' self might use! (1: 1–6)

Though the god of poetry did not try to win the mountain nymph Daphne with verses, his identity means that Waller can plausibly describe Thyrsis as wooing Sacharissa "With numbers such as Phœbus' self might use." Whereas Apollo, thwarted in his pursuit of Daphne by her mutation into a laurel tree, consoled himself by weaving from her leaves the sort of crown awarded victors in the Pythian games (held in his honor), and the ancient Greeks perceived such coronation as apt recognition of excellence in other pursuits (including literature), Waller could take for granted his earliest readers' familiarity with the postclassical tradition linking that same prize more exclusively with poets laureate. A fable "Applied" to Waller's own case therefore becomes wholly congruent with it:

> Yet what he sung in his immortal strain,
> Though unsuccessful, was not sung in vain;
> All, but the nymph that should redress his wrong,
> Attend his passion, and approve his song.
> Like Phœbus thus, acquiring unsought praise,
> He catched at love, and filled his arm with bays. (15–20)

The application made erases itself from the title onward, closing the distance between Apollo's experience and Thyrsis's until the god prefigures all poets parlaying erotic failure into artistic success.

Because "The Story" reverses how Waller-like poets become legendary, Apollo appears no more fabulous an ancestor than Petrarch, whose *Rime Sparse* so strongly shaped Renaissance love poetry, not only by spawning innumerable sonnet-sequences composed in their image, but also by conflating his beloved Laura with l'auro (gold), l'aura (inspiration), and lauro (laurel), influentially making her embody many kinds of value, including that of the wreath he wore as Europe's first poet laureate. But whereas Petrarch's poetry incorporates various legends recounted in Ovid's *Metamorphoses* by subjecting them individually and collectively to further transformations, Waller both emphasizes and minimizes his own contribution in an "Applied" version of just one such myth.[5]

In his poem "Upon His Majesty's Repairing of Paul's" (1645), Waller invokes Amphion as well as Orpheus to praise Charles I's attempts throughout the 1630s to renovate England's premier cathedral, then dilapidated: "Those antique minstrels sure were Charles-like kings, / Cities their lutes, and subjects' hearts their strings" (1: 15–16). Though no human has ever possessed the powers attributed to those legendary poet-musicians, many literary critics now assume that Charles I let himself be blinded on this point by throngs of flatterers writing verses to and about him. "Upon His Majesty's" prompts Gerald Hammond to reflect that "some poets could keep writing as if nothing were happening—not least Edmund Waller, whose capacity to fool himself into believing that all was going well became legendary"; as Martin Butler maintains, however, no "singleminded, monolithic court" expressed and perpetuated "royal myopia" through "escapism, idealisation and wishful thinking."[6] Moreover, "became legendary" better describes the focus of Waller's skepticism than the scope of his own gullibility. If the royal renovator had read "Upon his Majesty's" he would have found its chastened "exorbitancy" accomplished more than just extravagant praise: it demystifies legend as analogous to the flattering perspective of panegyric. As Orpheus dismembered represents an embellished poet whose works have been "scattered," so that same figure in his guise as miracle-working musician joins Amphion as a civilizing law-giver whose efforts "became legendary" as fond recollection over centuries turned history into myth.

Waller sometimes supplants "bold tales of gods or monsters" with "human passions" so seamlessly that this translation becomes all but invisible. In his poem "For Drinking of Healths" (1645), he promotes alcohol with a precedent from Greek mythology that retains sufficient "exorbitancy" to elevate the poem's tone, but confines itself to "actuall workes":

Deserted Ariadne, thus supplied,
Did perjured Theseus' cruelty deride;
Bacchus embraced, from her exalted thought
Banished the man, her passion, and his fault. (1: 13–16)

Waller preserves the essential outlines of the relevant myth: abandoned by Theseus after helping him negotiate her father's labyrinth and overcome the Minotaur, Ariadne then married Dionysus. But Waller also transforms this legend: "Bacchus embraced" conveys how Ariadne drowned her sorrows in drink.

Another example of Waller's sly adaptation of mythic material occurs in *A Panegyric to My Lord Protector* (1655). This poem initially appeared in two editions: a quarto with the byline "E. W. Esq." and a folio silent about its authorship except as attributed to "a Gentleman That Loves the Peace, Union, and Prosperity of the English Nation." Whereas the folio groups the poem's iambic-pentameter couplets in verse-paragraphs of varying length, the quarto arranges them in the rather unusual format of quatrains rhyming aabb. Judging the quarto "the first, possibly pirated, edition" (2: 195), G. Thorn Drury prints the folio as the more authoritative text, but retains the other version's extended title and format. In contrast, Griffin makes a case for the superiority of "the non-stanzaic" form, which she reprints, preferring it as "more fluent, less aphoristic" (159). The same wording thus features in the fifth and sixth couplets of Griffin's text and the third quatrain of Thorn Drury's: Waller assures his kinsman Cromwell that

> Above the waves as Neptune showed his face,
> To chide the winds, and save the Trojan race,
> So has your Highness, raised above the rest,
> Storms of ambition, tossing us, repressed. (2: 9–12)

Alexander Ward Allison judges Waller's imagery typical of how the "formal characteristics of his similes sometimes mark them as rather idly ornamental," because in such cases "He can insist too explicitly on correspondences between the terms."[7] Certainly, Waller leaves no doubt that "winds" and "waves" mirror "Storms of ambition." His lines accomplish much else, however, subtly representing a rhetorical device that Allison detects in another portion of *A Panegyric* and terms "an upside-down simile," for "comparing not England to Rome but Rome to England" (14). But whereas Waller spells out his inversion both in that case and in his "antique minstrels" couplet, his lines about Cromwell involve an allusion needing recognition before their "upside-down" character emerges.

The first book of Virgil's *Aeneid* relates how

> When rioting breaks out in a great city,
> And the rampaging rabble goes so far

That stones fly, and incendiary brands—
For anger can supply that kind of weapon—
If it so happens they look round and see
Some dedicated public man, a veteran
Whose record gives him weight, they quiet down,
Willing to stop and listen.
Then he prevails in speech over their fury
By his authority, and placates them.
Just so, the whole uproar of the great sea
Fell silent.[8]

As Griffin notes, *A Panegyric*'s couplets express a "double" vision: "Neptune . . . emerges . . . to calm the storm which is about to destroy Aeneas; Virgil compares his action to that of a great man who quells a riot by the force of his authority; Waller makes Cromwell a statesman who is like Neptune who is like a statesman" (160). Waller produces a far more commensurable analogy, whose net effect shows Neptune resembling the Protector (rather than vice versa): the foregrounded terms are now those drawn from Britain's recent disorders. T. R. Langley also finds merit in the allusion, observing that "Waller actively courts a parallel which not only confers a measure of respectability upon apologists for usurped power (Virgil's reputation was not that of an egregious toad-eater), but also implies affinities between the recipients of the respective panegyrics"; Waller alone, however, draws censure as always "ready . . . with a timeserving couplet."[9]

The *Aeneid*'s first book likewise plays a key part in Waller's poem *Of the Danger His Majesty [Being Prince] Escaped in the Road at Saint Andrews* (1645), which expresses the future Charles I's peril by cheekily claiming that

Great Maro could no greater tempest feign,
When the loud winds usurping on the main
For angry Juno, laboured to destroy
The hated relics of confounded Troy. (1: 85–88)

Together with the equivocal term "feign," Waller's comparison between literature and life allows him to write himself out of the picture: respecting the scope of Virgil's imagination, he makes no claims for his own artistry, while implying the superior merit of a "tempest" belonging among "actuall workes." Waller absolves himself of a hopeless task (emulating the peerless dynamism of Virgil's own "loud winds"), while evoking memories of a locus classicus for inspired writing about wild weather. Covert appropriation thus usurps the "usurping" itself.

III: "Light . . . tales"

If these various adaptations of myth exemplify a systematic approach paralleling or in most cases anticipating the Hobbes–Davenant goal of curbing "exorbitancy," then Waller's failures in the same kind should be as instructive as his successes. In his poem "Of Salle" (ca. 1637), Waller contrasts Charles I's "actuall workes" with fables dismissed:

> Of Jason, Theseus, and such worthies old,
> Light seem the tales antiquity has told;
> Such beasts and monsters as their force oppressed
> Some places only, and some times, infest. (1: 1–4)

But magnifying Charles I's efforts to curtail the piracy of Barbary corsairs from the North African seaport of Salé cannot diminish the acts of "worthies old" as merely provincial: Jason and Theseus exert a hold on the Western imagination not readily dislodged. In his poem *Instructions to a Painter* (1666), Waller makes this similarly unconvincing attempt to capitalize on the future James II's undeniable military prowess in the English naval victory over the Dutch at Lowestoft:

> The great Achilles marched not to the field
> Till Vulcan that impenetrable shield,
> And arms, had wrought; yet there no bullets flew,
> But shafts and darts which the weak Phrygians threw.
> Our bolder hero on the deck does stand
> Exposed, the bulwark of his native land;
> Defensive arms laid by as useless here,
> Where massy balls the neighbouring rocks do tear. (2: 127–34)

Readers still wedded to the myth that Tudor and Stuart monarchs were of Trojan descent might have balked at "weak Phrygians." Achilles fares ultimately no better, reluctant to fight until assured of insurmountable odds in his favor. Moreover, his "arms" must be special to further those odds, but cannot be "impenetrable," a "shield"-specific attribute. In travestying the terms of Homer's epic, Waller promotes the stature of his own champion, but sets a risky precedent: viewing Greeks and Trojans with Thersites's contempt takes a step toward extending the same treatment to the poem's English heroes—as in the savage parodies *Instructions* inspired. In addition, whatever local advantages Waller derives from extolling moderns at the ancients' expense cannot disguise how the English and Dutch navies both fought with the same postclassical artillery.

IV: "the inspirèd train"

Waller's premature attempts to lead the moderns into war against the ancients fail; but their aggressiveness shows that he did wish to level the playing field. When not engaging in full frontal attack and adopting a lighter touch, he draws strength from entrenched ancients, even as he transforms them, proving an unusually early exponent of neoclassicism. Though F. W. Bateson gives an overly schematic account of "the series of *surprises*" sprung by "The Story," which also has too even a texture to be characterized as featuring "acrobatics," he stresses that the poem shows "how far Waller is outside the Renaissance tradition," not least because "His love for Sacharissa and her rejection of it have been abstracted out of their human context and are here simply disembodied concepts that the mind can play with in the dry light of reason."[10] Waller was even sufficiently an eighteenth-century poet avant la lettre to style Thyrsis "a youth of the inspirèd train." Such poetic diction represents one of several traits in the poem suggesting that he may have been translating a Latin original of uncertain authorship.

Griffin claims of "The Story" that "Waller liked it enough to produce a Latin translation" (152). By contrast, Thorn Drury annotates "Fabula Phœbi et Daphnes" by reporting "a tradition that these lines were written by Sir John Suckling, and by him sent to Waller" (2: 178). Thorn Drury also records that "Fabula" when first printed with Waller's poems (1645) referred to Galatea (1: 53 n.1); later editions substituted Sacharissa's name. Inconceivable as a printer's error, the original reading possibly reflects reassignment of a poem initially concerning the same courtship featured in Waller's "Thyrsis, Galatea" (1645). If "The Story" preceded "Fabula," Sacharissa's name would have been changed and then changed back again. If "Fabula" came first, however, then "The Story" completes a reassignment that would have remained invisible except for the clash between the English version and the still unrevised Latin one. As an exile when his first collection appeared, Waller would have been unable to monitor its production very closely. In another seeming giveaway, "Fabula" lacks any equivalent of the English version's central image (Thyrsis compared to a deer), which makes no contribution to the application around it and probably illustrates the padding needed to switch from a more to a less concise language and from unrhymed lines to neoclassical distichs. The same pressure would account for Waller's poetic diction.

Though very little translation as such can have been involved in generating a second "Applied" text (whichever came first), Waller's "abstracted" and "disembodied concepts" vindicate Ruth Wallerstein's observations about the habits of thought and expression fostered by the extensive translating in England during the sixteenth and seventeenth centuries and associated by her with the formation of neoclassical distichs. Though she consistently disparages Waller as a poet by promoting Denham and Falkland at his expense, her otherwise valuable account of how neoclassical distichs evolved cannot disguise the high value that his contemporaries and immediate successors placed on his contribution. Chapter one quoted her views to suggest what Hobbes might have gained from his experience of translating Euripides, Thucydides, and possibly Tacitus: "a tendency to paraphrase and to sententious generalization" resulting from translation and paralleling similar characteristics in the emergent neoclassical distich offers one explanation for how Hobbes moved from producing versions of others' works to generating his own.[11] Hobbes's renditions of Thuycidides et al. encouraged an "Applied" mode of interpretation relevant to his own thought and equivalent to Waller's approach, as meeting "in the dry light of reason."

V: "commerce"

"For Drinking" describes this symbiosis:

> Bacchus and Phœbus are by Jove allied,
> And each by other's timely heat supplied;
> All that the grapes owe to his ripening fires
> Is paid in numbers which their juice inspires. (1: 17–20)

No legend or passage from classical literature portrays the two younger gods as closer than other pairs of siblings among Zeus's numerous offspring; Waller's poem creates a tighter bond between them by giving a new twist to the claim (standard in such an anacreontic) that poetry enjoys a special relationship with alcohol. Metonymy readily converts the god of wine into the drink itself, in his marriage to Ariadne as in his kinship with Apollo, who likewise shades from god of poetry to "numbers" themselves. But in this new context, Waller imports "exorbitancy" by assigning a mythic lineage to the reciprocity he presents. He simultaneously curbs this "exorbitancy," however, because the special relationship remains the same: mutual back-scratching. He offers his own equivalent of Davenant's verse-epistle to Dorset: an affinity with Hobbes's *De Cive* through the shared perception that "*benefit* and *gratitude* go together," in ties shaped not by sociability but by a quest "for honour or advantage."[12] "For Drinking" thus features two ways in which Waller's thinking, like Davenant's, could resemble Hobbes's. Thorn Drury offers unpersuasive grounds for ca. 1628 as a possible date of composition for the poem, while reproducing a manuscript version, not the shorter one that appeared during Waller's lifetime in successive editions of his works (2: 185); I quote only lines common to both versions, extant by 1645.

In his poem "Of English Verse" (1668), Waller produces couplet-quatrains resembling those of the quarto *Panegyric*, except in tetrameter; these stress the impossibility of achieving permanency in his own "daily changing tongue," insisting that poets "Must carve in Latin, or in Greek," for their work to endure (2: 6, 14). Such pessimism accords with Hobbes's *Answer:* "The languages of the *Greekes* and *Romanes* (by their Colonies and Conquests) have put off flesh and bloud, and are become immutable, which none of the moderne tongues are like to be" (54). Unlike Hobbes, however, Waller finds consolation: though lasting fame must elude poets writing in a mutable language, they can beguile women into exchanging sexual favors for prospective commemoration. Women hoping to see their beauty perpetuated in monuments more lasting than bronze create perishable trophies recording men's erotic triumphs:

> Verse, thus designed, has no ill fate,
> If it arrive but at the date
> Of fading beauty; if it prove
> But as long-lived as present love. (29–32)

Though such English poets as Waller have the upper hand in this scenario and are less deceived than women as to its nature, both parties can only bargain with such assets as they possess. Waller again discovers how "*benefit* and *gratitude* go together" and sociable dealings revolve around "honour or advantage" sought.[13]

In his three-canto mock-heroic *Battle of the Summer Islands* (1645), Waller recounts a protracted but indecisive struggle between inhabitants of the Bermudas and two whales (mother and cub) temporarily trapped in one of the islands' bays, only to conclude by anticipating a point elaborated in *Leviathan*: "To make Covenant with bruit Beasts, is impossible; because not understanding our speech, they understand not, nor accept of any translation of Right; nor can translate any Right to another."[14] When a conflict initially welcomed by the Bermudans as a source of gain and glory degenerates into a stalemated war of attrition, they ponder two alternatives: to engage in diplomacy with the mother whale or blow her and her cub to bits with "loud engines . . . / . . . framed to batter walls" (1: 3.84–85). Either option treats the whales as human adversaries: fellow-combatants open to parleying or obdurate occupants of a town not won unless first destroyed. The islanders do not immediately grasp that Waller's Leviathan lacks the resources of Hobbes's, those of "a COMMON-WEALTH" or "Artificiall Man" (81):

> Their courage droops, and, hopeless now, they wish
> For composition with the unconquered fish;
> So she their weapons would restore again[,]
> Through rocks they'd hew her passage to the main. (69–72)

Thorn Drury ends the third of these lines with a period, not a comma. Maclean prints a semicolon for Thorn Drury's period, and a comma for his semicolon (241). Both editors' punctuation obscures the conditional nature of the offer that the Bermudans would like to make. The mother whale cannot return the harpoons buried in her back or comprehend the terms of such an agreement, however, just as the Bermudans possess no means, with or without "weapons," of engineering her escape from the bay: "But how instructed in each other's mind? / Or what commerce can men with monsters find?" (73–74). Such limits preclude any possibility for "*benefit* and *gratitude*" to "go together"; and no other aim can usefully be served when the islanders' recourse to "loud engines" would merely heap smashed blubber. As "Great Neptune" intercedes with "A tide so high that" mother and cub return to the open sea, the Bermudans have failed to finish off the larger whale or strike a deal with her, and the sole transaction has involved shared damage rather than mutual benefit: "And thus they parted with exchange of harms, / Much blood the monsters lost, and they [the islanders] their arms" (87, 88, 89–90).

Even if Waller did not invent his quarto *Panegyric*'s extended title ("of the Present Greatness and Joynt Innterest of His Highness, and This Nation"), it summarizes the poem's content; here, "commerce" can occur as linking "men" alone and no "monsters."

> While with a strong and yet a gentle hand,
> You bridle faction, and our hearts command,
> Protect us from ourselves, and from the foe,
> Make us unite, and make us conquer too,

Waller assures Cromwell,

> Let partial spirits still aloud complain,
> Think themselves injured that they cannot reign,
> And own no liberty but where they may
> Without control upon their fellows prey. (2: 1–8)

James Garrison suggests that the opening couplet recalls a passage from Jonson's *Panegyre* (ca. 1603), written for the accession of James I, and thus from the outset evinces an "intention of dressing Cromwell in royal robes."[15] But Waller also depicts Cromwell as a true Protector, with potential to turn a body politic riven by civil wars into a nation united at home and powerful abroad. Those rejecting his rule on partisan grounds overlook the benefits of his protection, espousing a self-defeating conception of "liberty" whose triumph would unleash Hobbes's state of nature. Because prior commentators have shown little or no hesitation in classifying this passage from *A Panegyric* as a direct expression of Waller's indebtedness to Hobbes's political philosophy, I shall seem quixotic for introducing it as exemplifying an affinity between Waller and Hobbes that can now be identified as a shared propensity for articulating relationships based on "Joynt Innterest." But in thus suggesting Waller's general receptivity to the Hobbesian perspective that much life consists of mutual back-scratching, I do not exclude the possibility that in this case Waller was revealing his respect for Hobbes's conception of politics. Nor do I express unwarranted skepticism; rather, I am sufficiently persuaded of *A Panegyric*'s foundation in Hobbes's political philosophy to fill a void by establishing what Waller knew of that body of thought and how far he was redirecting or reinforcing its ideological thrust.

VI: "composition"

Differentiating *A Panegyric* from some of the literature generated by the Engagement controversy, Warren Chernaik draws this essentially negative conclusion: "Waller's defense of Cromwell is not, like the pamphlets I have quoted, mere watered-down Hobbes, arguing simple submission to power."[16] Jack Gilbert's interpretation of the poem likewise strikes an evasive note: "I am not now proposing Waller's ultimate agreement or disagreement with Hobbes." But as Gilbert clarifies, his noncommittal stance partly reflects his concern to demonstrate how *A Panegyric* draws on various arguments "to make a strong case with wide appeal."[17] Moreover, Chernaik educes a perceptive parallel: "Dryden's account of the genesis and moral of the *Aeneid* fits Waller at least as well as it does Virgil" (157). "But for the lesser scope of Waller's poem," Chernaik maintains, "Dryden could be discussing the *Panegyric*, with . . . its conscious idealization of the less-than-perfect, and its preference for 'the arts of peace' over those of war" (158). The resemblance between that "account" and *Upon the Beginning* (see chapter one) further enriches understanding of *A Panegyric* as a partly Hobbesian text and validates David Norbrook's focus on Waller's "project of Protectoral Augustanism" as "the pre-eminent Cromwellian Augustan."[18]

On the other hand, the preceding paragraph includes views that Chernaik has since repudiated, albeit in an essay citing them without caveat.[19] His more recent discussion of *A Panegyric* terms the poem "deeply conservative" because "the claim of 'liberty' (as in Hobbes) is simply a mask for selfish and disruptive ambition, and the power of the state exists to protect unruly subjects, fractious children, from the consequences of their folly" (196). This revised estimate reverts to the ahistorical name-calling typifying commentary predating Chernaik's first and better thoughts. Wallerstein classifies *A Panegyric* with Cromwellian poems by Marvell and Dryden as

> in harmony with that weary, practical belief in the absolute priority of order by which, partly through the medium of Hobbes, many even of the Royalists who had fought longest and given most were soon to be reconciled to the apparently accomplished fact of Cromwell's triumph and England's meteoric rise to international significance.[20]

Intrinsically evil, "order" as an "absolute priority" matches "deeply conservative"; "practical" proves a term of abuse when subject to a dismissal itself "weary."

As Wallerstein makes Hobbes only "partly" responsible for a view of life she finds unsympathetic, so Chernaik's essay ranks *Leviathan* with *The Case of the Commonwealth Stated* as expressing an equally crude outlook: "the argument for transfer of allegiance by conquest, as developed by Hobbes in 1651 and by Marchamont Nedham in 1650, is independent of any particular form of government, largely ignoring constitutional issues along with qualms of conscience" (198). These words make too little allowance for the contrast between Nedham's frankly opportunistic approach to politics and Hobbes's system-building, which disabled him from jumping any bandwagon without taking a great many bricks with him. Moreover, most Hobbes scholars attribute at least some of *Leviathan*'s motivation to its author's concern to show how his long-time employers the Cavendishes might view the requirements of duty and honor in the political landscape of the post-regicide period, a line of interpretation hardly consonant with his "largely ignoring constitutional issues along with qualms of conscience."[21] Nonetheless, Chernaik's lumping of *Leviathan* with Nedham's *Case* reflects a current trend in literary studies toward subsuming Hobbes's thought within the Engagement controversy, while selectively emphasizing areas of disagreement.

Norbrook claims that Hobbes's political philosophy, produced by a figure "who was . . . to return voluntarily to acknowledge the *de facto* power of the republic, could be used to legitimize any established regime" (278). This statement misleadingly implies some necessarily close correlation between Hobbes's actions as a would-be citizen of Interregnum England and the overall meaning of his political philosophy; it also fails to address whether he himself would have sanctioned so wide a range of applications for his words. Norbrook, too, suggests that default more than authorial agency or even the disposition of Hobbes's original interpreters shaped *Leviathan*'s politics: "Had events worked out differently, the speech-act of its publication might have been strongly royalist; but the failure of the royalists to regain ascendancy left the work as a legitimation of the republic's *de facto* power" (212). This beaching makes *Leviathan* a mere hostage to fortune, contradicting the terms on which Norbrook praises Nedham's *Case:* "The second edition added extracts from Salmasius and from Hobbes, both strong supporters of absolute monarchy, to defend submission to the Commonwealth," an instance of its author's "characteristic relish in the effrontery of mustering the republic's enemies in its defence" (222–23). But if Hobbes's theory "could be used to legitimize any established regime," through the example he set in "voluntarily" taking the Engagement, or because *Leviathan* ended up being rewritten by historical contingency, then the witty and versatile Nedham cannot be supposed half so clever in appropriating the arguments of two "strong supporters of absolute monarchy." Not finding friends among enemies' enemies, Hobbes in *Behemoth* equally derided Salmasius the opponent of regicide and Milton its advocate.[22]

I do not deny that the ideological contexts in which Hobbes's works initially appeared influenced how they were read; nor do I seek to return him to the splendid isolation in which he used to be studied. Johann Sommerville sheds doubt on whether *A Panegyric*'s opening argument reflects an indebtedness to Hobbes's thought in particular, classifying his "doctrine" about the "mutual link between protection and obedience" as a "notion . . . well-known before 1650" and "one of the least innovatory parts of his system," in addition remarking that the same author's "comments on the horrors of life in the state of nature are amongst the most famous passages in his works," but "also amongst the least original."[23] Moreover, Chernaik grounds his revised estimate of *A Panegyric* on "The standard treatment of conquest theory in Hobbes and his contemporaries," a classic essay by Quentin Skinner (212 n.9). This point of inspiration has nonetheless been subject to debate and modification, involving not only other scholars but also Skinner himself.[24] Furthermore, Waller's general familiarity with the literature of the Engagement controversy is uncertain, whereas his attested admiration for *De Cive* establishes a verifiable source for *A Panegyric*'s perspective on the wisdom of obedience to a protector capable of averting anarchy.

Langley ignores this principle of economy: though he usefully cross-references *A Panegyric* with contemporary texts less often discussed, his appraisal of Waller as merely one of several authors who variously "adapted Hobbist ideas to suit the situation in which they . . . found themselves" strands them all in an indeterminate sea ("It would be surprising if the drift of their thoughts had not been, now and then, concurrent") (16), but still entails insisting on Waller's acquaintance with a text he is not known to have read—if "It is . . . a matter of reading *Leviathan*" registers such a claim (56). The same principle of economy furnishes a relatively stable basis on which to assess the relationship between *De Cive* and *Leviathan*, and more especially whether Waller's familiarity with the former would have sufficed for his *Panegyric* to acclaim Cromwell in plausibly Hobbesian terms. In turn, such a discussion sheds light on the extent to which Waller's poem was thereby conforming with the logical implications of its presumed model or extrapolating from them in a manner consistent with *Leviathan*, and thus on the vexed question of how far Hobbes himself was conscious of having created a political philosophy whose scope ultimately sanctioned Cromwell's rule, either on the initially unwitting basis of its core principles or as subsequently developed in a somewhat calculated way by its author, regardless of how much room for denial he retained.

VII: "so great a master"

In the earlier of two extant letters that they exchanged (one from each hand), Hobbes wrote from Rouen (August 8, 1645) to assure Waller that

> I was told you had an inclination to put a booked Called de Cive into English. I can not hope that it should have that honor, and yet now I thinke of it, the honor will come all to the English booke, when it is of your doing, but so will the envy also. I will not presse you to it but I must thanke you for having once entertayned the thought, wch alone I esteeme as a great obligation.[25]

Aubrey records Waller's account:

> I have heard him say that he so much admired Mr. Thomas Hobbes' booke *De Cive*, when it came forth, that he was very desirous to have it donne into English, and Mr. Hobbes was most willing it should be done by Mr. Waller's hand, for that he was so great a master of our English language. Mr. Waller freely promised him to doe it, but first he would desire Mr. Hobbes to make an essaye; he (T. H.) did the first booke, and did it so extremely well, that Mr. Waller would not meddle with it, for that nobody els could doe it so well. Had he thought he could have better performed it, he would have himselfe been the translator. (2: 277)

Whereas the letter professes a distant-sounding "esteeme" prompted by "a great obligation" incurred by a mere "inclination," Aubrey terms the mooted translation a "freely promised" offer eliciting Hobbes's praise of Waller as "so great a master of our English language." Hobbes's reluctance to "presse" Waller beyond "having once entertayned the thought"—of which he had only been "told"—seems to rule out the back-and-forth reconstructed by Aubrey. The letter gives no hint that Waller desired or Hobbes would undertake "an essaye" as a model.

Philip Wikelund judges that the letter evinces "beyond the graceful compliment to a friend, the tough-minded thinker's characteristic inclination to retain control of his philosophical property, even when that friend was a poet of talent with an amateurish inclination toward philosophy." Though Aubrey's account contradicts this reading of the evidence, which promotes Hobbes's purported "inclination" over that he attributed to Waller, Wikelund quotes it entire, as additional context to supply for the letter's first publication.[26] In their edition of *De Cive*, Richard Tuck and Michael Silverthorne gloss Aubrey's testimony with "This may be true, but we do possess Hobbes's actual reply." Aubrey's words lack the authority of first-hand evidence, as their fidelity to Waller's own words cannot now be determined. Even so, the introduction just quoted concludes "Either way, it is clear that the project lapsed" (xxxvi).

But the two apparently conflicting reports can be reconciled quite simply. Having only heard of Waller's "inclination," Hobbes had no means of assessing it. Assuring Waller that he was under no pressure to translate *De Cive*, Hobbes inoculated himself against any disappointment if the project should founder, as it did, and guaranteed that under these circumstances his prospective translator would suffer no loss of face. Such an assurance offered both parties some protection and need not have signaled to Waller that his "inclination" was unwelcome. Rather, and albeit with the utmost tact, it required him to insist on the strength of his proposed commitment. With this preliminary sounding accomplished, the negotiations could then proceed along the lines described by Aubrey, in a summary overview that appears to hold no place for the episode represented by Hobbes's letter because it refers to a later and more complex interaction made possible by that necessarily tight-lipped response.

Aubrey cannot be right that Waller admired *De Cive* "when it came forth": it first appeared in Paris in a very small edition. But this error strengthens the impression that Waller's interest in the work was genuine: when the revised edition had yet to be written, he can only have had access to a copy of the first after arriving in France as an exile (November 1644) and must have sought out a rare volume or obtained it from someone else (perhaps even Hobbes himself). The second letter from their extant correspondence (July 1656) registers Waller's pleasure on receiving from its original author an English translation of Hobbes's *De Corpore* published with *Six Lessons to the Professors of Mathematicks of the Institution of Sr. Henry Savile, in the University of Oxford.*

Furthermore, Hobbes's letter and Aubrey's testimony overlap concerning Waller's literary prowess. Either "so great a master" or some similarly glowing view of *De Cive*'s potential translator must underlie Hobbes's prediction that "the honor will come all to the English booke, when it is of your doing." Hobbes had to show some deference toward a friend who was always his social superior and then his employer too. As Noel Malcolm's commentary to Hobbes's correspondence explains, Hobbes was tutoring "Robert Waller, who died young," and also another of the poet's dependents—"probably a son of Waller's brother-in-law Nathaniel Tomkins" (125 n.1 and n.2).

Even as Waller's wallah, however, Hobbes had no need to grovel and possibly regarded his employer's literary stature as germane to the potential of an English *De Cive:* "so great a master" would bring to the project his own eminence as a stylist and a much higher reputation in his native land than Hobbes could then claim. The bookseller Humphrey Moseley partly attributed his publication of Milton's debut volume to "that incouragement I have already received from the most ingenious men in their clear and courteous entertainment of Mr. Wallers late choice Peeces."[27]

VIII: "Those who speak like this"

For Hobbes, Waller's eloquence would have had a sinister dimension, too: he was noted for his skills as an orator in parliament and suspected in that capacity of polishing his language "to make it as ornate and attractive as possible to the audience, in order to win a reputation" (*De Cive*, 123). Whereas Hobbes linked the oratory of members of parliament with the preaching of his *Answer*'s "Unskillful divines" (48), as demagoguery molding public opinion to ends he deplored, Waller's earliest readers encountered his political speeches as literature, printed with his first collection of poems. According to Clarendon, Waller

> had been even nursed in parliaments, where he sat when he was in his infancy; and so when they were resumed again, (after a long intermission and interdiction,) he appeared in those assemblies with great advantage, having a graceful way of speaking; and by thinking much upon several arguments, (which his temper and complexion, that had much of melancholic, inclined him to,) he seemed often to speak upon the sudden, when the occasion had only administered the opportunity of saying what he had thoroughly considered, which gave a great lustre to all he said; which yet was rather of delight than weight.[28]

Though Mark Kishlansky reports that "About half of all members of the House of Commons served in one parliament only," Waller's parliamentary speech-making continued into his second childhood: through much of the post-Restoration period, he complacently out-Nestored Nestor.[29] Insisting that age proved no handicap to an orator who remained "the delight of the House," because "even at eighty he said the liveliest things of any among them," Gilbert Burnet, bishop of Salisbury, nonetheless shared Clarendon's misgivings: "He was only concerned to say that which should make him be applauded. But he never laid the business of the House to heart, being a vain and empty, tho' a witty, man."[30] Both historians' grudging view of Waller's speech-making reveal an exceptional member of parliament whose name Hobbes took to be legion.

Whereas Hobbes would have had to revise his conception of parliamentary oratory if he had known or thought enough about Waller's singularity in the Commons as an aspirant Demosthenes or Cicero, Waller must have seen how portions of *De Cive* unambiguously constituted his own and a great many other people's worst nightmare. In particular, Hobbes's views on personal property rights were, as A. P. Martinich notes, "the source of much of the opposition to his political philosophy" (*Dictionary*, 236). According to *De Cive*, "a citizen has nothing which is properly *his own*, against the will of the *commonwealth*, or of the holder of sovereign power" (104). In a passage especially relevant to Ship Money, the controversial tax whose legality Waller's kinsman John Hampden challenged (1635), this text stresses the sovereign power's entitlement to demand supply as the need is perceived to arise, rather than to obtain it only when the need becomes apparent to those making the payments: "Those . . . who think it is time enough to extract the funds for provisioning the troops and other army expenses when danger begins to appear, are surely failing to consider how difficult it is to scrape together such an amount of money all at once; people are so tight-fisted" (145). *De Cive* parrots the language of reluctant tax-payers, explaining why their position is unconstitutional and self-defeating:

> *we know that money is sometimes necessary for the public defence, but those who exact it must demonstrate the need and take the money on the basis of consent.* Those who speak like this fail to realize that the procedure they suggest has already taken place at the beginning when the commonwealth was being formed; by speaking as if they were still in a disorganized crowd and no commonwealth were yet formed, they are undermining the commonwealth that has been formed. (136–37)

Translating *De Cive* on personal property rights, Waller would have had to repudiate in every instance, sometimes by parodying, views he had expressed earlier: opposing Ship Money, he had figured prominently among "Those who speak like this." Far from crediting the "necessity" of Ship Money as "present," he had construed it as "feigned," "suppositious," and a mere "visour."[31] Far from accepting the imposition of this tax as authorized "when the commonwealth was being formed," he had taken exception to Ship Money as "a Right so inhærent in the Crowne, that it would not be in the power of an Act of Parliament to take it away" (7).

Norbrook nonetheless suggests that Waller's defense of Strafford at that figure's trial "may have been hinting at a Hobbesian scepticism about the status of laws when the traditional political framework had broken down" (106). But Norbrook does not establish whether Waller would have been familiar with Hobbes's thinking at this juncture and in any case makes too much of an interchange reported in Thorn Drury's introduction as follows: "It being alleged that the Earl had attempted to subvert 'the fundamental laws of the realm,' Waller characteristically asked in the House, what these 'fundamental laws' were, and was told . . . that if he did not know, he had no business to sit there" (1: xxxiii). Thus, Waller was outwitted in his attempt to divide Strafford's opponents by tempting them to confront their diverging opinions in other matters.

Likewise making no attempt to document a purported influence on Waller exerted before 1645, but also offering a less strained reading of the available evidence, Langley speculates that Waller's conduct during his own trial "befitted a disciple of Hobbes," for he might not then have been aware that his strenuous efforts to save his life illustrated Hobbes's view of humans as dedicated to self-preservation (15). In May 1643, Waller's colleagues in the Commons learned of his covert diplomacy with the royalists at their headquarters in Oxford. For Robert Ashton, these clandestine negotiations "aimed almost certainly at a concerting of efforts to bring about a successful peace."[32] But Waller's conduct did not look so benign to his fellow members of parliament: they heard of his unofficial correspondence from John Pym, the hawkish leader of the Commons, who strategically conflated it with an unrelated project discovered at the same time—a royalist plan to spark an insurrection in the parliamentarian stronghold of London. Pym thus hatched what he now exposed as Waller's Plot—a treasonous offense putting its supposed author at risk of execution. Through various means generally interpreted to his utmost discredit, but most effectively through a speech equivalent to Davenant's "Humble Remonstrance" in the aftermath of the Army Plot, Waller escaped with a fine of £10,000 and banishment for life (repealed after eight years). His one attempt to impose his political views without recourse to his skills as an orator (except in the last resort), the whole episode proved worse than a failure, as Ashton explains:

> Pym's version . . . which deceived not only the middle and war groups at Westminster but also many of the peace group, not to speak of generations of subsequent historians, put paid to any possibility of coordinating

a drive for peace from both Oxford and Westminster, and gave a
notable fillip to the opponents of the peace groups in both places. (210)

That his own attempt at peacemaking had backfired this badly might
have disposed Waller to embrace the doctrine of a thinker so distant
from the political mainstream that he considered peace a bargain at
any price and civil war a far greater evil than any ills invoked by his
compatriots as a reason for challenging the authority of the crown.
But then again, Waller did not have to agree with every tenet of
De Cive to admire it.

Conversely, Hobbes did not have to approve of every form that
Waller's eloquence took to appreciate having "so great a master of our
English language" as a prospective translator. Howard Warrender
argues that the first part of *Philosophical Rudiments* differs markedly
from the second and third in representing a translation of *De Cive* so
free as to be irresponsible if undertaken by anyone other than
Hobbes.[33] Warrender nonetheless equivocates as to what this contrast
means in relation to Aubrey's testimony. He treats both pieces of
evidence as proof of Hobbes's substantial involvement in the entire
translation, but recognizes that his textual findings only corroborate, at
most, Aubrey's report of how "he (T. H.) did the first booke" (8, 8 n.1).
If Hobbes "did the first booke," however, he might well have tackled
it as "an essaye" at Waller's request. The liberties he then permitted
himself in translating his own words could mean that he wished the
English *De Cive* to be freely rather than literally rendered, suiting "so
great a master" as Waller. Though Malcolm in championing Cotton's
authorship of *Philosophical Rudiments* rejects as "a strange convo-
lution of his argument" the conclusion that Warrender draws, he does
not say whether he perceives any stylistic contrast within that English
text, only remarking that "Aubrey's account . . . does not imply that
Hobbes completed the translation."[34]

If David Johnston correctly surmises that Hobbes came to recognize
during the 1640s a need for a more overtly persuasive style than he had
adopted in his self-consciously scientific *Elements*, an English *De Cive*
rendered freely by an eminent stylist with a high reputation would have
edged it closer to *Leviathan* by boosting its rhetorical qualities and
bringing it to a wider audience than it might otherwise have reached.
The translation that Waller failed to produce thus possibly helped create
Leviathan by leaving a role for it to play. On this logic, however, the
fullest expression of Hobbes's own prowess as "so great a master"
should have made an English *De Cive* redundant, whereas *Philosophical
Rudiments* appeared in print shortly before *Leviathan* did.

IX: "every commonwealth"

Unhesitatingly identifying the English *De Cive* as Hobbes's "own translation," Langley ignores a debate having a complex bearing on the relationship between Hobbes's thought and the literature of the Engagement controversy (205 n.16). Martinich doubts that Hobbes authored or authorized *Philosophical Rudiments* and notes how this translation was unique among the various versions of his political philosophy in being "published by Richard Royston, a royalist" (*Dictionary*, 320). Tuck imparts a different spin: after the regicide, "Hobbes's early works began to be pirated by English publishers, anxious to use them to establish a wholly royalist case against the new republican regime," whereas its author "quite clearly and deliberately refused to allow *Leviathan* to be used in this way."[35] But whether Hobbes failed to retain ownership of *De Cive* or successfully shielded *Leviathan*, both works in their English versions reached market within a month of each other as perceived competitors, commercially and ideologically.

That many readers saw or were encouraged to see *Philosophical Rudiments* as specifically royalist is strange: the revised *De Cive* incorporates a striking admission when Hobbes defines as one of his aims

> not to give the impression that citizens owe less obedience to an Aristocratic commonwealth or a Democratic commonwealth than they owe to a Monarchical commonwealth. For though I have deployed some arguments . . . to press the point that Monarchy has more advantages than other forms of commonwealth (the only thing in this book which I admit is not demonstrated but put with probability), I say everywhere explicitly that every commonwealth must be allowed supreme and equal power. (14)

Though these words did not appear in the version of *De Cive* that Waller first read, they illustrate why he needed to know only that text (assuming he understood its overall import without such additional clarification), not *Leviathan* as well or instead, for his *Panegyric*'s opening argument.

But if *Philosophical Rudiments* still served as royalist propaganda, an ironic scenario results: four years after the appearance of an English *De Cive*, the author who had initially contemplated making such a book published a justification of Cromwell's rule that apparently reflected continuing admiration for a thinker suspected of having changed his tune in such a way as to set *Leviathan* in stark opposition to its newly translated precursor. Conversely, the translator to whom Malcolm attributes *Philosophical Rudiments* also wrote a philippic, "To Poet E. W., Occasion'd for His Writing a Panegyric on Oliver Cromwell" (1689), convicting Waller of a self-damning "Treason in rhyme" by pointedly denying him any intellectual pedigree: "Each sentence in thy poem is thine own."[36]

X: "in conscience . . . justified"

Refuting charges leveled by Wallis, *Considerations* in effect maintained that Hobbes had only ever portrayed Cromwell in a manner opposite to *A Panegyric*'s:

> he wrote and published his *Leviathan*, far from the intention either of disadvantage to his Majesty, or to flatter Oliver, who was not made Protector till three or four years after, on purpose to make way for his return. For there is scarce a page in it that does not upbraid both him, and you, and others such as you, with your abominable hypocrisy and villainy.[37]

But whereas all versions of Hobbes's political philosophy denounce rebels of every stripe, denying them any conceivable warrant, *Leviathan* never rebukes Cromwell by name. Once the future Protector had established himself as a successful usurper, too, he no longer ranked among rebels, whatever taints of "abominable hypocrisy and villainy" still clung to him. As just "a page" in *Leviathan* concedes of a ubiquitous paucity more persuasive than that alleged by *Considerations*, "there is scarce a Common-wealth in the world, whose beginnings can in conscience be justified" (722).

Implying that *Leviathan* cannot have "justified" any "Common-wealth" whose "beginnings" postdated its own appearance, *Considerations* is disingenuous: one intended merit of Hobbes's political philosophy had always been its comprehensiveness in addressing a wide range of constitutional issues, some of which might have seemed merely theoretical at the time of writing, but later acquired practical relevance. *Elements* and *De Cive* in its first edition were most immediately topical concerning obedience: the Civil Wars were impending or still young. Later editions of *De Cive* overlapped with the drafting and publication of *Leviathan*, when years of internecine conflict had made the more pressing question where Hobbes's readers could find security. Every version of his political philosophy nonetheless foregrounded a point expressed by *Considerations* as "Protection and obedience are relative" (421). With or without *Leviathan*, the importance of that relationship would have made his work relevant to the political conditions of the Interregnum, notwithstanding his inability to predict that a commoner would one day assume the title of Protector, exacting obedience in return. Even so, *Leviathan*'s publication during the final stages of Cromwell's improbable ascent helped ensure that Hobbes's political philosophy would not be overshadowed by tracts seemingly more up-to-date than *De Cive*.

Clarendon remembered demanding "why" Hobbes "would publish such doctrine" as *Leviathan* contained, eliciting "a discourse between jest and earnest upon the Subject" concluding "*The truth is, I have a mind to go home.*"[38] For Richard Peters,

> although there is abundant evidence that Hobbes wanted to go home, it is absurd to take his reply to Clarendon too seriously and suggest, as his opponents did later, that Hobbes hoped to work his passage home by writing the *Leviathan*. It seems probable that Hobbes wrote the *Leviathan* much more in order to instruct his countrymen how best to reconstruct English civil society so that it was a fit place for sensible people like himself.[39]

"That Hobbes went to the trouble of arranging the printing of the work in London confirms the essential validity of the joking remark he made," Malcolm judges, but then stresses how

> It would . . . be too limited an explanation to say that Hobbes wrote *Leviathan* merely to ease his passage to England. Certainly he was keen—and entitled—to point out that his theory of political authority based on necessary consent (and necessary consent based on a rational understanding of ultimate self-interest) was not inherently pro-royalist. ("Summary Biography," 31, 32)

Nonetheless, the point that Hobbes had "much more" motivation than just "*a mind to go home*" does not detract from the "essential validity" of that as part of a not exclusively "joking remark." Moreover, Peters writes as if "*home*" and "English civil society" were different places, as if the projects to gain "passage" to the first and "to reconstruct" the second were unrelated. On the other hand, even a small dose of "ultimate self-interest" acknowledged "between jest and earnest" sufficed to doom Hobbes in the eyes of Clarendon, an inter-locutor whose rectitude could assume a humorlessly priggish cast and whose own principles would not permit him *"to go home"* until after the Restoration (thus not before ending a lengthy and uncomfortable period of exile). If Hobbes deliberately goaded an old friend, however, he recklessly disregarded what Clarendon would make of such a rationale for *Leviathan*'s existence and poisoned his own well.

Asserting Hobbes's nominalism, *Leviathan* explains how

in reasoning, a man must take heed of words; which besides the signifi-cation of what we imagine of their nature, have a signification also of the nature, disposition, and interest of the speaker; such as are the names of Vertues and Vices; For one man calleth *Wisdome*, what another calleth *feare*; and one *cruelty*, what another *justice*; one *prodigality*, what another *magnanimity*; and one *gravity*, what another *stupidity*, &c. And therefore such names can never be true grounds of any ratiocination. (109–10)

Hobbes thought that his philosophy had overcome language's unstable "signification" because he had subjected his "ratiocination" to the rigors of a scientific methodology based on definitions. But insofar as he drew attention to his own "nature, disposition, and interest" as a "speaker," he sacrificed every gain he had made as a science-minded philosopher, becoming a further example of how "one man calleth *Wisdome*, what another calleth *feare*."

Hobbes had no need to poison his own well, however, for it to appear toxic in the eyes of many. Noting various reasons why *Leviathan* gave offense, Tuck reports how its author had become so repugnant even to "men who had once been his friends":

They believed that the book was in many ways a repudiation of all that Hobbes had formerly stood for, and in particular a piece of treachery to the cause of royalism in England—a cause which was in need of redou-bled support after the execution of Charles I in January 1649. After the restoration of the monarchy in 1660, Hobbes persistently denied these charges, but they were not wholly unfounded. (27)

Clarifying for Wallis's benefit, *Considerations* explains how "He that says a man may submit to an enemy for want of protection, can never be construed, but that he meant it of the obedient," and therefore concludes that "this submission to Oliver, or to your then masters, is allowed by Mr. Hobbes his doctrine only to the King's faithful party, and not to any that fought against him, howsoever they coloured it, by saying that they fought for the King and Parliament" (421, 423). But Wallis and other parliamentarians did not require Hobbes's sanction to engage in a "submission to Oliver" (however little this corresponded with their original aims), whereas "the King's faithful party" represented at least one source of sustained opposition to Cromwell (however little resistance it could offer on the battlefield). If those loathing Cromwell had reason to throw in their lot with those merely tolerating him and those genuinely admiring him, then, even by default, he had the basis for implementing an effective regime.

In his *Dialogue between a Philosopher and a Student of the Common Laws of England* (1681), Hobbes reflects how

> The late long Parliament that . . . Murdered their King (a King that sought no greater Glory upon Earth, but to be indulgent to his People, and a Pious defender of the Church of *England*) no sooner took upon them the Sovereign Power, then they Levyed Money upon the People at their own Discretion. Did any of their Subjects Dispute their Power? Did they not send Souldiers over the Sea to Subdue *Ireland*, and others to Fight against the Dutch at Sea, or made they any doubt but to be obeyed in all that they Commanded, as a Right absolutely due to the Sovereign Power in whomsoever it resides? I say not this as allowing their Actions, but as a Testimony from the Mouths of those very Men that denyed the same Power to him, whom they acknowledged to have been their Sovereign immediately before, which is a sufficient Proof, that the People of *England* never doubted of the Kings Right to Levy Money for the Maintenance of his Armies, till they were abused in it by Seditious Teachers, and other prating Men, on purpose to turn the State and Church into Popular Government, where the most ignorant and boldest Talkers do commonly obtain the best preferments; again, when their New Republick returned into Monarchy by *Oliver*, who durst deny him Money upon any pretence of *Magna Charta*, or of . . . other Acts of Parliament . . . ?[40]

Here, Hobbes chiefly denounces a level of hypocrisy that never ceased to amaze him when he contemplated the conduct of Charles I's opponents; but conflicting currents appear, too, making this passage an especially valuable guide to the complexities or contradictions in Hobbes's conception of "Sovereign Power."

In his startlingly casual reference to a "New Republick returned into Monarchy by *Oliver*," Hobbes relishes the irony that this should be the bitter outcome for rebels allegedly aiming at "Popular Government"; but he cannot gloat without also acknowledging Cromwell as a head of state entitled to command resources essential to the performance of this role. Even more striking, perhaps, is Hobbes's prior concession that at some point (necessarily vague) the members of the Long Parliament "took upon them the Sovereign Power" and enjoyed accordingly "the Kings Right to Levy Money," even though Charles I himself had been "denied the same." Hobbes raises a larger issue than he implicitly answers when his rhetorical question about the members of the Long Parliament demands "Did any of their Subjects Dispute their Power?" This tactic fudges what it meant to be "the People of *England*" when rival governments offered competing claims to authority but equally demanded obedience from "their Subjects." Mired in the same ambiguity is Hobbes's stress that his remarks are not tantamount to "allowing . . . Actions" undertaken by the Long Parliament, which clashes with his simultaneous conviction that there is "a Right absolutely due to the Sovereign Power in whomsoever it resides." If this last point holds, then whether Hobbes personally is "allowing" certain "Actions" becomes irrelevant and by his own standards absurd. "Actions" of "Sovereign Power" are authorized in advance by all persons represented by that rule; sentimental asides about Charles I's character and intentions merely digress. As Jean Hampton notes, Hobbes "argues against the legitimacy of initiating a rebellion, but his conservative critics angrily appreciate that he also condones (and must condone) as rational the continuation of rebellious activity once it has begun"; she sees Hobbes as "essentially . . . admitting that the self-defense right retained by each subject in the common-wealth is equivalent to the *entire* right of self-preservation and hence makes the subjects the judges of whether or not they will obey *any* of the sovereign's laws."[41]

As Hampton convicts Hobbes of "essentially . . . admitting," so Malcolm detects in his answer to Clarendon an "essential validity," and Tuck judges "charges" leveled against him as "not wholly unfounded." Such formulations allow wiggle room, without clarifying for whom. Annabel Patterson deems Hobbes the equivocator in claiming that "an attack on the notion that history afforded an argument for republicanism" formed a part of his "project in re-laying the theoretical grounds for absolute sovereignty (while hedging his bets on who might most successfully embody it in England: Cromwell or Charles II)."[42] Though Hobbes had the right to deny holding views he had never explicitly voiced, prudence also dictated his sometimes disavowing opinions his earliest readers found implicit in his work. At least to their ears, his silences could seem as eloquent as Homer's. Derek Hirst supposes as much when he summarizes *Leviathan*'s meaning for its original audience: "given the essential egotism of mankind, it is protection that all need. This—Hobbes left unspoken—the Rump as the sitting tenant could provide."[43] But any prior or subsequent "tenant" had potential to "provide" in such a manner, and by the same "unspoken" logic, which had become a cornerstone of Hobbes's political philosophy well before Pride's purge (1648) had reduced the Long Parliament to its "Rump" version, as Waller for one would have known.

XI: "proportioned to . . . inclination"

Waller's continuing admiration for Hobbes and Cromwell emerges from his letter responding to the augmented English *De Corpore*. His awareness that his correspondence might be subject to governmental scrutiny possibly motivated some of the fervor with which he styled Cromwell's institution of provincial rule by Major Generals "a perfect foundation of Government," approvingly citing it as evidence that "his Highnes . . . sees a good way before him"; but Waller also sounds like (or excellently mimics) a concerned patriot and loyalist when fretting about how "fayling of the good succes hoped for abroad, & these arrears & want of Mony att home, may perhaps give occasion & oportunity to such as are enemys to a settlement to retard & shocke his desseins" (1: 296). As for Hobbes's latest volume, Waller counts it "a present of the best kinde," as "preferring wth soloman wisdome to any other treasure," and on the principle of "gifts being proportioned to the use & inclination of the receaver," but disingenuously claims that "Had I gonn (as by this tyme I had donn) to the greene-dragone to fetch it, I could not have written *ex dono Authoris* upon it, as a wittnes to posterity that I was not only in y^r favor but in y^r esteeme too," whereby "that wch bought would have ben my cheifest delight only, is now that & my honor too" (294, 295, in mosaic). If Waller had not been so proleptically challenged in getting to "the greene-dragone" (not a pub but the same bookshop selling *Leviathan*), he should have ended up with two copies of Hobbes's most recent publication: the gift plus the one that "by this tyme" he would have purchased already. As he sped forward in the manner of Zeno's arrow, he was apparently overtaken by Hobbes, who may have been amused by his friend's sophistry. But if Waller was slow to obtain by his own means Hobbes's latest volume, he was swift to assure him concerning the effectiveness of its "Six Lessons" directed at two of his greatest rivals: "Wallis & his fellowe [Ward] (you have handeled . . . so well already) that I will say nothing of them, for if I should say all I approve in you or finde ridiculous in your adversarys I should requite y^r booke wth another" (295, square brackets added). Waller never did "requite" the augmented English *De Corpore* with such a defense, however; his "should" expressed not a sense of obligation but a hypothetical condition—one permitting him at present to "say nothing."

Perhaps only a rash author would have attempted to support Hobbes in his acrimonious disputes with the leading mathematicians of his day: his efforts to achieve such feats as squaring the circle were wrongheaded and rejected with much ridicule. On the other hand, Waller could conceivably have written on Hobbes's behalf without embroiling himself in the details of the mathematical disputes themselves: he gave in this same letter a taste of what more he could have accomplished in such a vein, expressing his contempt for a diatribe entitled *Examinations, Censures, and Confutations of Divers Errours in the Two First Chapters of Mr. Hobbes His "Leviathan"* (1656). Written by William Lucy, future bishop of St. David's, *Examinations* had appeared under the pseudonymous surname Pike. Noting that this soubriquet derives from a feeble pun, Waller mocks it in its own right and as a rhetorical gaffe: "it is ominous that he will prove but a pike to a leviathan, a narrowe river fish to one wch deserves the whole ocean for his theater" (295). Possibly expressing Waller's admiration for the sheer scope of *Leviathan*, this comment certainly confirms his ability to make witty capital of its title. Waller also responds to two related statements made by Lucy in his preface: that *Leviathan* is a "book I find admir'd by many Gentlemen," and that such persons, when "meeting with new opinions, and some shew of reason for them, are by that means furnished the next table-meeting to surprize a poor Country-Parson, such as I" (quoted, 296–97 n.5). Waller remarks of himself and his fellow "country-gentlemen" that

> sure, if wisdome comes by leasure, we may possibly be as good judges of philosophy as country-parsons are, all whose tyme is spent in saluting those wch come into the world att gossipings, takeing leave of those that goe out of it att funerals, & vexing those that stay in it with longwinded harangs. (295)

Waller demonstrates his class-solidarity, but not necessarily his inclusion among the "many Gentlemen" whom Lucy deemed *Leviathan*'s most likely devotees.

Whereas Waller's interest in translating *De Cive* possibly reached the point of requiring its author to furnish "an essaye," the additional Hobbes-related work that he did not produce to "requite" the augmented English *De Corpore* was by his own admission a purely notional expression of his continuing respect, so perhaps the two authors' friendship had dwindled since 1645. But the second of their extant letters to each other only came into existence because, as Waller explains at the beginning, he had originally meant to convey his gratitude for Hobbes's gift in person: "On Saterday last I was att y^r lodging by 9 a clocke in the morning (having ben by some urgent occasions prevented in my intention to wayt on you the day before) but came a little too late to tell what I hope you will admit this to doe" (294). Moreover, Hobbes's willingness to present Waller with a copy of his latest publication must mean that he was anxious to offload it on anyone who might take it or considered it somewhat "proportioned to the use & inclination of the receaver."

XII: "afrayd of the churchmen"

Though no more can be made of Waller's inaugural membership of the Royal Society than can be made of Cowley's, Aubrey's recollections suggest that Waller had at least some understanding of Hobbes's place in the history of ideas. Recalling the generosity that Newcastle had displayed during the later 1640s, Waller told Aubrey that "the lord marquisse of Newcastle was a great patron to Dr. Gassendi, and M. Des Cartes, as well as Mr. Hobbes, and that he hath dined with them all three at the marquiss's table at Paris" (1: 366). Given that Newcastle had ruined himself supporting Charles I, his largesse on this score was all the more impressive, especially in contrast to Waller's failure to make any such use of his own wealth, which remained considerable, even after payment of the fine that preceded his exile. Unless Waller was merely striving to impress Aubrey, however, he seems to have appreciated the significance of such a meeting of minds, even if his appreciation stopped well short of acting as "a great patron" himself. Waller's recognition of where Hobbes stood in relation to his intellectual peers likewise informs the last known contact between these sometime neighbors. Aubrey reports that Waller inquired through an intermediary about Hobbes's reaction to Spinoza's *Tractatus Theologico-Politicus* (1670); the answer returned apparently expressed Hobbes's frustration as a muzzled author: he felt "cut thorough . . . a barre's length, for he durst not write so boldly" (1: 357). Precisely what Hobbes intended by this last comment is hard to say, as Martinich insists.[44] Hobbes's notoriety as a suspected atheist removed the need to exercise caution in a context where he could not possibly give greater offense than he had already given. But the denunciations he had already received for expressing his views as a professed Christian and his partial silencing by Charles II meant that he could scarcely proceed at all, regardless of whether he had proceeded too "boldly" in the past.

The outrage Hobbes had stirred and the constraint he experienced as a muzzled author limited how "boldly" Waller himself felt he could venture when deliberating whether to pay him a tribute after his death. Though Aubrey then invited Waller to write "some verses" in Hobbes's "praise," the poet declined: "he was afrayd of the church-men" (1: 358). Even in itself, this refusal could be construed as an act of homage. In addition to owning a motive whose prominence in human affairs Hobbes had always maintained as a staple feature of his thought, Waller might have been echoing more specifically and to self-consciously witty effect the paradoxical pride with which Hobbes referred to his own fear. I thus go further than Gilbert, who merely remarks that "The basis of Waller's caution—fear—was certainly one Hobbes would have accepted" (27). Waller also refrained from commemorating Hobbes both despite and because of this conviction, reported by Aubrey: "what was chiefly to be taken notice of in his elogie was that he, being but *one*, and a private person, pulled-downe all the churches, dispelled the mists of ignorance, and layd-open their priest-craft" (1: 358). These words pay at least a portion of the tribute their speaker chose not to put in writing; they also echo the sardonic tone often heard in Hobbes's own remarks about religious issues, which have led some commentators to see as mere window-dressing the minimalist Christianity he professed.

Waller's praise for "a private person" who had succeeded in dismantling "all the churches" nonetheless remains elusive: such words might or might not correctly identify Hobbes as an atheist; their out-look could be interpreted as Hobbesian or Hobbist. Whereas Hobbists "boldly" profess in words and deeds an allegiance probably spurious, their Hobbesian counterparts confine themselves to verbal expression and tend to be Nicodemites. As Warrender notes, "while Hobbes had many admirers, very few identified themselves wholeheartedly and unambiguously with his thinking, or stood up with him to be counted," attributing this timidity to "the hazards of the political scene" and the degree to which even those readers of Hobbes who "approved his political insight" also in many cases "had reservations in matters of religion."[45] Though Waller cannot be counted among the "very few" who embraced Hobbes's thought "wholeheartedly and unambiguously," his off-the-record paean to the exposer of fraudulent "priest-craft" appears to express no "reservations" except concerning the prudence of committing such an opinion to print. His esteem for *De Cive* might not have been restricted to its "political insight," for he contemplated translating the entire volume, whether or not he agreed with all of it; and "the hazards of the political scene" had no apparent share in that project's demise. Moreover, even if he proved a Nicodemite when he failed to "requite" Hobbes's then latest volume with a "booke" documenting "all" he could "approve" in its author and found "ridiculous" in that figure's already numerous "adversarys," Waller was still an admirer who had maintained his respect over at least a decade that included his publication of an original poem incorporating a Hobbesian perspective on the relations between protection and obedience.

XIII: "private interest"

Though the zeitgeist of post-Restoration England possibly determined Waller's refusal to pen Hobbes an elegy and his informal appraisal of him as most notably a demolisher of "all the churches," he knew him in ways impossible for Hobbist or Hobbesian authors who had become such through an influence exerted quite recently and perhaps only at second hand. As I have argued elsewhere, however, this period's mutually sustaining extremes of piety and impiety had a decisive impact on Waller's final phase as a self-consciously reborn poet of sacred verses, beginning with *Of Divine Love* (ca. 1680).[46] According to this line of thought, Anne Wharton inspired much of Waller's slim volume *Divine Poems* (1685), as an exemplary author of pious verses in her own right and as Rochester's niece. Her uncle's dramatically penitential end in the summer of 1680 had transformed him from the greatest sinner of the age to the greatest reformed one. But this new identity still depended on the old. Allying himself with Rochester through Wharton, Waller benefited from the family connection, while keeping a safe distance. Though his sacred verses wage no war against the impiety formerly associated with Rochester, an already extant conflict declares their presumed allegiance, and the earliest of them explicitly rejects Epicurus (a libertine hero) and appears to disparage Hobbes—another such hero, via Hobbism. But whereas Waller confronted an apparently simple task in generating verses of orthodox piety (if that was his entire aim), or in doing so as a means of discrediting Hobbist-libertine values (a further ambition requiring little extra effort, given the cultural context), he showed incompetence in these areas that I take as evidence of his being in two minds about the validity of Hobbes's ideas.

Especially revealing are passages from Waller's last poetic effort of any kind, *On the Fear of God* (ca. 1687), where transparently pious intentions collide with a Hobbesian conception of the poem's subject instead of colluding with one based on orthodox faith: "Though the word fear some men may ill endure, / 'Tis such a fear as only makes secure," because "Where that fear is, there's nothing to be feared"; moreover, "Tranquillity and peace this fear does give; / Hell gapes for those that do without it live" (2: 1.3–4, 13, 15–16). The last of these sentiments appeals to self-interest by reversing the position that *Of Divine Love* establishes: "The fear of hell, or aiming to be blessed, / Savours too much of private interest" (2: 2.1–2). I stand by my case as originally stated down to the point that all of Waller's feelings about fear in his final poem are consonant with "Rationall Worship" as defined in *Leviathan*—"to speak Considerately of God," because this "argues a Fear of him, and Fear, is a confession of his Power" (404)—for I should have laid more stress on why such conceptions of fearful worship diverge from orthodox Christianity.

As Martinich notes (*Thomas Hobbes*, 59), the philosopher cited the Psalms' "the beginning of wisdom is fear of the Lord" when criticized for *Leviathan*'s controversial definition of "RELIGION" as "*Feare* of power invisible, feigned by the mind, or imagined from tales publiquely allowed" (124), a viewpoint whose various possible meanings Martinich then discusses at some length (59–63). But Hobbes's critics were not objecting simply because "the word fear some men may ill endure." Rather, his outlook appeared to deny Christianity any special status and to express the skeptical detachment of an observer for whom all religions are equally valid—or not. Waller could more justly have invoked the Psalmist's words to explain the focus of his last poem, except that—damningly—he did not seem to think he had any such sanction. Thus, Waller and Hobbes in presenting their religious views both addressed a topic (fear) with ample warrant in scripture, but gave grounds for suspecting that their thinking was unorthodox. Waller furthermore mingled his "fear of the Lord" with "private interest"—a motivation associated with Hobbes's account of human nature, as *Of Divine Love* seemed to acknowledge in opposing it.

Rejecting Warrender's much-discussed interpretation of Hobbes's philosophy, Sommerville observes that it generates an "entire system of obligation . . . grounded . . . upon God's commands, or perhaps upon fear of the penalties for breaking these commands" (76). If Warrender is correct, Hobbes little merited his contemporary reputation as an atheist, and the equivocation as to whether "commands" or "penalties" chiefly oblige in his philosophy overlaps with the same gray area charted by Waller's final poem. Conversely, if Sommerville is right in his critique of Warrender's thesis, then "The Idea that all obligation in Hobbes stems from God's will cannot be vindicated," and his "conception of morality is reducible to calculations of self-interest" (79), which does not make him an atheist, but helps explain why so many of his earliest readers took him to be one, and illustrates another way in which his thinking is paralleled in Waller's work. That such starkly opposed accounts of Hobbes's thought should yield two different versions of the same result does not doubly ascertain that *On the Fear* consciously or unconsciously draws on his ideas. Rather, it highlights the wide range of understandings that Hobbes's views on religion have promoted through his witting or unwitting failure to be less ambiguous on key points. Still, Waller the reborn author of sacred verses should have had little trouble skirting such treacherous reefs; his inability to stay clear of them seems to me a symptom less of his scant talent for this type of poetry than of the extent to which Hobbesian ideas had found a permanent lodging in his mind.

Chapter Five

"Absurd and Foolish Philosophy": *Hobbes and Rochester*

I: "long conservation"

When the reborn Waller made the penitent Rochester a talisman, he belatedly returned a compliment: Rochester had openly revealed his high regard for Waller, whose devotional phase and muted reciprocal gesture he did not live to see. In *An Allusion to Horace 10 Sat: 1st Book* (1680), Rochester proclaims Waller one who "In Panegyricks does excell Mankind."[1] Dorimant, the hero of Etherege's comedy *The Man of Mode* (1675), then and now thought to be based on Rochester, quotes Waller several times with evident relish.[2] As John Dennis records in *A Defence of "Sir Fopling Flutter," a Comedy* (1722), the traditional identification of Dorimant reflects Rochester's known habit of "repeating, on every Occasion, the Verses of *Waller*."[3] But according to Burnet, the satirically inclined Rochester "admired most" Nicolas Boileau and Cowley "among the *French*, and . . . *English* Wits"; and Aubrey relates how Waller maintained that "men write ill things well and good things ill; that satyricall writing was downhill, most easie and naturall; that at Billingsgate one might hear great heights of such witt; that the cursed earth naturally produces briars and thornes and weeds, but roses and fine flowers require cultivation."[4] "Panegyricks" and "satyricall writing" only meet as polar opposites.

Even so, Robert Parsons when preaching Rochester's funeral sermon claimed that the dead man might have penned "as excellent an Idea of Divine Poetry, under the Gospel, useful to the teaching of Virtue, especially in this generation, as his profane Verses have been to destroy it," because he had already demonstrated his innately "diligent and industrious" disposition when misapplying his gifts to produce "Panegyricks upon Vice."[5] Waller's poem *Of Divine Poesy* (1682) partly vindicates such logic, as inspired by Wharton's paraphrase of Isaiah 53, a chapter that her uncle, Rochester, cited as occasioning a spiritual breakthrough when he heard it read by Parsons, who explains how that author of "profane Verses" then "declar'd that *the mysteries of the Passion appeared so clear and plain to him, as ever any thing did that was represented in a Glass"* (24). The prophet's words thus acquired a powerful new significance because of their reputed impact on a figure previously noteworthy for so assiduously undermining virtue.

As Larry Carver maintains, prodigal sons outrank the life-long devout, as paradoxically valued according to the duration and degree of their waywardness.[6] By contrast, only blame attaches to the factors held responsible for such protracted wallowing in sin. Parsons reports that Rochester's reformation included this admission: *"that absurd and foolish Philosophy, which the world so much admired, propagated by the late Mr. Hobbs, and others, had undone him, and many more, of the best parts in the Nation"* (26). If Rochester here only renounced his past way of life, it bore so little relation to Hobbes's thought that it destroyed him at an early age. Burnet remembered Rochester confessing that "for five years together he was continually Drunk: not all the while under the visible effect of it, but his blood was so inflamed, that he was not in all that time cool enough to be perfectly Master of himself. This led him to say and do many wild and unaccountable things" (50–51). Hobbes so firmly opposed self-destructive behavior that John Bramhall, bishop of Derry, objected how "He maketh the only end of all the laws of nature to be *the long conservation of a mans life and members."*[7] This rebuke offers a notable exception to the rule that Hobbists espouse Hobbes's ideas in their denounced form alone. Hobbes himself did not suppose that he had emphasized the merits of self-preservation to the exclusion of all other considerations, including pious ones (albeit in this case smacking of redundancy): *De Cive* opposes "drunkenness" not only "because it impedes the use of reason" but also because "holy scripture forbids it for the same reason."[8]

II: "Extravagance . . . publiquely seen"

" 'Tis not consistent with an harmonicall soul to be a woman-hater, neither had he an abhorrescence to good wine," Aubrey records of Hobbes, stressing that "He was, even in his youth (generally) temperate, both as to wine and women," for "I have heard him say that he did beleeve he had been in excess in his life, a hundred times; which, considering his great age, did not amount to above once a yeare" (1: 350). Not everyone would now accept that limiting "excess" to an average of "once a yeare" constitutes abstemiousness, or that casual consumption of "women" is "consistent with an harmonicall soule," if similarly subject to moderation. Burnet employed phrasing like Aubrey's in explaining that Rochester justified "the gratification of our natural Appetites" because "It seemed unreasonable to imagine these were put into a man only to be restrained, or curbed to . . . a narrowness," which doctrine "he applied to the free use of Wine and Women" (57). Hobbes was clearly no alcoholic, however; and Aubrey perhaps oversells his claim that this donnish bachelor (for one) proved no misogynist. Sir Leslie Stephen notes that Aubrey's "arithmetic is erroneous," but adds of Hobbes's excesses that "twice a year would hardly bring him up to the average of his time."[9] Moreover, Aubrey describes how Hobbes even approached his own bingeing from a characteristically health-conscious standpoint:

> When he did drinke, he would drinke to excesse to have the benefitt of vomiting, which he did easily; by which benefit neither his witt was disturbt longer then he was spuing nor his stomach oppressed; but he never was, nor could not endure to be, habitually a good fellow, i.e. to drinke every day wine with company, which, though not to drunkennesse, spoiles the braine. (1: 350)

In addition, as Aubrey records, Hobbes's "dyet, etc., was very moderate and regular" during his "last 30+ yeares" (equivalent to Rochester's entire lifetime), as part of a regimen including "dayly walking," a determination "twice or thrice a yeare" to "play at tennis," and singing "when he was abed, and the dores made fast, and was sure nobody heard him . . . for his health's sake," because "he did beleeve it did his lunges good, and conduced much to prolong his life" (1: 350, 351, 352). Thus, wine, women, and song all figured in Hobbes's personal example of how to live in a "harmonicall" manner more hobbit than Hobbist.

Leviathan hints at another consideration possibly helping Hobbes keep his own drinking under control, for it explains that

> the variety of behaviour in men that have drunk too much, is the same with that of Mad-men: some of them Raging, others Loving, others Laughing, all extravagantly, but according to their severall domineering Passions: For the effect of the wine, does but remove Dissimulation; and takes from them the sight of the deformity of their Passions. For, (I believe) the most sober men, when they walk alone without care and employment of the mind, would be unwilling the vanity and Extravagance of their thoughts at that time should be publiquely seen: which is a confession, that Passions unguided, are for the most part mere Madnesse.[10]

Whereas Hobbes had not needed to "have drunk too much" himself to know of the "variety of behaviour" he describes, he can only have vouched for his second example of "Passions unguided" from his own experience. He gives the "vanity and Extravagance" of daydreaming no more than a horrified glance and should have known that, especially compared with the scope of minds not tethered by "care and employment," drunkards' "variety of behaviour" is quite limited. He might also have pondered why drunkards no longer having "sight of the deformity of their Passions" should worry so little about being observed, as their daydreaming counterparts are not. The answer must be that sufficient alcohol will "remove Dissimulation" and other forms or effects of inhibition, and that drunkards simply do not care how their conduct appears to sober and possibly reproving eyes. Less absolute today, the disparity in rank between tapsters and their loftiest clientele was virtually unbridgeable in Hobbes's lifetime, and also tended to "remove Dissimulation."

Such reflections are vital to an understanding of Rochester's capacity for scandal: he was never subject to the restraints implied by Hobbes's brief regression into a humors-based psychology, whereby "variety of behaviour" results from sundry individuals succumbing through intoxication to "domineering Passions" peculiar to each. A tavern unto himself, Rochester was not restricted to "Raging" rather than "Loving," or "Loving" instead of "Laughing"; he pursued "all" permutations so "extravagantly" that his "vanity and Extravagance of . . . thoughts" in every context exhibited the apparent freedom of one "alone" and "without care and employment of the mind," except that having such pub-like conduct "publiquely seen" would have been the whole point.

III: "a perfect *Hobbist*"

As David Farley-Hills stresses, Rochester "was a rebel whose pranks in defiance of conventional morality and manners have been chronicled almost to the obliteration of both man and poet," but "also very much an aristocrat, a man of immense social privileges, and these could only be upheld by an insistence on the traditional forms and ceremonies which articulated a complex and age-old social hierarchy."[11] Anthony à Wood nonetheless attributed Rochester's profligacy to his bad company: "he . . . frequented the Court (which not only debauched him but made him a perfect *Hobbist*)."[12] On this account, Rochester merely imitated others whose "debauched" and *"Hobbist"* conduct amounted to much the same thing, in their own eyes and those of contemporary observers. But even if Rochester began as a fellow traveler in creating scandal, he swiftly surpassed his peers in the impact he made, which sometimes set him at odds with the king. For James Turner, Rochester's turbulent relationship with Charles II exemplifies how "Libertine rebelliousness is a kind of dramatic testing procedure, like a child's testing of the boundaries of parental tolerance."[13] Even illustrating a type, however, Rochester characteristically pursued such "testing" to the furthest extreme imaginable: the "parental" authority he challenged was a king's. Moreover, though the association between high social rank and perceived or professed Hobbism has become a staple feature in discussions of the post-Restoration zeitgeist, chapter four records how Lucy before the end of the Interregnum had already noted or claimed that *Leviathan* found favor with gentlemen in particular; and Rochester the Hobbist still seems an exceptional figure compared with even the most dissolute of his high-born companions, if only because his own leanings in that direction received a more profound literary expression. Recent commentators on his work have tended to see it as a late-seventeenth-century equivalent of Donne's recognition of how "new philosophy calls all in doubt," thus viewing his ultimately rescinded investment in an *"absurd and foolish Philosophy"* as more significant than just an acknowledgment of the cost exacted by a principled devotion to sensational excess.[14]

Perhaps Rochester thereby disowned his best work: John Adlard "is sad . . . to see him surrendering, in his sickness, to a second-rate debater like Burnet."[15] On the other hand, Jeremy Treglown emphasizes how Rochester "was under intense pressure to repent and to be seen to do so," whereas Jeremy Lamb depicts a dying alcoholic simply incapable of knowing his own mind.[16] By further contrast, Carver maintains that Rochester's oeuvre "everywhere reflects his Christian and God-fearing upbringing and provides evidence, if anything, of an excessive preoccupation with and acceptance of Christian orthodoxy which Rochester, for all his efforts, could never banish with pagan reasons" (89–90). Rochester's well-documented love of dressing up had an intellectual counterpart in the variety of personae and points of view adopted in his poetry, none pursued by halves. "The ability to assume another's role is a striking feature of his poetry, as of his life," observes Keith Walker.[17] As with his "testing," so here, Rochester typifies and takes to a characteristic extreme a general tendency noted by Turner, who comments that "libertinism was not so much a philosophy as a set of performances," with "defining 'properties'. . . better understood as theatrical props than as precise attributes."[18]

Insofar as "philosophy" entered Rochester's work, it did so quixotically, according to Thomas Rymer, whose "Rochester Preface" of 1691 claimed that "No Imagination cou'd bound or prescribe whither his Flights would carry him: were the Subject light, you find him a Philosopher, grave and profound, to wonder: Were the Subject lumpish and heavy, then wou'd his Mercury dissolve all into Gaity and Diversion."[19] Possibly anxious to establish Rochester as no mere peddler of smut, however, most recent commentators have tended to "find him a Philosopher" everywhere, not slighting his propensity for "Gaity and Diversion," nor stressing his own capacity to be "grave and profound," but attributing his ideas and phrases to a variety of intellectual stimuli, including Hobbes's influence.

IV: "but *Lucretius* enlarg'd"

Though his only evidence consists of more limited assertions by Parsons and Wood that I have already quoted, Vivian de Sola Pinto asserts that "Rochester read Hobbes's books with enthusiasm in his early youth and accepted his philosophy wholeheartedly."[20] "It is unlikely that Rochester had merely imbibed a few catch phrases from a popular 'philosophy' of his day, Hobbesian materialism or Epicureanism," Dustin Griffin more circumspectly remarks.[21] However, Griffin also classifies *Leviathan* as a book "that Rochester very likely read," adding that "There are a few statements by contemporaries to suggest that he knew Hobbes well," though instancing only Wood, introduced as "not a careful witness," and in connection with words interpreted "more likely" to convey not that Rochester was "a disciple of Hobbes" but that he "had adopted the bold but fashionable view that all knowledge derives from sense" (15). Though "unlikely" and "very likely" point in the same direction, the difference in their intensity lacks sanction in the available evidence; and they are contradicted by "more likely," which collapses the distinction between "a popular 'philosophy' " and a "fashionable view." Given how much else Rochester reputedly "imbibed," the odds are he had little opportunity to become acquainted with more than "catch phrases." But we simply do not know about the scope of his reading except where it left discernible traces in his work. Rochester was surely steeped in the history of ideas when writing *A Satyre against Reason and Mankind* (1679) if it merits Walker's description of it as "deeply influenced by Hobbes and Montaigne" (282); but this summary formulation exaggerates the tenor of a tradition of commentary about the poem that is itself based on overstatement and largely indifferent to the question of how Rochester reconciled two or more such immersions, if these were indeed profound.

Observing that "The male speakers in Rochester's poems can be ranged on a spectrum of identities," David Vieth deems a "strident hedonist and Hobbist" the narrator "who declaims most of 'A Satyr,' " but does not otherwise descend to particulars or explain the interrelationship of the sources perceived as informing a poem "indebted to Hobbes, Montaigne, and the tradition of *le libertinage* generally."[22] Rightly suggesting Rochester's broad scope of expression, Vieth misleadingly narrows the intellectual heritage of *A Satyre* to a smooth continuum of thought with no disjuncture between Hobbes-derived attitudes and those characterizing a Hobbist. Similarly, Farley-Hills explains that Rochester's *Satyre*

> is essentially a poem in the tradition of philosophical scepticism that aimed to demonstrate the limitations of the human mind in solving metaphysical problems. This scientific scepticism was, of course, very influential during the Restoration period and informs, for instance, Hobbes' philosophical work and much of Cowley's poetry.
>
> The tradition of philosophical scepticism, however, is also represented among the French satirists, where it derives in part from Montaigne. (165)

Though Pinto accepts Vieth's conjectural date of composition for *A Satyre*, he differs from both that commentator and Farley-Hills in the conclusions he reaches about the poem's significance as a guide to the workings of Rochester's mind:

> Hobbes's materialism had appealed to him at first because of its boldness and the justification that it offered for the life of pleasure. But the *Satyr against Mankind* shows that by the spring of 1675–6 he was outgrowing that "seducing system", and it was natural that he should turn to the other unorthodox creeds which were current at the time in Western Europe. As he was often in Paris, it is highly probable that he knew something of the works of the French "libertins." (186)

These words show how the same pieces of evidence patterned in one way by Vieth and Farley-Hills can yield an exactly opposite picture, where "unorthodox creeds" can be differentiated rather than lumped together as "*libertinage* generally" or a "scepticism" at once "philosophical" and "scientific" (as well as literary, and more especially satirical). But Pinto's analysis depends on a chronology no longer regarded as valid by most Rochester scholars; and no writer's movements of thought can be reconstructed with such assurance on the basis of so little evidence. Moreover, the "natural" progression charted means that even Rochester's "outgrowing" of Hobbes or Hobbism marks no real break.

Pinpointing the issue at stake here, Griffin remarks of *A Satyre*'s view of reason that "Rochester no doubt derived his conception from the climate of free thought all around him, in which Hobbism and Epicureanism were prominent. Since the poem alludes throughout to complex philosophical ideas, it is impossible to say whether the allusions are specific or general" (170). In this disarming admission, an inability to differentiate between "allusions" of a "specific" and a "general" kind nowhere impedes the perception that they relate to "complex philosophical ideas." Because both sorts of intellectual legacies equally well define the perceived texture of Rochester's work, they prove mutually reinforcing when taken together, as merely entering the same endless loop at different points. Thus, the consensus that his thought has roots in a very rich soil considerably broadens his possible reading while paradoxically minimizing the actual variety of his concerns: in each of his imputed allegiances, he simultaneously proves loyal to all of them.

Hobbes's younger contemporaries certainly sensed overlaps between his thinking and that of such libertine heroes as Lucretius and Epicurus. In the preface he wrote for his own translation of the Roman philosopher (1681), Thomas Creech managed to conflate him with the Greek and English one as well, stressing how "the admirers of Mr. *Hobbes* may easily discern that his *Politics* are but *Lucretius* enlarg'd; His state of *Nature* is sung by our *Poet*; the rise of *Laws*; the beginning of *Societies*; the *Criteria* of *Just* and *Unjust* exactly the same; and natural *Consequents* of the Epicurean Origine of Man."[23] Whether Creech was promoting Lucretius at Hobbes's expense or forging an alliance between them, he exaggerates their similarities and concludes ambiguously: does his casual phrasing mean that "the Epicurean Origine of Man" is a matter of fact with certain "natural *Consequents*" or that those results will infallibly follow from any thinker's adopting such a conception of humanity for a starting point? Hobbes wasted his life if he generated a philosophy "exactly the same" as Lucretius's, whose thought he could more economically have "enlarg'd" as a translator. Though Samuel Mintz cannot resist perpetuating the tradition whereby "it is certain Rochester had read and admired Hobbes," his main point rests on a worthwhile distinction: Hobbes's role "in shaping [that poet's] intellectual outlook is small when contrasted with the influence of Seneca and Lucretius."[24] These words serve as an apt corrective to Lamb's claim that Rochester's version of a chorus by Seneca reveals "more clearly" than any of his other poems "the influence of Hobbism," implausibly construed as a "sensual brand of atheism" derived directly from Hobbes's own work (74, 32).

Addressing the one poem of Rochester's most commonly interpreted as substantially indebted to Hobbes's thought, Thomas Fujimara's analysis of *A Satyre* attempts to define where such influence begins and ends. For Fujimara, "the first section of the poem" combines "support of right reason (limited to practical concerns)" with an "attack on speculative reason (dealing with nonsense)," prompting these conclusions: "The main concern is epistemological, and the basic ideas are largely paralleled by those in Hobbes's *Leviathan*."[25] By contrast, the remainder of *A Satyre* focuses on "ethics" and differs from Hobbes's thinking in tone and content, to the point where "the voice of the poet is clearly heard" (210). But if the limits Fujimara sets to Rochester's borrowing from Hobbes's work offer a refreshing alternative to more sweeping assertions made in that regard, the echoes he retains depend too heavily on tidy partitioning. Griffin rightly dissents because "The conception of right reason presented by the poem insists on our considering epistemology and ethics together," and furthermore stresses that *A Satyre*'s "power and appeal . . . depend less on its derived philosophical content than on its vigorous surge and flow . . . and the consequent ambiguity of its argument" (199, 197). Whereas Griffin's own derivation of "complex philosophical ideas" from "allusions" both "general" and "specific" exemplifies the type of approach tending to muffle the centrifugal energies released in Rochester's best work, his reading of *A Satyre* remains an especially helpful guide to the poem's unpredictable shifts of tone and viewpoint.

V: "an Ignis fatuus"

A Satyre's radical contempt for humanity sometimes overwhelms the logical structure of its argument, which begins by assailing the first of its twin targets, and then, only after rehearsing the objections raised by "some formal band and beard," clarifies that "Tis not true Reason I despise, but yours" (46, 111). In overstating a case whose scope it thereafter restricts, Rochester's poem adopts a rhetorical strategy often deployed in *Leviathan*. As Ralph Ross observes, the author of that text will routinely be found

> stating a case as directly and unequivocally as possible to make an immediate impact on the reader. Once the impact has been made, however, the qualifications follow. If the qualifications meet all the objections that came to the reader's mind when he recovered from the shock of the first statement, he may be persuaded. But the qualifications take much away from what Hobbes said originally, and may even convert it into something else. When the qualifications do not follow at once on a statement, but come later, sometimes much later, Hobbes seems inconsistent even when he is not.[26]

But this point of resemblance also brings out the contrast in intensity between Rochester's "qualifications" and Hobbes's, always less dramatic, just as his "immediate impact" never hits so hard. Though Farley-Hills stresses that *A Satyre* "is, paradoxically enough, conceived in syllogistic form and Rochester's chief scorn is often reserved for the stupid and the irrational" (172), its overall volatility and recourse to "shock" tactics more extreme than Hobbes's underscore the implausibility of Fujimara's assessment of the poem's "epistemological" character. But Pinto flies too far in the opposite direction when terming *A Satyre*'s opening lines "an attack on Reason, the idol of Hobbes and the freethinkers of the age," constituting "in some measure a recantation, a turning-back of Rochester on himself" (152): such an argument subordinates the omni-directional reversals of the poem to a relatively ordered intellectual progression (assumed rather than demonstrated) in which Hobbes, previously embraced, is then renounced.

When *A Satyre* deems "Reason" (retroactively redefined as the abuse of that faculty) "an Ignis fatuus of the Mind, / Which leaving Light of Nature, sense, behind," travels through "Pathless and dangerous wandring wayes" (12–14), it possibly recalls how *Leviathan* condemns proponents of *"School-Divinity"* because their teachings "make men mistake the *Ignis fatuus* of Vain Philosophy, for the Light of the Gospell" (708), as Harold Love suggests in the edition quoted (385). But Hobbes himself perhaps drew on Bramhall's *Defence of True Liberty* (1655), part of their controversy over free will (originating in debates conducted a decade earlier): "He who leaves the conduct of his understanding to follow vulgar notions shall plunge himself into a thousand errors, like him who leaves a certain guide to follow an *ignis fatuus* or a will-with-the wisp."[27] These remarks would have made an impression on Hobbes, as directed against him by a proponent of that *"School-Divinity" Leviathan* derides, making "the *Ignis fatuus* of Vain Philosophy" a plausible return of serve. As Griffin shows, however, Rochester could have found his imagery in many places besides the pages of Bramhall and Hobbes (211–13); Walker sees *A Satyre*'s wording at this juncture as most closely anticipated in the poetry of Francis Quarles (283). Love nonetheless observes (386) that Rochester's "Ignis fatuus" departs from a "Light of Nature" possibly echoing *Leviathan:* "there is no conception in a mans mind, which hath not at first, totally, or by parts, been begotten upon the organs of Sense" (85). In itself, though, this potential link offers too slender a basis on which to concur with Fujimara's view of the "epistemological" relationship between Rochester's thought and Hobbes's, or to disagree with Griffin's suggestion that Rochester only resembled Hobbes on the very limited and indirect dimension of having "adopted the bold but fashionable view that all knowledge derives from sense."

Moreover, *A Satyre* diverges so sharply from Hobbes's perspective that at an early stage it buries homo sapiens with this epitaph: "Hudled in dirt the reasoning Engine lies, / Who was so proud, so witty and so wise" (29–30). Love glosses Rochester's "Engine" by referencing Descartes and Robert Boyle (387), but not Hobbes, a mechanistic philosopher whose significance for the poem is assessed otherwise, in the claim that *A Satyre*'s "ideas stand in a tradition of reductive naturalism to which Boileau was explicitly opposed, and which found its most influential English exponent in Hobbes" (383). But whereas Hobbes portrayed humans as mechanical beings capable of malfunctioning, often dramatizing the perversely self-destructive fate incurred by "the reasoning Engine," his builders of civil society had accomplished much, and certainly enough to make wholly regrettable any relapse into the state of nature. By contrast, *A Satyre* denies all but superficial achievements to civil society, hardly spares even "true Reason" from its all-encompassing scorn, and so strongly asserts the merits of nature (as embodied in animals other than humans) that rationality and mechanism receive a disdainful treatment at odds with Hobbes's emphasis.

VI: "Man or Beast"

"I'de be a Dog, a Monky, or a Bear," *A Satyre*'s speaker professes, "Or any thing but that vain Animal / Who is so proud of being Rational," further explaining with respect to "Man" that "For all his Pride and his Philosophy, / Tis evident Beasts are in their degree, / As wise at least, and better farr than he" (5–7, 112, 114–16). Stuart Sherman even suggests that *A Satyre* could be voiced by "a satyr."[28]

Questioning "Which is the Basest Creature, Man or Beast," the poem leaves no doubt, stressing that

> Birds feed on birds, Beasts on each other prey,
> But savage Man alone does man betray:
> Prest by necessity they kill for food,
> Man undoes Man to do himself no good.
> With teeth and claws by nature arm'd, they hunt
> Natures allowance to supply their want.
> But man with smiles, embraces, friendship, praise,
> Inhumanly his fellows life betrayes. (128–36)

This outlook has less in common with Hobbes's than with Waller's poem *Of Divine Love*, which possibly echoes Rochester's *Satyre* in noting now

> greedy wolves unguarded sheep devour
> But while their hunger lasts, and then give o'er;
> Man's boundless avarice his want exceeds,
> And on his neigbours round about him feeds.
> His pride and vain ambition are so vast,
> That, deluge-like, they lay whole nations waste.[29]

Marianne Thormählen comments that Waller's "observation of men and animals leads him to comparisons resembling those of Rochester's satirist," only to dismiss "These resemblances" as "surely coincidental."[30] An avowed student of context, she here succumbs to a pressure she partly resists (to gloss *A Satyre* wholly in terms of its presumed indebtedness to Hobbes and "*libertinage* generally"), eschewing a link departing too abruptly from this tradition of commentary, though it had occurred to her in an unforced way as an apparently authentic response.

In contrast to Rochester and Waller, *De Cive*'s dedicatory epistle maintains that

> There are two maxims which are surely both true: *Man is a God to man*, and *Man is a wolf to Man*. The former is true of the relations of citizens with each other, the latter of relations between common-wealths. In justice and charity, the virtues of peace, citizens show some likeness to God. But between commonwealths, the wickedness of bad men compels the good too to have recourse, for their own protection, to the virtues of war, which are violence and fraud, i.e. to the predatory nature of beasts. (3–4)

Uncharacteristically, Hobbes implies that "bad men" reduce "good" to their own level in "relations between commonwealths," whereas "the virtues of war" prove the same for all nations. He tacitly corrects himself in his next sentence: "Though men have a natural tendency to use rapacity as a term of abuse against each other, seeing their own actions reflected in others as in a mirror where left becomes right and right becomes left, natural right does not accept that anything that arises from the need for self-preservation is a vice" (4). Because no supranational agency regulates "relations between commonwealths," states fight each other under the same circumstances in which individuals battle in the state of nature, and "rapacity" can only be "a term of abuse," unless accounted one of "the virtues of war": either way, the words have no meaning in the absence of international laws defining what combatants are permitted to do. The constraints that protect members of a civil society from each other no longer apply when some of them fight individuals from another body politic: as in *Leviathan*'s "warre of every man against every man," so in such a conflict, "nothing can be Unjust," because "notions of Right and Wrong, Justice and Injustice have there no place," as impossible without the intervention of some "common Power" (188).

Hobbes's confused assimilation of *"Man"* and *"wolf"* suggests that the concept of warfare troubled him: he wavers between condemning it and exonerating it as "natural." *Leviathan* likewise stumbles, albeit in a different way: here, "the virtues of war . . . are violence and fraud" becomes "Force, and Fraud, are in warre the two Cardinall vertues" (188). Whereas this later formulation works on its own terms, Hobbes misleadingly embeds it in his account of the state of nature, as if it were context-specific; he does not spell out that this typifies how "left becomes right and right becomes left" under conditions of "natural right," or that his words apply not only to "warre of every man against every man" but also to conflict between civil societies. At least no "predatory nature of beasts" comes into play, however.

If Hobbes's attempted equation of *"wolf"* and *"Man"* misrepresents his thought, this rare instance of his placing people and "beasts" on an equal footing still conveys a difference between his own perspective and that of Waller and Rochester: whereas *De Cive* distinguishes the mutual relations of citizens from those of commonwealths when defining the circumstances under which humans should rightly be bestial (and then, of necessity), *Of Divine Love* deplores international conflict as a gross repudiation of the example set by its subject—apt to "make inward peace, / And foreign strife among the nations cease" (2: 5.45–46)—and *A Satyre* views civil society as mere anarchy periwigged.

VII: "every man's hand against
every man"

For Warren Chernaik, however, such a vision of post-Restoration society marks no departure from Hobbes's state of nature but rather a distinctively libertine way (not confined to Rochester) of drawing on it. "The state of nature, which Hobbes depicts . . . as an intolerable condition from which man, by the iron laws of self-preservation, must seek at all costs to escape," according to Chernaik, "the libertine poets and playwrights of the Restoration period present as 'the way of the world', an empirical description of the life around them."[31] In itself, *The Way of the World* (1700) opposes this approach, for Chernaik explains how Congreve here "employs a method akin to the reductio ad absurdum of satire: the libertine interpretation of Hobbesian principles, in which life is seen as unlimited, deadly competition, is shown to be self-defeating and inimical to civilised life" (40). Such an "interpretation" reverses Hobbes's meaning: he encouraged readers to embrace their not "unlimited" condition as law-abiding citizens so that they might continue enjoying the benefits of a "civilised life" rather than sinking back into the "deadly competition" of universal conflict. Though Chernaik claims to reconstruct a reading of Hobbes produced by post-Restoration libertines, his own misrepresentation of *Leviathan* permits his verdict that "Dorimant's unscrupulousness . . . equips him for success in a world where, as Hobbes puts it, force and fraud are the cardinal virtues" (12). Chernaik invents "deadly competition" by applying a comment on warfare to "a world."

Not all of Chernaik's evidence takes so weak a form. He explains how "a rather battered, disreputable rake says in Sir Charles Sedley's *Bellamira* (1687), paraphrasing Hobbes: 'In matter of Women, we are all in the State of Nature, every man's hand against every man. Whatever we pretend' " (214). Moreover, Chernaik acknowledges that the adaptation of Hobbes he attributes to his libertine writers involves strain: he recognizes "the problems which arise when ideas originally developed in a political context by such authors as Hobbes and Locke are applied to the domestic sphere, and in particular to the conduct of sexual relationships inside and outside the constraints of marriage" (18). But these words point up one of numerous ways in which Hobbes's state of nature cannot be "precisely the world depicted in many Restoration comedies," as Chernaik maintains (35): "constraints of marriage" represent a form of social organization incompatible with primal anarchy. As *Bellamira*'s rake surely knew, the womanizers whose outlook he expresses cannot occupy and opt out of society in pursuing any object of desire. Even when most energetically stealing each other's sexual partners, members of any community can no more reside in the state of nature than fallen humanity can return to Eden. The failure to distinguish between civil society and its absence that Chernaik would attribute to his libertine writers takes a self-evidently absurd turn with his "Hobbesian nightmare, chapter XIII of the *Leviathan* brought to life"—in a park (37).

Such an environment ill suits Chernaik's "central tenet" of "Hobbesian . . . psychology," one that "leads to a radical ontological insecurity and an ethic of ruthless egoism, seen both as necessary for survival in the jungle of the world and as emotionally intolerable" (61). But unlike a "jungle," Hobbes's state of nature was an environment to which humans could not and did not adapt, and from which they had to escape by producing an alternative setting still less susceptible to characterization in such terms. In taking this step, Hobbes's early humans made choices that Chernaik denies them: he insists that "In the Hobbesian world of human relationships . . . the only options open are victory or defeat" (155). The very existence of civil society as a compromise solution indicates that even the state of nature offered other "options" than just those two. The choice exercised in contracting to leave behind the state of nature generated communities capable of fostering additional alternatives.

Nonetheless, Chernaik is no more idiosyncratic in seeking to collapse any distinction between civil society and the state of nature than in claiming that Hobbes presents either or both sets of circumstances in terms of a "jungle," or in stressing that he posits a crudely dichotomous model of human interaction in which, wherever they find themselves, people must pair up as winners and losers, predators and prey, bullies and wets. In substantiating how often Hobbes has been misunderstood in one or more of these ways, I note the further and likewise popular misconception that he loathed nature as a sort of anti-Romantic.

VIII: "the Created state"

Fujimara comments that, for Rochester, and "Despite the existence of a human society, the state of war is maintained, though now through subterfuge; instead of open acts of aggression, men hypocritically undermine and destroy other men, through 'smiles, embraces, Friendship, praise.' " Hobbes did not suppose that only "open acts of aggression" occurred in the state of nature, however; he left room for "subterfuge" too ("fraud"). Fujimara attempts to justify his position by arguing that "the most vainglorious" individuals in Hobbes's state of nature "must, if they be possessed of power, feel considerable confidence of success in their aggression against their weaker neighbors" (213). But such logic ignores Hobbes's point that people in the state of nature are more alike than different; their mutual relations can only be fluid or uncertain, which explains the impossibility of any sovereign power's emergence through a process of natural selection. As John Laird observes, Hobbes believed that in the state of nature "nearly any weakling, given a favourable opportunity, was strong enough to hurt . . . and even to *kill*."[32] Because might alone cannot prevail under such circumstances, acts of "subterfuge" potentially threaten even the most seemingly powerful or militant individuals, who likewise remain vulnerable to fleeting coalitions of forces, based however temporarily on "smiles, embraces, friendship, praise." Whereas anarchic conditions could yield a given day's top dog, however, they could not result in unchecked mastery or abject subjection for any one kind of protagonist.

Tom Sorell therefore has no case when he concludes that

> Hobbes cannot make great claims for the power of the state to transform people for the better, and hold at the same time that were the state to dissolve, its people would immediately revert to savagery. If competitiveness and the hunger for glory are causes of quarrel indelibly engraved in human nature, then there cannot be a state made up of men who are free of the hunger or of the urge to compete. Either the truths about men that Hobbes states are scientific, or they are not. If they are not, they cannot endow an argument for absolutism in sovereignty and quiescence in subjection with any scientific authority. If they *are* scientific truths, on the other hand, then . . . they must hold no matter what political arrangements men live under.[33]

Though Hobbes possibly exaggerated the extent to which civil wars entail an abrupt reversion to the state of nature, he looked to government to restrain people rather than "transform" them, and thought a high level of power necessary to do so, but not because of their propensity for "savagery." Hobbes's state of nature gave people no meaningful choice of how to behave because their prospects under such circumstances were so bleak. According to Hobbes, traits conceivably filling some productive function in civil society ("competitiveness and the hunger for glory") could only heighten the conflict and uncertainty in the state of nature. Acknowledging that "The state can inhibit . . . dispositions, make it dangerous for people to behave aggressively," and thus need not "transform" them, Sorell nonetheless insists that Hobbes's analysis means that "at bottom subjects in the commonwealth must always be the savage and warlike creatures they start out as" (125). But Hobbes's state of nature itself is "warlike," not the "uncivilized . . . creatures" within it, who simply have no opportunity to transcend their conditions, and therefore are equally hapless whether they engage in "open acts of aggression," or "subterfuge," or any behavior not conducive to the formation of civil society.

Revealingly, the weakness of Sorell's analysis leads him to maintain that Hobbes's philosophy envisions humans in a manner akin to *A Satyre*'s outlook: he speculates that "perhaps their nature is so unfortunate that their being left free to kill themselves off in the state of nature would be, from a sufficiently detached point of view, no bad thing," for they "deep down are only arrant wolves," and "discoverably unattractive as specimens of living creatures" (125, 126). Concerning the state of nature, *Leviathan* makes the crucial point that

> WARRE, consisteth not in Battell onely, or the act of fighting; but in a tract of time, wherein the Will to contend by Battell is sufficiently known: and therefore the notion of *Time*, is to be considered in the nature of Warre; as it is in the nature of Weather. For as the nature of Foule weather, lyeth not in a showre or two of rain; but in an inclination thereto of many dayes together: So the nature of War, consisterth not in actuall fighting; but in the known disposition thereto, during all the time there is no assurance to the contrary. All other time is PEACE. (185–86)

Thus, Hobbes's precivilized humans are neither "arrant wolves" nor outright lambs, but equally prey to chronic insecurity, having zero "assurance to the contrary." Again illustrating Whiggism's parodic relation to Hobbes's thought, Crane Brinton finds "several faults" in the figurative use of "storm" by analysts of political crisis, commenting that it "is too literary and too dramatic for our purposes, too close altogether to the metaphor as used by prophets and preachers," but cannot refrain from making the Civil Wars inevitable by characterizing the years of Charles I's personal rule (1629–40) as "the calm before the storm."[34]

Reporting how "In Rochester's view, the commonwealth— Hobbes's system of political restraints and protections—is no less brutish or insecure than the state of nature it was designed to escape," Griffin dramatizes the divergence between *A Satyre*'s concerns and Hobbes's (237). Elsewhere, however, Griffin makes the contrasting and more general point that "Rochester's world is like the Hobbesian state of nature: war of all on all. Victory goes not to the wits, but to the cheats, crafty and self-interested, and to women" (133). If this resemblance held true, then "Victory" would belong to nobody: Hobbes described a primal anarchy with no settled outcomes. Maximilian Novak perpetrates the same error in this reading of *A Satyre*:

> Influenced by Hobbes's concept of the state of nature, a state in which humankind live in fear of the depredations of those willing to use their power against the weak, Rochester extended the state of nature into society itself, which he viewed as dominated by the "knaves"—those who are willing to use their abilities to dominate the "fools" of the society.[35]

Any such extension makes nonsense of the very "concept" at issue, again betraying the common but false assumption that Hobbes's state of nature features a static conflict between distinct types of beings. Pinto offers another kind of false extension in reflections arising from his claim that whereas Hobbes's "young readers cared little for his political philosophy," they were attracted by "the reasoned defence of sensuality" that he also offered:

> It is true that Hobbes had gone on to argue that laws were necessary to put an end to the "state of nature" when man was governed only by his desires, but his philosophy implies the notion that sensuality is the natural state of man and that laws are merely man-made conveniences necessary for the preservation of society. Rochester with that logical directness which was characteristic of his mind tried the experiment of putting the "state of nature" to the text [*sic*] of practice. (29)

Hobbes had sought to convince his audience of the need for obedience to law as essential to and co-extensive with the creation of civil society. Though Rochester was free to pick and choose among Hobbes's arguments, he would have been strikingly naïve if he thereby thought that while retaining an especially privileged position in civil society he could simultaneously revive a state of nature requiring an alteration in everyone else.

In his interpretation of Rochester's poem "*The Fall*" (1680), Pinto again claims that for Hobbes "sensuality is the natural state of man."

> How blest was the Created state
>   Of Man and Woman er'e they fell
> Compar'd to our unhappy Fate:
>   Wee need not feare another Hell.

Naked beneath coole shades they lay:
   Enjoyment waited on desire.
Each member did their wills obey
   Nor could a wish sett pleasure higher.

But we poore slaves to hope and fear
   Are never of out Joyes secure:
They lessen still as they draw nere
   And none but dull delights endure. (1–12)

According to Pinto, Rochester here "contrasts the 'state of nature' before the introduction of 'law' in the sense of Hobbes, with the incapability of man to find complete pleasure in the life of the senses now" (31). But whereas a parodic and possibly ambivalent response to scripture typifies Rochester's writing and that of other exponents of "*libertinage* generally," Hobbes reconstructed the state of nature without reference to Genesis; and *Leviathan* sanctions neither the drudgery of "poore slaves" addicted to unfulfilling sex nor its paradisal reverse when contending that "because the constitution of a mans Body, is in continuall mutation; it is impossible that all the same things should alwayes cause in him the same Appetites, and Aversions" (120). At the opposite extreme from Pinto, Farley-Hills explains why Rochester would not wish to reconstruct Hobbes's state of nature, summarizing *A Satyre*'s "Hobbesian argument" as the proposition that "In his natural state man is far more vicious and 'unnatural' than other animals" (184). But Hobbes had made no comparison of this kind: he did not refer to "other animals" in such a context or characterize as "vicious" a mode of existence in which neither virtues nor vices figured, having yet to be defined in so purely "natural" a setting.

Whatever merit informs his reading of Rochester's *Letter from Artemiza in the Towne to Chloe in the Countrey* (1679) as "a vision of man's predicament as . . . caught in a Hobbesian search of power after power" (205), Farley-Hill's reflection that this poem shows how "Hobbesian 'natural' man is ironically more likely to be found in the town than in the country" assumes that a rural location ought to approximate Hobbes's state of nature (209). Similarly, Jessica Munns remarks that "Hobbes's defence of singular, and distinctly urban, authority to control a warlike and savage state of nature severs nature from law, as nature can only negatively justify civic society"; not Hobbes but Davenant defined "Cities" as "Wall'd-Parks of Hearded Men."[36] A rural community sufficiently organized to lay down and uphold laws would prove Hobbes's point: leaving the state of nature does not mean forsaking country life. Conversely, modern commentators sometimes invoke his state of nature to describe urban districts where spiraling poverty and crime eliminate most forms of security. Maintaining that "For Hobbes the pristine land was a disgusting wilderness," Turner neglects to acknowledge that Hobbes meant not to bury the countryside but to praise human work, including *Leviathan*'s "Culture of the Earth" (186), as permitted under conditions of ordered peace.[37]

Confirming that Hobbes's thinking about the state of nature is one of the least well-understood aspects of his philosophy, Derek Hughes links the heroes of Dryden's plays *The Conquest of Granada* (1670) and *The Indian Queen* (1664, written with Sir Robert Howard), observing that Almanzor "was brought up outside the limits of civilization" and that Montezuma was "brought up outside civil society," classifying each as "a noble savage" illustrating how "the heritage of the Hobbesian savage is a persistent and disruptive one."[38] Though the state of nature depicted in *Leviathan*'s thirteenth chapter is certainly a savage environment, it features no noble savages, which can only be registered as such from the perspective of an outsider for whom such evaluative terms have become meaningful. As Philip Parsons maintains, "Hobbes's 'state of nature'. . . precedes all law and all moral value."[39] Perhaps Hobbes's bold thought-experiment in imagining the primal anarchy of a world without the first trappings of civilization gave some impetus to the cluster of Enlightenment ideas involving noble savages. But it cannot have done more than that, if the relevant portion of *Leviathan* offers any guide in its remarks about Native Americans' "brutish manner" of living (187). In quoting this passage in chapter two, I noted that Hobbes half-heartedly makes an unwarranted concession without securing any advantages; this is the worst of both worlds, rhetorically, but not one inhabited by noble savages.

Conversely, ignoble savagery preoccupies Hughes when he comments that "In examining humanity in the state of nature" the Davenant–Dryden adaptation (1667) of *The Tempest* "portrays not the regenerative nature of Shakespeare but the nature of Hobbes," because "The most common images of nature in the play are of predatory beasts and of poison, and there is no masque of reapers."[40] Concurring with Chernaik, this comment supposes that Hobbes conceived the primal anarchy of an uncivilized world as a "jungle" environment where humans act as "predatory beasts" (or serve as their prey). But Hobbes did not share the perspective expressed by the natural or illegitimate son Edmund in *King Lear* (1604–05): "Thou, Nature, art my goddess."[41] Though Edmund can hope to resemble the alpha male dominating many communities of beasts, Hobbes's humans in a precivilized world are too much alike for any self-selecting leader to emerge and begin imposing order. Richard Strier rightly distrusts James Black's claim that Nahum Tate's adaptation (1681) of *King Lear* makes a "Hobbesian 'natural man' " out of Edmund, and could have rejected it more forcefully if it did not treat the first of these epithets as interchangeable with "Hobbist"; again rightly, he also dismisses Nancy Klein Maguire's interpretation of "the political position of the play as a whole" as "Hobbesian."[42] Mary Ann Radzinowicz suggests that Milton portrays Nimrod as having "brought about a condition very like Hobbes's 'state of nature' "; she even compares Hobbes himself with this first ruler, as thinking "he can make names mean what he wills them to mean."[43] But Hobbes emphasized the importance of definitions because he wished to avoid the common tendency for people to use words in a self-servingly inconsistent way; he also sought to illustrate how conflict alone could not generate the means of its sudden resolution with the emergence of a winner taking all: some incipiently political mechanism was required to halt an otherwise endless war. In the words of Thomas Spragens, Hobbes shows how "Nature, which presents man with his political predicament, will not save him from it. It will not do so, first, because it does not possess a principle of order, and second, because it has no principle of creativity."[44] These points clarify how the nature Hobbes describes is "not the regenerative" one of Shakespeare, but do not establish him as thinking in terms of "predatory beasts" and "poison." As François Tricaud notes, "competition and diffidence (the former entailing the latter)" serve in Hobbes's state of nature to "operate like an infernal machine, without anyone's responsibility being really involved."[45]

IX: "Base Feare"

Further underscoring its divergence from Hobbes's thought, *A Satyre*'s vilification of "the Basest Creature" insists on his "responsibility" with another invidious comparison involving animals other than humans, because

> For hunger or for Love they fight and teare,
> Whilst wretched man is still in arms for Feare:
> For feare he Arms, and is of arms afraid,
> By fear to fear successively betray'd. (139–42)

Though Rochester here foregrounds a trait accorded a comparable prominence in Hobbes's thought, he differs by disparaging it as "Base Feare" (143). As Fujimara notes, Rochester implies a "standard of good or evil . . . more or less absolute," which means he "is not relativistic like Hobbes" (215). Blurring this critical distinction, Love claims that "Rochester reverses Hobbes's priority by making fear the origin of power rather than power the origin of fear" (393). Likewise strained is Griffin's speculation that "if Rochester departs from Hobbes, he may in his own mind have thought he was following him the better" (173). Equally wide of the mark, Thormählen offers this reading: "The all-pervading fear that prompts human action in Rochester's *Satyr* is of an aggressively worldly kind. The 'security' it compels man to strive for is a comfortable position in this life, not in a subsequent existence. Its materialistic nature may make it seem natural to associate it with fear as discussed by Hobbes." Rochester hardly describes "a comfortable position," however; and Hobbes's philosophy was not "materialistic" in this sense. But Thormählen invests little in her comparison between Rochester and Hobbes; it only arises in passing when she reflects how "it would be hard to find two more dissimilar attitudes to fear than those put forward by Waller . . . and the speaker in Rochester's *Satyr*," because *On the Fear of God* presents its theme "as a means to escape damnation." Nonetheless, she then contrasts Waller's position and "A nobler attitude" struck by Sir Thomas Browne's *Religio Medici* (1642), which is to say that *On the Fear* addresses a "Base" emotion, of the type scorned by Rochester's *Satyre* (221). Recognizing the fear of which he writes as different from any sanctioned by orthodox piety, Waller, too, acknowledges it as "Base." Instead of directing satire against so abject a trait, Waller resembles Hobbes in offering to defend a concept (not, as he claimed, a "word") that many "men" (rather than the "some" alleged) "may ill endure" (2: 1.3).

Whereas Fujimara rightly dismisses the opinions of W. J. Courthope (who traces *A Satyre*'s "emphasis on fear to Rochester's reading of *The Leviathan*") and John Moore (who in discussing the same poem "speaks of the 'highly rhetorical presentation of the Hobbesian conception of the role of fear in human existence' "), he introduces inaccuracies of his own when seeking to set the record straight: "In place of Hobbes's more complex analysis of human motivation, Rochester offers just one dominant motive, the base passion of fear" (212, 213). Though the epithet "Base" has no counterpart in Hobbes's conception of fear, that emotion nonetheless plays a more "dominant" role in his philosophy than Fujimara acknowledges, and precisely because his "analysis of human motivation" is "complex."

In Fujimara's summary of Hobbes's views as a social-contract theorist, self-preservation proves a decisively "strong motive" prompting humans "to give over those aggressive actions which will prove mutually destructive" and elect a sovereign power whose rule ensures that "security will supplant fear." By contrast, "a state prior to the establishment of a commonwealth" is one that, according to Fujimara, features "warfare among men, in which condition fear becomes a strong motive" (213). Such an overview divorces one "strong motive" (fear) merely responsive to barbaric conditions from another (self-preservation) leading to productive results (the formation of a commonwealth). But Hobbes did not isolate fear from self-preservation, either in general, or when stressing fear's inducement to seek both peace and the social structures capable of sustaining it.

Similarly, Fujimara falsely insists that Hobbes makes fear "a secondary motive," as stimulated by the heightened vainglory of a few bold aggressors (212). As I have already explained, the supposed impact of this mighty minority holds no place in Hobbes's state of nature and therefore cannot serve as evidence that "not all men will be equally motivated by fear" in his account (213). As Laird again clarifies, "The most striking piece of sustained psychological description in all of Hobbes's writings was his attempt to show how human nature was compounded of fear and weakness in varying degrees," inasmuch as "every minor and petty apprehension or precaution had the fear of death behind it, if not immediately, yet at no very distant remove" (173). Therefore, "not all men will be equally motivated by fear" (because that would deny "varying degrees"); but every person is still "equally" subject to that emotion in some measure. Fujimara's remarks about vainglory as "one of the strongest motives in human behavior" for Hobbes likewise mislead in generating the conclusion that he presents a universal bully ("an aggressive, predatory creature with strength and will"), whereas Rochester depicts a wet ("a wretched, miserable creature, eternally on the defensive for fear of other men"). Though vainglory in *A Satyre* "is considerably de-emphasized, if not denied," as Fujimara states, this is but one of several points on which Rochester and Hobbes comprehensively differ (212).

X: "If upon Earth"

A Satyre begins building toward its conclusion by defining an ideal figure such as Hobbes could have approved: "a meek humble Man of honest sense, / Who Preaching peace does practice Continence," and one "Whose pious life's a proof he does believe / Mysterious Truths, which no man can conceive" (216–19). But if Burnet's recollection has any validity, Rochester in his final thoughts found the incomprehensible nature of God a recipe for despair rather than the simple fact Hobbes took it to be. According to Burnet, Rochester "thought our Conceptions of God were so low, that we had better not think much of him," especially in that "to love God seemed to him a presumptuous thing, and the heat of fanciful men," though he "acknowledged that he thought they were very happy whose Fancies were under the power of such Impressions; since they had somewhat on which their thoughts rested and centred" (60). Moreover, as holds consistently true for every other portion of *A Satyre*, any such momentary resemblance between its own doctrines and those of Hobbes immediately yields to a stronger impression of their contrasting characters.

Whereas Hobbes defined an ideal within the reach of every citizen, and thus a potential source of stability for all civil societies, *A Satyre* emphasizes the extreme unlikelihood that its own epitome of excellence will ever be realized, and so justifies rejecting the outward conformity with civic norms that Hobbes encouraged:

> If upon Earth there dwell such God-like men,
> I'le here Recant my Paradox to them;
> Adore those Shrines of Virtue, homage pay,
> And with the rabble World, their Laws obey. (220–23)

Love claims that Thormählen interprets the second of these couplets "as a parody of a Hobbesian social contract" (395). In fact, she explains how

> The idea of an entire population voluntarily subordinating itself to the rule of a sovereign power is a central Hobbesian conception. In my view, few *Satyr* passages come as close to the ideas of Hobbes as lines 222–3. As previous lines of argumentation in the poem have suggested, the speaker's view of mankind in general cannot be characterised as "Hobbesian". Here, though, the *Satyr* speaker seems to move close to Hobbes' ideas on the establishing of a commonwealth. He clearly has not accepted the civilisation he is actually living in as an improvement on the "state of nature". But these men, he seems to say, would be my sovereigns. They would be heartily minded to the common weal, each in his own way, supplementing the other; they would rule justly and in a spirit of peace. Show them to me, and to the world at large, and we will submit to their sway. (237)

Here is no "parody," or accurate paraphrase of Rochester's meaning either. As Griffin notes, "A conditional recantation . . . is offered only to make the satire more relentless" (240). Rochester's willingness to extend a hand into the void proves him no alienated misanthrope; but this show of fellowship merely emphasizes the appalling point that humankind encompasses not even a single individual capable of meeting the terms of the "contract" proposed. In that sense, at least, the couplet at issue (but not Thormählen's reading of it) furnishes "a parody of a Hobbesian social contract." Insofar as this is "as close to the ideas of Hobbes" as *A Satyre* approaches, her unpersuasive paraphrase only reinforces her own skepticism about the extent to which such thinking figures in the poem. But her impulse to make the propounded affinity "as close" as she can suggests that she is as much inclined to exaggerate Hobbes's importance for an understanding of Rochester's *Satyre* as those previous commentators who in her view have both understated "differences" and overstated "similarities" between the two men's work (175). The inconsistencies and contradictions of this tradition she half-heartedly resists are especially clear in Adlard's overview of Hobbes's perceived influence on Rochester.

XI: "continuall mutation"

Linking Rochester's "Dialogue between Strephon and Daphne" with his "Song" beginning "Absent from thee I languish still" (both 1691) and his lyric "*Love* and *Life*" (1677), Adlard (10) proposes that all three poems address an issue phrased by the male speaker of the first as "tis Natures Law to Change" (31), thus weaving variations on *Leviathan*'s statement that "because the constitution of a mans Body, is in continuall mutation, it is impossible that all the same things should alwayes cause in him the same Appetites, and Aversions." Rochester's "Dialogue" likewise strikes Lamb as significant for "the emphasis he places in it on change, which, to the Hobbist, was integral to a proper understanding of life" (76). But as Walker notes, "tis Natures Law to Change" expresses "A common sentiment" (231). Moreover, the final two stanzas of "Absent from thee" invoke the constancy of a fixed point in the beloved they address:

> When weary'd with a world of woe
> To thy safe bosome I retire
> Where love and peace and truth doe flow,
> May I contented there Expire

Least once more wandring from that heav'n
I fall on some Base heart unbles'd,
Faithless to thee, false, unforgiv'n
And loose my everlasting rest. (9–16)

Unperturbed by the clash between "continuall mutation" and "everlasting rest," however, Adlard (11) also associates these lines with a passage from *Leviathan* explaining that

> Men measure, not onely other men, but all other things, by themselves: and because they find themselves subject after motion to pain, and lassitude, think every thing els growes weary of motion, and seeks respose of its own accord; little considering, whether it be not some other motion, wherein that desire of rest they find in themselves, consisteth. (87)

Hobbes makes these points because he denies that "motion" ever ceases for living beings, which find "repose" only in death. Moreover, as Adlard himself acknowledges, Rochester invokes the concept whereby "Love is presented as a recurring death-wish, every orgasm being, in a stock seventeenth-century witticism, a death" (10). Insofar as this form of "repose" has some claim to be considered a phenomenon and not just the expression of a "stock . . . witticism," Hobbes perhaps should have given it some thought; but he paid very little attention to the mechanics of lovemaking.

Whereas Adlard combines the final two stanzas of "Absent from thee" with Hobbes's explanation of how "men measure . . . by themselves" on the circumspect basis that the poem's "background seems to be in *Leviathan*" (11), he abandons such caution in reconstructing the process whereby Rochester "read" (9) a passage from that same text—"There be also other names, called *Negative*; which are notes to signifie that a word is not the name of the thing in question; as . . . *Nothing*" (108)—and then wrote a poem "Upon Nothinge" (1679) featuring this triplet: "Great Negative, how Vainely would the wise / Enquire, defyne, distinguish, teach, devise, / Didst thou not stand to pointe their blind phylosophyes" (28–30). Thormählen almost goes so far concerning "Upon Nothinge": she claims that "The affinity between . . . *Leviathan* . . . and Rochester's poem . . . seems too great for coincidence," citing the amount of evidence she withholds: "much more material could be adduced" (145). By contrast, Adlard merely backpedals to clarify how "Upon Nothinge" draws on Hobbes only inasmuch as "words rather than ideas are carried over," and "naturally enough since Rochester was not a philosopher but a poet" (9).

Even so, Adlard then stresses that "The same is not true of another sentence in *Leviathan*," quoting "The *Present* onely has a being in Nature; things *Past* have a being in the Memory onely, but things *to come* have no being at all" (97). In Adlard's blunt formulation, "This became" Rochester's opening lines from "*Love* and *Life*:"

> All my past Life is mine no more,
>   The flyeing houres are gone
> Like Transitory dreams given o're
> Whose Images are kept in store
>   By memory alone.
>
> What ever is to come is not:
>   How can it then be mine?
> The present moment's all my Lott. (1–8)

Treglown shortly preceded Adlard in positing a connection between Rochester and Hobbes on this dimension; but his influential case has failed to convince even some commentators quite open to envisaging such a link. "As often with Rochester's borrowings . . . it is the differences that prove more significant than the similarities," Farley-Hills generalizes on this score, nonetheless failing to explain why a debt transformed can still be so readily identified (85); more genuinely skeptical, Thormählen insists that "Hobbes' discourse on prudence, experience and expectation does not have a great deal to do with the situation outlined in *Love and Life*" (69); and Love spins differently the influence proposed by Treglown and seconded by Adlard, suggesting that *Leviathan* itself echoes Saint Augustine's "Those two times therefore, past and to come, in what sort are they, seeing the past is now no longer, and that to come is not yet?" (358).[46]

XII: "men are . . . equall"

The most clear-cut instance of a passage in Rochester's work resembling and possibly drawing on a comment by Hobbes occurs when the poet ponders "providence" in his *Epistolary Essay, from M. G. to O. B. upon Their Mutuall Poems* (1680):

> In wit alone 't ha's been magnificent
> Of which so just a share to each is sent
> That the most avaritious are content.
> For none er'e thought (the due Division's such)
> His own too litle, or his Freind's too much. (60, 64–68)

According to *Leviathan*,

> such is the nature of men, that howsoever they may acknowledge many others to be more witty, or more eloquent, or more learned; Yet they will hardly believe there be many so wise as themselves: For they see their own wit at hand, and other mens at a distance. But this proveth rather that men are in that point equall, than unequall. For there is not ordinarily a greater signe of the equall distribution of any thing, than that every man is contented with his share. (184)

In their editions, however, Vieth (146) and Love (430) parallel Rochester's lines with this passage from Descartes's *Discours de la Méthode* (1637), which Vieth gives in English: "Good sense is, of all things among men, the most equally distributed; for every one thinks himself so abundantly provided with it, that those even who are the most difficult to satisfy in everything else, do not usually desire a larger measure of this quality than they already possess." Hobbes would have been appalled to see his arch-rival Descartes given such credit, as apparently first in the field; and if Rochester did not arrive independently at the insight in question, he might just as plausibly have derived it from Descartes as from Hobbes. Unlike the text cited by Love, which refers to "Le bon sens," but like Hobbes's, the poem concerns "wit"; on the other hand, Descartes in "les plus difficiles a contenter" supplies a counterpart to "most avaritious," as Hobbes does not. On biographical grounds, there is little to choose between Pinto's claims that "Rochester read Hobbes's books with enthusiasm in his early youth" and that "As he was often in Paris, it is highly probable that he knew something of the works of the French 'libertins' " (which would of course vouch equally well for his knowledge of Descartes).

XIII: "To vice enslav'd"

Possibly *"M. G.,"* certainly a fellow peer and poet vilified by Rochester in his satirical "My Lord *All-Pride*" (1679), Mulgrave wrote in his poem "On Mr. Hobbes":

> While in dark ignorance we lay, afraid
> Of fancies, ghosts, and every empty shade,
> Great Hobbes appear'd, and by plain reason's light
> Put such fantastic forms to shameful flight.
> Fond is their fear, who think men needs must be
> To vice enslav'd, if from vain terrours free;

The wise and good morality will guide,
And superstition all the world beside.[47]

Those few commentators who quote this poem often misrepresent it by
giving the first two pairs of Mulgrave's couplets but not the second.[48]
In themselves, the lines about the routing of "fantastic forms" could be
construed as either Hobbesian or Hobbist. Hobbes did promote "plain
reason's light" at the expense of "dark ignorance"; but "every empty
shade" is a formulation sufficiently open-ended to encompass all the
additional restraints from which Hobbists supposed themselves
liberated by their understanding of his work. When Mulgrave opposes
"all the world" and "The wise and good," he recognizes only two
categories of people: those rejecting Hobbes's achievement and so
continuing to take "superstition" for their "guide" and those embracing
that same achievement as fully compatible with "morality." Though
Mulgrave does not specify what "morality" he has in mind and could
be a Hobbist dismissing the "vain terrours" of conventional piety, his
hostility toward "vice" looks straightforwardly Christian.

On this score, Mulgrave flies in the face of most contemporary
opinion (at least as recorded in print), which polarized quite differently, celebrating or censuring Hobbes because "every empty shade"
included "morality" itself. Ridiculing the second of these positions,
Mulgrave does not thereby endorse the first. Exposing the "Fond . . .
fear" of Hobbes's critics as groundless, Mulgrave denies not only the
existence of Hobbists but also the validity of their creed, which
assumes that banishing "vain terrours" discards "morality" as well, or
otherwise legitimizes a disposition "To vice." In writing as if Hobbism
were no more than a projection of "Fond . . . fear," Mulgrave possibly
sought only to discredit Hobbes's critics as strongly as he could. But
whether he intended as much, his approach has the additional consequence of exposing the spurious freedom claimed by libertines (as "To
vice enslav'd"), and of treating Hobbists as either unworthy of notice
or beneath contempt. He must have known that the "Fond . . . fear"
of Hobbes's critics mirrored the very tenets of perceived or professed
Hobbists. Rochester's animosity toward Mulgrave (reciprocated)
should have made him conscious on some terms of that figure's reputation as both "a perfect *Hobbist*" and a repentant sinner purported to
have renounced "*that absurd and foolish Philosophy . . . propagated
by the late Mr. Hobbes*," though only after writing many "Panegyricks
upon Vice."

Even if not understood as a veiled attack on Hobbists as a group,
and more specifically on a "perfect" representative whom Mulgrave

had reason to detest, however, the couplets discussed illustrate why Christopher Hill has no strong case when he implicitly qualifies the excessive certainty of his claim that "Rochester had no doubt read *Leviathan*" with these additional points: "but Hobbes's ideas were in the air, particularly among court wits. It was difficult to avoid them."[49] The greatest currency of Hobbes's thought coincided with its utmost travestying by foe and professed friend alike, who mainly agreed in caricaturing him as a propagator of Hobbists, to the degree that Mulgrave's dismissal of those in the first category serves equally well as a dismissal of those in the second. Though Rochester himself might not have shared this caricaturing perspective (inasmuch as the *"absurd and foolish Philosophy"* he was heard as renouncing could have been attributed to Hobbes by Parsons, in the honest if mistaken belief that any repudiation of dissolute conduct had to entail a rejection of libertinism, and thus of Hobbism, and thus of the thinker perceived as responsible for the popularity of such modish ways), that poet offers few if any counter-balancing instances of distinctively Hobbesian ideas incorporated in his own work with fidelity to their source.

Chapter Six

"Common Passions": Hobbes and Suckling

I: "all the excellent of that peaceable time"

Though Suckling apparently committed suicide soon after he fled into exile to escape the arraignment suffered by his friend and co-conspirator Davenant on the discovery of the Army Plot (not in 1642, as sometimes reported), C. V. Wedgwood speculates that "Had he lived to the Restoration he would have been in his element," expressing the widespread and plausible perception that his work anticipated or influenced the literature of a period beginning more than a decade after his death.[1] If he had been contemporary with Rochester (who as Dorimant quoted him), then affinities between his thinking and Hobbes's would partly reflect the influence of ideas widely circulating as he wrote, except that I have already downplayed the significance of that diffusion, because of the adulteration and dilution accompanying it.[2] Alternatively, if the character and composition of the Great Tew circle that flourished during Suckling's own time could be reconstructed with certainty, this might establish him in a setting where he had opportunities to become acquainted with Hobbes's thought, as expressed in person rather than encountered through any less reliable process of transmission.

The group in question takes its name from the Oxfordshire estate of its host Falkland; throughout the 1630s it convened there, with perhaps occasional meetings in London too. Though Aubrey represents Great Tew as "like a Colledge, full of learned men," he also sets virtually no limit to the savants assembling in that setting: his roll-call includes Hobbes, Jonson, Waller, and "all the excellent of that peaceable time."[3] A similar formula concludes the list of visitors to Falkland's estate compiled by Clarendon: "all men of eminent parts and faculties in Oxford, besides those who resorted thither from London."[4] Aubrey and Clarendon assign such importance to the Great Tew circle's distin-guished membership ("excellent" or "of eminent parts") that the group itself becomes indistinct (a catch-"all"). Noel Malcolm generalizes that "the intellectual and social world of early seventeenth-century England was so closely knit that one has only to begin pursuing possible connections to see any neat pattern of separate 'circles' break up before one's eyes." Though Malcolm's skepticism incongruously denies the existence of "separate 'circles' " while reifying one of them to banish Hobbes, Clarendon, and Waller to its circumference, as "peripheral" or "London-based" members of Falkland's group, he queries whether a coherent identity of its own can be ascribed to so fluid a series of overlapping associations.[5]

At the opposite end of the spectrum, Hugh Trevor-Roper boldly recreates the Great Tew circle on the view that Falkland shared with his friends a degree of intellectual freedom unusual for the time: "it was this taste for heresy, this willingness to dissent from received opinion, rather than any common opinion received by them, which united the whole circle, in varying degrees of intimacy, around their host." For Trevor-Roper, such heterodoxy in no way impeded a high level of inclusiveness: "Of the members of this wide circle Aubrey and Clarendon between them give a long list. But even that list is not complete. As each says, there were others."[6] Where Malcolm sees unremarkable open-endedness, Trevor-Roper thus sees exceptional open-mindedness.[7]

Suckling endorses neither of these rival approaches when his poem *The Wits* (ca. 1637) portrays a score or so of such figures competing for the poet-laureateship (possibly not then vacant, but occupied by Jonson, here a contestant nonetheless); the majority are usually now considered members of the Great Tew circle or courtiers close to the queen.[8] The fiction that such proceedings occurred let Suckling twit the pretensions of people he knew, many no longer recognized as even occasional poets, but only establishes the range of his own acquaintance. It does not sanction Trevor-Roper's generalization that of the Great Tew circle "Suckling remembered chiefly the poets," questionable in itself and misleadingly confident about his membership in a group he deemed a distinct entity (170). Nor is Richard Tuck justified in making John Selden's inclusion in *The Wits* "evidence" of that figure's "association with Tew," as part of his larger claim that the members of Falkland's circle were "Seldenians"—thus displacing Hugo Grotius, whom Trevor-Roper names "the greatest of all influences on the . . . group" (192).[9] Falkland's "taste for heresy" would have had to overcome his fervor as a Son of Ben if he welcomed into the Great Tew circle a poet whose pronounced irreverence toward Jonson was not confined to *The Wits*.[10] On the other hand, the Socinianism of

Suckling's *Account of Religion by Reason* (ca. 1637) accords with the theological outlook usually ascribed to that group; and whereas Johann Sommerville denies that Hobbes rationalized faith in quite the same way, bringing out additional points of contrast, he also maintains that Hobbes's "minimalist interpretation of Christian fundamentals, and his arguments in favour of tolerating harmless though heterodox opinions, are close to attitudes expressed by members of Falkland's Tew Circle."[11] But if broadly Socinian thinkers in seventeenth-century England were often tarred with the same brush as figures upholding the most controversial doctrines of Faustus Socinus, only Hobbes among conjectured members of the circle ever faced prosecution for indulging a "taste for heresy."[12]

II: "bayted"

Unlike Davenant, Suckling expressed no political views meriting comparison with Hobbes's. Rather, his statements took various forms while remaining consistently remote from Hobbes's perspective. In a letter (June 6, 1639), he explained his participation in the first of the Bishops' Wars against the Scots for rejecting Charles I's new prayer book and its bid to impose uniformity of worship throughout Britain, tacitly accepting the characterization of all such volunteers as "Cavaleirs that studied not the Cause bur came for honor and love to the king" (145). But if such a quasi-feudal sense of obligation had been more widespread at the time, Charles I's position would not have been so dire as it was becoming and Hobbes might have had less incentive to develop an alternative conception of obedience. By contrast, a letter that Suckling addressed toward the end of 1640 to Jermyn illustrates how he had a gift for political analysis when he "studied . . . the Cause," in this case by candidly acknowledging Charles I's difficulties and proposing a Machiavellian solution: the willing and prompt sacrifice of "suspected Instruments"—Strafford the unnamed prime candidate (166). Suckling's shrewd points here embody a freewheeling pragmatism foreign to Hobbes's theoretical approach. Suckling's subsequent engagement with Jermyn in the Army Plot to spring Strafford from jail suggests another transition in his political outlook, except that his earlier proposal for that figure's sacrifice had reflected no personal hostility (such as informs Davenant's ode "To the King on New-Yeares Day 1630"), and his motive for military service might once more have been "honor and love to the king"; either way, however, there is again no appreciable overlap with Hobbes's perspective. But if Suckling's political outlook differed from Hobbes's because he expressed a soldier's ethos or "studied" to cut rather than untie any Gordian Knot, the two men were also veterans of another theater of conflict testing their abilities in much the same way and to much the same effect.

According to Aubrey, drawing on Davenant, Suckling "grew famous at court for his readie sparkling witt which was envyed, and he was (Sir William sayd) the bull that was bayted. He was incomparably readie att repartying, and his witt most sparkling when most sett-upon and provoked" (2: 240). Of Hobbes, Aubrey likewise reports that "The witts at Court were wont to bayte him. But he feared none of them, and would make his part good. The king would call him *the beare*: 'Here comes the beare to be bayted!' " (1: 340). The difference between "bull" and "beare" is negligible: Aubrey depicts a capacity for survival based on gifts of "repartying" or an ability to "make" one's "part good" such as no beasts have ever possessed. Still, Aubrey's analogy in both cases conveys the cruelly competitive environments in which Suckling and Hobbes were "bayted," even though the two courts in question are usually remembered as different, with each mirroring the disposition of its central figure (fastidiousness in the case of Charles I, licentiousness in that of his successor).

III: "the life of man"

Aubrey's account of court life vindicates *Leviathan*'s dictum that "Competition of Riches, Honour, Command, or other power, enclineth to Contention, Enmity, and War: Because the way of one Competitor, to the attaining of his desire, is to kill, subdue, supplant, or repell the other."[13] Hobbes nonetheless made this claim in establishing "for a generall inclination of all mankind, a perpetuall and restlesse desire of Power after power, that ceaseth onely in Death" (161); he did not restrict his comments to court life here or when maintaining that "the Businesse of the world . . . consisteth almost in nothing else but a perpetuall contention for Honor, Riches, and Authority" (717–18). If "almost" carries enough weight, or occupants of every social rank can be envisaged as pursuing some version of the goals identified, then Hobbes might well describe a universal competitiveness; but his words seem most obviously applicable to the sort of hothouse environment where he and Suckling were "bayted."

Moreover, this apparent imbalance is not local or momentary but a consistent feature of his philosophy, beginning with *Elements*' "comparison of the life of man to a race," where

> To endeavour is appetite.
> To be remiss is sensuality.
> To consider them behind is glory.
> To consider them before is humility.
> To lose ground with looking back vain glory.
> To be holden, hatred.
> To turn back, repentance.
> To be in breath, hope.
> To be weary despair.
> To endeavour to overtake the next, emulation.
> To supplant or overthrow, envy.
> To resolve to break through a stop foreseen courage.
> To break through a sudden stop anger.
> To break through with ease, magnanimity.
> To lose ground by little hindrances, pusillanimity.
> To fall on the sudden is disposition to weep.
> To see another fall, disposition to laugh.
> To see one out-gone whom we would not is pity.
> To see one out-go we would not, is indignation.
> To hold fast by another is to love.
> To carry him on that so holdeth, is charity.
> To hurt one's-self for haste is shame.
> Continually to be out-gone is misery.
> Continually to out-go the next before is felicity.
> And to forsake the course is to die.

For Hobbes, this contest has "no other goal, nor no other garland, but being foremost."[14]

According to Thomas Spragens, these words demonstrate how "At the very outset of the modern era, Hobbes has produced the model of the 'rat race,' and he has done so within the context of a world view which provides it with a profound cosmological foundation."[15] The same association strikes J. C. A. Gaskin, to opposite effect: his introduction to *Elements* instances Hobbes's "picture of . . . the rat race" in reproving him because his "account of ethics seems to reduce apparently altruistic virtues, including some conspicuously Christian virtues, to egoism or exercises of covert self-interest" (xxx, xxix). But the phrase invoked in both cases did not become current until ca. 1939. Apparently sideswiping a strawman woven from Camus and Sartre in caricature, A. P. Martinich proves no less anachronistic when conveying how "The whole thrust of Hobbes's psychology is reductionistic" by smelling another "rat" in the "comparison" at issue: "These sentiments exude the stink of existential absurdity."[16] Perhaps via Camus's treatment of Sisyphus, Spragens assimilates his own "rat race" perspective with Martinich's in stressing that "The modern Sisyphus pushes his boulder across an endless plain" because "An irremediable anxiety . . . is the overriding subjective attribute of the man caught up in the paradigmatic race. His life is one of ultimate and endless striving, without any *telos* to fulfill his quest" (190). But no mortal "plain" can ever be "endless"; and staying alive seemed precious to Hobbes, though the primary importance of self-preservation did not blind his everyman from pursuing a wide range of satisfactions before death sealed the "race." Because "it is impossible that all the same things should always cause in him the same Appetites, and Aversions" (*Leviathan*, 120), Hobbes's everyman shouldered no single "boulder." Though "Power after power" restricts that everyman's "quest" to one predominant purpose, and though I have already suggested that only a few individuals could feasibly seek "Honor, Riches, and Authority," Hobbes's universalizing sought to acknowledge the underlying similarity and surface variety of all ways of "being foremost."

The disparity between these "modern" interpretations and the words inspiring them is all the greater, too, in that Hobbes recalled a distant past. Whereas the ancient Greeks sometimes competed for lavish prizes, as in the games held in Patroclus's honor near the end of the *Iliad*, they also gave the Western world its ideal of amateur sports; they ordinarily raced or otherwise tested their bodies with no more than a "garland" in prospect. Though Hobbes only invokes that sort of token trophy to stress that winning is its own reward, his wording shows what else was on his mind. Pessimistic enough to count no man happy until dead, and even though only after an Odyssey of struggles, the ancient Greeks also recognized this world of pain as affording gratifying opportunities for displays of individual prowess such as harried commuters and the smelliest embodiments of "existential absurdity" never encounter. Tennyson grasped as much when he included these "comparison"-like infinitives in his dramatic monologue "Ulysses" (1842): "To strive, to seek, to find, and not to yield."[17]

Such boundless possibilities nonetheless fell to aristoi rather than hoi polloi, who scarcely exist in the literature of the culture invoked by Hobbes's "garland," except insofar as they lend substance to Achilles's dilemma: to be a short-lived hero or a long-lived nonentity. Suckling on Aubrey's report could not reap the advantages of his mental sharpness without paying a price: in a cruelly competitive environment, "his readie sparkling witt . . . was envyed," which meant that "he was . . . bayted"; but he also proved "most sparkling" in this capacity when "most sett-upon and provoked," and thereby "grew famous at court," a high-stakes setting best suited to revealing and rewarding such luster while surrounding him with rivals predisposed "to kill, subdue, supplant, or repell" him. The same point would hold true for Hobbes's own experience of being "bayted," except that he had formulated his "comparison" at least two decades before having any known first-hand exposure to the risks and rewards of court life; and by that later time he was an old man not especially concerned with making a good showing in such a setting, unlike the exemplary courtier-poet Suckling.

Moreover, Hobbes's "comparison" belies itself: *Elements* nowhere acknowledges his own "race." Only when semi-seriously attributing *Leviathan* to his own desire *"to go home"* (reported by Clarendon and discussed in chapter four) would Hobbes admit to self-interested motives that he routinely ascribed to everyone else.[18] Though his modern biographers concur in depicting him as competitive, most notably in his rivalry with Descartes, he generalized that "Continually to out-go the next before is felicity" without addressing how such an assertion applied to its own formulation. But part of *Elements'* character as the most self-consciously scientific expression of his political philosophy is that such a "comparison" marks a rare excursion into figurative language and includes no admission at odds with his making the work's professed objectivity as convincing as possible. Even to conceptualize such a "race," Hobbes had to take himself out of it, to obtain a view from the stands—a scientific, if not Olympian perspective, but not that of a sweaty and short-breathed runner half-blinded by dust. The nature of his enterprise dictated that he be an exceptional case, even in consulting his own experience to express truths about human nature that he expected his readers to confirm by inspecting themselves in the same way. What he wrote about everyman could not have been written by every man. He was doomed to resemble the Cretan classifying all Cretans as liars, with generalizations true only if false, or false only if true.

I do not share M. M. Goldsmith's skepticism about Hobbes's "comparison," however:

> Is life, the race itself, pleasant? Is all activity pleasurable? Hobbes does not say whether action is itself pleasant or unpleasant. For every satisfaction energy must be expended. The expenditure of energy could be regarded as a pleasure itself. Motion occurs in a world of other motions and resistances. Action seems therefore to have an unpleasant aspect; it is an effort, a struggle, in a recalcitrant environment. Hobbes does not

seem to think that activity is pleasant in itself. Should he not have asked of any activity, "Is the game worth the candle?" Struggle does not seem to make victory sweeter, for magnanimity is to get what one wants with ease.[19]

Because Hobbes took life to be coextensive with "activity" and being as superior to nothingness, there was no other "game" but burning the one "candle"; he supposed any doing better than none, because "to forsake the course is to die." As for "magnanimity," we all like easy victories once in a while. Some weight, too, should be given to the circumspect way in which Hobbes introduced his "comparison," admitting that "it holdeth not in every point" (59).

But such considerations do not explain why Hobbes's account of "perpetuall contention" still rings more true of court life than of his rivalry with Descartes or of agricultural laborers barely subsisting. According to Norbert Elias,

> It is particularly in the circles of court life that what we would today call a "psychological" view of man develops, a more precise observation of others and oneself in terms of longer series of motives and causal connections, because it is here that vigilant self-control and perpetual observation of others are among the elementary prerequisites for the preservation of one's social position.[20]

This emphasis on vigilance explains the link between "perpetual observation" and "perpetuall contention," though Hobbes's " 'psychological' view" partly confirms and partly denies Elias's point: he cannot have fashioned it on his own experience of such "circles," but possibly had been influenced by what he had read or heard about them. Conceding that Hobbes had an aristocratic model of human nature in mind when generalizing about everyman's competitiveness, I do not thereby retract my disagreement with those commentators who suppose that Hobbes always or chiefly takes his cues from the outlook of a social and political elite. However unconvincing in this or that instance, his attempt to pin down "a generall inclination of all mankind" strikes at the heart of aristocratic exceptionalism: the belief that persons of high rank or birth are morally as well as socially superior to those less privileged than themselves, but also just so different as to constitute a breed apart. Hobbes's inconsistency when picturing everyman in terms that sometimes seem caste-specific is not self-serving, moreover; this distinguishes his approach from Suckling's where they agree in their psychological views, for Suckling often fostered a unique identity by contrasting himself with "all mankind" (even, if not especially, his peers at court), whereas Hobbes only distanced himself from the common herd in attempting to address human nature (including his own) from a position of analytical detachment.

IV: "trump on every occasion"

Though Hobbes sometimes wrote as if "bayted" beyond endurance (in controversies with the leading mathematicians of his day, for instance), Suckling cultivated a cavalier persona giving free rein to his "readie sparkling witt" while removing him from any competitive arena in which he could be "sett-upon and provoked." In the contest dramatized by *The Wits*, Suckling himself figures only through what Thomas Clayton terms a "presence in absentia" trope: because he "Prized black eyes, or a lucky hit / At bowls, above all the Trophies of wit," he "did not appear," and "of all men living . . . cared not for't" (77–78, 73, 75).[21] Like the Cheshire Cat, Suckling disappears, leaving only his smile. But he remains in attendance throughout, responsible for the wit and *The Wits*. Furthermore, he dedicated significant effort to his negligent ease, skilful and reckless enough to gain and lose large sums through serious play.

Aubrey styles him "the greatest gamester, both for bowling and cards, so that no shopkeeper would trust him for 6*d*., as to-day, for instance, he might, by winning, be worth 200 *li*., the next day he might not be worth half so much, or perhaps be sometimes *minus nihilo*" (2: 240–41). Fortune nonetheless favors the well-prepared: Aubrey relates that Suckling "played at cards rarely well, and did use to practise by himselfe a bed, and there studied how the best way of managing the cards could be," putting this idle research to good use: he "invented the game of cribbidge" and "sent his cards to all gameing places in the country, which were marked with private markes of his," with the result that "he gott 20, 000 *li*. by this way" (2: 241, 245). Though Aubrey also characterizes Suckling as "one of the best bowlers of his time in England," the tools of this trade were too cumbersome for preparation "a bed," which would partly account for Aubrey's report of "His sisters comeing to the Peccadillo-bowling-green crying for the feare he should loose all <their> portions" (2: 241). In writing poetry, as in playing cards, Suckling enjoyed a wider range of options: he could stack the deck, raise or lower the ante, and choose his game. He could also invent his own sport, as in the "two 'major' " poems identified by Clayton—cribbage-equivalents that "introduced minor genres into English verse, 'The Wits' as a 'trial for the bays' of poetry . . . and 'A Ballad upon a Wedding' as a burlesque, rusticated epithalamion."[22]

Only in poetry, however, could Suckling refuse to compete, while guaranteeing his own supremacy in the manner of those, denounced by *Leviathan*, who "use for trump on every occasion, that suite whereof they have most in their hand" (112). These words pinpoint the self-serving inconsistency of Suckling's cavalier persona because they convey by analogy the "intolerable" nature of a widespread abuse of rhetoric: "when men that think themselves wiser than all others, clamor and demand right Reason for judge; yet seek no more, but that things should be determined, by no other mens reason but their own" (111). Thus exemplifying *De Cive*'s case of how "a man . . . gives a different judgement of an action when he does it than when someone else does the very same thing," Suckling presents himself as an exceptional figure, most notably among his peers, by turning the tables on them in every conceivable way; but he takes as his point of reference laws of human nature resembling those propounded by Hobbes.[23]

Most frequently, Suckling creates his cavalier persona by contrasting his apparent insouciance with the behavior of all others, including gentlemen much like himself in birth and education, but governed by psychological laws from which he alone stands exempt. At other times, though, he depicts himself as a driven mechanical being; on these occasions, he distinguishes himself through the Hobbesian manner in which he identifies traits that all humans share but many would wish to characterize in a more sentimental or idealistic way. Most extremely, Suckling sometimes acts the part of a rude mechanical whose behavior—rude in its simplicity, mechanical in its predictable expression of humble drives—could not differ more from the refined conduct of a gentleman. This style of presentation appears to fly in the face of the others: as Suckling himself noted in the letter to Jermyn quoted above, "the People are naturally not valiant, and not much Cavaleir" (165). But identifying with the humbly born is one of the ways in which he adopts a cavalier stance. Understanding this form of his persona entails recognizing the aristocratic composition of Suckling's presumed audience: he offers a version of pastoral by affirming the security of his elite status through the confidence with which he disguises it and the humor with which he mocks those less assured than himself. Long after his death, his distinctive urbanity, paradoxically defined by its freedom from artifice, still dazzled Millamant in *The Way of the World*: "Natural, easie *Suckling!*"[24]

The exceptionally complex range of self-presentations that Suckling fashioned in connection with his play *Aglaura* (ca. 1637) illustrates how the artful cultivation of his "Natural, easie" persona involved Hobbesian conceptions of human nature.

V: "hopes, and feares"

Sir Anthony Van Dyck's portrait of Suckling shows him outdoors, perusing the opening scene of *Hamlet* (ca. 1600) in a second Shakespeare folio resting on a boulder inscribed "NE TE QUAESEVERIS EXTRA." Malcolm Rogers translates this motto from Persius's *First Satire* as "Do not seek outside yourself" and explains its resonance for Suckling: "first, that he must ignore those who criticise him for his love of Shakespeare; secondly . . . he must, like Shakespeare, remain free of sevile Classical imitation in his own writing, and thirdly—Persius's basic advice—he must ignore those who criticise his own writing."[25] Persian another way, Suckling sports garb associated with *Aglaura*'s setting. He stands with distant snow-capped peaks to his right; rocks surround him in the foreground, including a shadowed outcrop behind and above him setting off his reddish hair, but also serving as a dark thought-bubble. Combining Bardolatry, exoticism, sublimity, rugged nature, and pathos, this image strikingly anticipates the values of nineteenth-century Romanticism. But it also documents its own time (ca. 1637) and Suckling's investment in *Aglaura*, which cost him a lot of money and at least some effort: a reworking of his unfinished *The Sad One*, it was itself revised to have two conclusions (tragic and tragicomic); subsequently performed in the public theater, it was first enacted at court in lavish productions funded by the author, who also undertook the expense of its publication in folio and its presentation for the royal collection in an elaborate manuscript. Two first tries, two fifth acts, two performance-settings, two costly printings—these features of *Aglaura* agree with Van Dyck's portrayal of Suckling as a theatrical son of Shakespeare sufficiently proud of his first complete play to risk comparison with *Hamlet*.

Suckling conveys a very different impression in the prologue written for court performances of tragic *Aglaura*:

> Those common passions, hopes, and feares, that still
> The Poets first and then the Prologues fill,
> In this our age, hee that writ this, by mee,
> Protests against as modest foolerie.

Hee thinks it an odd thing to be in paine,
For nothing else, but to be well againe.
Who writes to feare is so; had he not writ,
You nere had been the Judges of his wit;
And when hee had, did hee but then intend
To please himselfe, hee sure might have his end
Without th'expence of hope, and that hee had
That made this Play, although the Play be bad.
Then Gentlemen be thriftie, save your doomes
For the next man, or the next Play that comes;
For smiles are nothing, where men doe not care,
And frownes as little, where they need not feare. (1–16)

L. A. Beaurline plausibly suggests that "still" in the first of these lines abbreviates "instill" (263). But Suckling possibly wished to make two related points otherwise impossible to express so concisely: that "hopes" and "feares" explain why dramatists write prologues, but that in both cases the motivation remains continuously apparent— "still" a factor because authors cannot escape from their "common passions" merely by expressing them, and because prologues, though they cannot relieve authorial anxiety, become permanent records of it. Either way, Suckling stands aloof from dramatists who make themselves sick by caring what an audience thinks. Would-be critics should save their strictures for others, not to spare his feelings, but to avoid wasting their breath.

Even so, Suckling was sufficiently aware of his audience to write different prologues and epilogues for the various versions of *Aglaura*, each time framing his words to separate audiences—spectators at court and those in public theaters. Indeed, his awareness of audience was so acute that, aside from tragic *Aglaura*'s court epilogue (clearly marked for Charles I alone), he subdivides his court prologues and epilogues into portions for the court at large and portions for the crown alone. Because Suckling's dismissive view of anxious writers stems from a dismissive view of his audience, he must renounce his manifesto of carelessness when addressing the occupants of the throne:

This (Sir) to them, but unto Majestie
All hee has said before, hee does denie.
Yet not to Majestie: that were to bring
His feares to be, but for the Queene and King,
Not for your selves; and that hee dares not say:
Y'are his Soveraignes another way:
Your soules are Princes, and yee have as good

A title that way, as yee have by blood
To governe, and here your powers more great
And absolute, than in the royall Seat.
There men dispute, and but by Law obey,
Here is no Law at all, but what yee say. (17–28)

Suckling must now acknowledge his own "feares" and confess things "hee dares not say." But he can still purge himself of literary ambition: rather than express "hopes" that the crown will judge his play favorably, he identifies it as the sole authority applicable in his own case. Stressing his obedience to Charles I and Henrietta Maria as persons, he removes from the realm of literary criticism how his play will be judged: "although the Play be bad," he does not "care," provided he has been a good subject. The king and the queen in one way, Suckling in another, stand aloof from a court where anxious authors compete for approval from an audience whose opinion is not worth anything.

VI: "to *Contemne*"

In *Leviathan*, "*Appetite* with an opinion of attaining, is called HOPE," and "*Aversion*, with opinion of *Hurt* from the object, FEARE" (123). "DELIBERATION" occurs "When in the mind of man, Appetites, and Aversions, Hopes, and Feares, concerning one and the same thing, arise alternately" (127, 126–27). In focusing their own "hopes" and "feares" on "one and the same thing," Suckling's foolish authors merely impale themselves on the horns of a dilemma, remaining in a neurotic impasse. They lack the freedom of action *Leviathan* assigns to "DELIBERATION," albeit via a bogus etymology, on the grounds that "it is a putting an end to the *Liberty* we had of doing, or omitting, according to our own Appetite, or Aversion" (127). In contrast, Suckling entirely enjoys "the *Liberty* . . . of doing, or omitting": free even of "Appetites" and "Aversions," subject only, through love, to royalty, he can more truly do whatever he likes. Those authors worrying about audience reaction suffer from "PUSILLANIMITY" as defined by *Leviathan*: "*Desire* of things that conduce but a little to our ends; And fear of things that are but of little hindrance" (123). Suckling, however, illustrates *Leviathan*'s "MAGNANIMITY" or "*Contempt* of little helps, and hindrances," for

Those things which we neither Desire, nor Hate, we are said to *Contemne*: CONTEMPT being nothing else but an immobility, or contumacy of the Heart, in resisting the action of certain things; and proceeding from that the Heart is already moved otherwise, by other more potent objects; or from want of experience of them. (123, 120)

Presumably, the "more potent" object moving Suckling away from either desiring his general audiences' approval or hating their disapproval was a pose of apparent insouciance insulating him from the ambition placing foolish authors at others' mercy.

Though Suckling disguises his own priorities, they supply the entire basis of his generalization about "common passions": in lumping together all his fellow authors because of their concern about audience reaction and belittling them because he himself has no such cares, he guarantees his own high status: "although the Play be bad," its author could not have done better in terms of his sprezzatura in putting on both play and self-presentation. The pawn of the play's reputation constituted a strategically worthwhile sacrifice from the larger perspective of the game in which Suckling was engaged. Distancing himself from "common passions," he establishes himself as a gentleman writing over the heads of mere members of court to a more fitting audience— royalty itself.

Suckling's analysis of "common passions" would be more universal if covering all authors including himself, not all except himself. His own "hopes" and "feares" take an unusual and complex form, even in a context occupied by other cavalier poets; but those motivations can be deduced from what he achieves in demonstrating his own superiority with the unsurpassable sprezzatura of not competing in a competitive environment, a pointless style of self-presentation if not designed to impress an audience. Frank Whigham clarifies the strenuous nature of such effortlessness:

> one must exhibit sprezzatura about the exercise of sprezzatura. Planned or subsumed mistakes, inefficient casualness, can demonstrate freedom from the competitive telos of sprezzatura itself; insofar as the principle of grazia distinguishes the elite from those below, one may appear indifferent to the distinction, treating it as a trivial matter not worth attention. Substantive inadequacies can be viewed as insignificant, not worth hiding, indicating a position above concern for the possible disapproval of those present, who are thereby revealed as inferiors whose judgment is immaterial.[26]

Such mind games require the right audience, which explains why the "sparkling" of Suckling's "witt" was partly the cause but even more the effect of his being "bayted" in a setting occupied by the "foremost" in "being foremost."

Suckling confirms that such "freedom from the competitive" could only be temporary, and that he was not contemptuous "in resisting the action of certain things . . . from want of experience of them," in the general prologue to the tragicomic *Aglaura*, where he assumes that female viewers will approve the play's variety, but concludes of the male that " 'twould be vaine for mee now to indeare, / Or speake unto my Lords, the Judges here," because

> They hold their places by condemning still,
> And cannot shew at once mercie and skill;
> For wit's so cruell unto wit, that they
> Are thought to want, that find not want i'th' play. (5–10)

Repetition of "want" deftly conveys how male author and male audience cannot both be winners in a competitive battle of wits. Here Suckling accepts that the laws governing a Hobbesian social context of "perpetuall contention" apply to himself too.

He offers another different reading of his circumstances in the court epilogue for tragic *Aglaura* (addressed to the king alone), where he and his proxy clarify

> That th'abusing of your eare's a crime,
> Above th'excuse any six lines in Rhime
> Can make, the Poet knowes: I am but sent
> T'intreat hee may not be a President,
> For hee does thinke that in this place there bee
> Many have done't as much and more than hee;
> But here's, hee sayes, the difference of the Fates,
> Hee begs a Pardon after't, they Estates. (1–8)

Suckling once more adopts a cavalier persona: he distinguishes his own ends from those of frankly mercenary authors engaged in a Hobbesian "Competition of Riches." Not seeking "Estates" for himself and generalizing that other authors do seek them, Suckling establishes his superiority in two ways. But then Suckling could afford to be indifferent about "Estates": as his gambling illustrated, he had money to burn.

The funds he lavished on the production and printing of *Aglaura* prove the same point, or that as a playwright he had ambitions different from the self-consciously serious Jonson's, but sufficient to warrant the assumption of a cloaking cavalier persona. Though *The Wits* mocks Jonson by making him claim that "he deserv'd the Bayes, / For his were call'd Works, where others were but Plaies" (19–20), a not-new joke alluding to Jonson's much ridiculed inclusion of plays in his volume *Workes* (1616), *Aglaura* itself incurred charges of pomposity: Clayton prints three of the lampoons it inspired (201–03); and Beaurline comments of its 1638 folio edition that "The format was pretentious for a single play, as if it were a poem or a literary 'work,' " featuring "extra large paper, conspicuously wasted by wide margins, unused spaces at the top and bottom of certain pages, and duplicate title-pages" (257).

VII: "Th' observed of all observers"

Though the easiest resolution of the stark contradiction between Van Dyck's Suckling and that of the "common passions" prologue would see the former as his real self and the latter as a giveaway case of protesting too much, an anecdote of Aubrey's furnishes a richer understanding of these strikingly different representations: Davenant "would say that Sir John, when he was at his lowest ebb in gameing, I meane when unfortunate, then would make himselfe most glorious in apparell, and sayd that it exalted his spirits, and that he had then best luck when he was most gallant, and his spirits were highest" (2: 241). The "glorious . . . apparell" apparently borrowed from the wardrobe of *Aglaura* and the cavalier persona donned in the "common passions" prologue can both be understood as instances of theatrical self-invention where the costume changes but the motivation remains essentially the same.

In this connection, Suckling's identification with Hamlet assumes a new significance. Though Suckling the stereotypical playboy of standard accounts holds nothing in common with Hamlet the philosophical soliloquist, Van Dyck's Suckling embraces him—eerily, for some version of "To be, or not to be" must have run through Suckling's mind before he killed himself.[27] Conversely, Hamlet, as "The courtier's, soldier's, scholar's, eye, tongue, sword, / Th' expectation and rose of the fair state, / The glass of fashion and the mould of form," has an obvious relevance for Suckling and his commitment to sprezzatura; and Charles I's court did not need to house "Something . . . rotten" to make being "Th' observed of all observers" a stressful prospect, as well as a highly appealing one (III.i, 151–53; I.iv, 90; III.i, 54).

VIII: "low Words"

Suckling cared enough about tragic *Aglaura*'s court audience to emphasize in his "common passions" prologue his lack of concern on that score, while offering an altogether more polished expression of carelessness than the run-of-the-mill self-deprecation presented in the merely offhand-sounding prologue written for public performances of the same version:

> I've thought upon't; and cannot tell which way
> Ought I can say now, should advance the Play.
> For Playes are either good or bad; the good
> (If they doe beg) beg to be understood.
> And in good faith, that has as bold a sound,
> As if a beggar should aske twentie pound.
> ——Men have it not about them:
> Then (Gentlemen) if rightly understood,
> The bad doe need lesse Prologue than the good:
> For if it chance the Plot be lame, or blinde,
> Ill cloath'd, deform'd throughout, it needs must finde
> Compassion,—It is a beggar without Art:—
> But it fals out in penny-worths of Wit.
> As in all bargaines else, Men ever get
> All they can in; will have London measure,
> A handfull over in their verie pleasure.
> And now yee have't; hee could not well deny'ee,
> And I dare sweare hee's scarce a saver by'ee. (1–18)

Perhaps Suckling regarded these various stops and starts (including an unrhymed and metrically incomplete seventh line) as an extension of his dramatic mode, which approximates naturalism in reproducing the spasmodic rhythms of colloquial speech. Beaurline notes of the characteristic versification of Suckling's plays that

> His impulse was lyric and consequently he wrote a peculiar kind of dramatic line, varying between three, four, and five feet, usually ended by the completion of a short grammatical unit and signalled by a mark of punctuation. This habit made it easy for him to adapt lines from his poems . . . . He could write blank verse when he wanted to, but frequently, in the less formal and more conversational passages, he chose three- and four-foot lines. The effect is similar to that of the old fourteeners. (viii)

The same commentator sees *Aglaura*'s plot as solving "Suckling's problem with *The Sad One*, a lack of an interesting complication" (254);

the prologue just quoted exhibits a comparable deficiency, too closely resembling merely slapdash writing for its professed carelessness to achieve significance.

In contrast, the "common passions" prologue exemplifies a studiously polished negligent ease. "And ten low Words oft creep in one dull Line," remarks Pope's *Essay on Criticism*, illustrating and censuring an especially artless approach to diction and versification.[28] When boundaries of words and metrical feet frequently coincide, they make a poem seem halting; this amateurish effect is inevitable in lines of exclusively monosyllabic words. Though Suckling was far from dull, it often suited his cavalier persona to versify as if he belonged in Pope's *Dunciad*. Whereas just two of the general prologue's eighteen lines exhibit such dullness, a quarter of the lines in Suckling's "common passions" prologue are exclusively monosyllabic, indicating his more strenuous cultivation of an artless manner there. Though Suckling creates monosyllables through contractions, he more often does so by prosaically spelling out a meaning easily expressed with fewer and less humble words. The lame pedestrianism of "In this our age, hee that writ this, by mee," apparently rather than actually dull, introduces another "presence in absentia" trope: Suckling brings himself forward by stressing his removal, asserting his superiority to anxious authors and their "common passions" by seeming to take his own writing and audience so much less seriously.

IX: "most Poet"

Illustrating the link between ironically antipoetic matter and manner, Suckling's dialogue-poem "Upon My Lady Carliles Walking in Hampton-Court Garden" (1646) assigns Thomas Carew a high-flown response to the subject directly opposed by Suckling's mental undressing: "I had my Thoughts, but not your way, / All are not born (Sir) to the Bay" (22–23).[29] Other factors besides his penchant for such low thoughts expressed in exclusively monosyllabic lines help divorce Suckling from "the Bay": his poems minimally feature figurative language and musical effects, avoiding inversions and dense or other-wise complex syntax. His apparent artlessness occupies the opposite end of the stylistic spectrum from the baroque architecture of Miltonic blank verse, achieving an unadorned directness of expression exceeding even that of the Jonsonian plain style, which verges on seeming as "Natural," but never proves so "easie," for its hard-won home truths are badges of integrity proudly displayed.[30] In overall irreverence,

Suckling's antipoetic vein resembles Donne's in "The Triple Fool" (1633): "I am two fools, I know, / For loving, and for saying so / In whining poetry."[31] Closest to Suckling's particular kind of lowness, however, are portions of Sidney's *Astrophil and Stella* (1591) and Herbert's *Temple* (1633) that sponsor the homeliest truth in the homeliest garb: "looke in thy heart and write"; "Shepherds are honest people; let them sing."[32]

Though Suckling places many more eggs in the basket of an artless-seeming rusticity of expression than either Sidney or Herbert, he shares with them in contributing to a tradition of ironic commentary on the paradox most famously noted by Touchstone in Shakespeare's *As You Like It* (1599–1600): "the truest poetry is the most feigning" (III.iii, 19–20). According to Suckling's "Answer to Some Verses Made in His Praise" (1646),

> The antient Poets, and their learned rimes,
> We still admire in these our later times,
> And celebrate their fames: Thus though they die,
> Their names can never taste mortalitie:
> Blind *Homer's* Muse, and *Virgil's* stately Verse,
> Whilst any live, shall never need a herse.
> Since then to these such praise was justly due
> For what they did, what shall be said to you?
> They had their helps; they writ of Gods and Kings,
> Of Temples, Battels, and such gallant things:
> But you of Nothing; how could you have writ,
> Had you but chose a Subject to your Wit?
> To praise *Achilles*, or the Trojan crew,
> Shewed little art, for praise was but their due.
> To say she's fair that's fair, this is no pains:
> He shews himself most Poet, that most feigns:
> To find out vertues strangely hid in me,
> I, there's the art and learned Poetrie;
> To make one striding of a Barbed Steed,
> Prancing a stately round: (I use indeed
> To ride *Bat Jewels* Jade;) this is the skill,
> This shews the Poet wants not wit at will.
>   I must admire aloof, and for my part
>   Be well contented, since you do't with art. (1–24)

But Suckling here begins to leave the values of the Renaissance behind with a ridicule of the high flown, a consciousness of the gulf dividing classical antiquity from the modern world, and an ambiguous estimate of "The antient Poets" all having counterparts in Hobbes's own *Answer*.

Whereas Suckling's dialogue-poem mentally undresses Lucy Hay, countess of Carlisle, he denudes himself when his "Answer" rejects praise promoting him: he would sooner control his presentation and be "Nothing" than be praised extravagantly on someone else's terms. Sancho Panza to his admirer's Quixote, Suckling insists he has known no Pegasus save "*Bat Jewels* Jade" (a mount mocking the feigning of an author who fain would praise), distinguishing the "Barbed Steed" mode of poetry from his own hobbling gait. Quoting in context the exclusively monosyllabic lines from "An Answer" illustrates once again their halting character and confirms how their apparent artlessness debunks the poetic. Having established in relatively lofty terms the high status enjoyed by authors of classical antiquity, Suckling lowers his diction for a twofold deflation; "Since then to these such praise was justly due / For what they did, what shall be said to you? / These had their helps; they writ of Gods and Kings." Ridiculing his admirer's choice of subject, he rates the ancients themselves as no better than their material—"their helps"—for the reason given in the third of his exclusively monosyllabic lines: "To say she's fair that's fair, this is no pains." Such content happened to be the stuff of epic, though, and lacks any true counterpart in the modern world, even given efforts to transform its inhabitants through flights of fancy: those transports cannot fool a skeptical eye focusing on the gulf between actuality and the poetic. "He shews himself most Poet, that most feigns" has become so ironic as to verge on asserting with Hobbes's *Answer* that "the Resemblance of truth is the utmost limit of Poeticall Liberty."[33]

X: "native easiness"

In Clayton's reading of "An Answer," Suckling "merges aesthetic and philosophical concerns with colloquial familiarity through the intermedium of a social genre tinged with the shades of Great Tew" because his poem "is a formal mimesis of a spontaneous conversational expression of gratitude and admiration; refined into graceful informality, it complements the praised work of a translating rustic equitation into Cavalier urbanity, giving to airy nothing a knightly bearing and a place" ("At Bottom," 227). This overcooked reference to Great Tew makes sense given Suckling's circle of acquaintances; but his style also links him with the emerging discourse of science. "Natural, easie *Suckling*" proved so current more than half a century after his death because his language anticipated the standards established for the Royal Society in a self-consciously novel development. According to Sprat's history of that institution, all participants were expected to use "a close, naked, natural way of speaking; positive expressions; clear senses; a native easiness: bringing all things as near the Mathematical plainness, as they can: and preferring the language of Artizans, Countrymen, and Merchants, before that, of Wits, or Scholars."[34]

Suckling had very different reasons for his "native easiness"— unscientific ones keyed to the self-serving needs of his cavalier persona and to his own elaboration of "the truest poetry is the most feigning." But Quentin Skinner could also be referring to Suckling when he characterizes Hobbes as "conspicuously fond" of "aphorisms and commonplaces," and judges that "he makes considerable play with maxims and expressions of a proverbial kind."[35] Beaurline remarks "Suckling's interest in proverbs," suggesting that "His wit seems to lie in the elegant variation on commonplaces" (viii). On the other hand, chapter two noted the resemblance between Hobbes's rhetoric as described by Skinner—"commonplaces . . . reversed in every case" (306)—and Davenant's as described by James Winn—"challenging assertions" disguised as "principles everyone accepts"—to suggest that Davenant on this dimension sounds even more like Hobbes than he does Bacon.[36] The same cannot be said for Suckling's "elegant variation on commonplaces." Moreover, that "common passions" tend to receive commonplace expression renders insignificant the overlap between *Leviathan*'s "Hopes, and Feares," and Suckling's "hopes, and feares," considered merely as phrases.

Though Suckling's own wording on this point required no precedent, literary or otherwise, he possibly knew Donne's verse-epistle "To Mr. T. W." (1633), which begins "Pregnant again with th' old twins hope, and fear" (1). This line might also have played some part in the formation of Hobbes's quip about being coeval with fear (quoted and discussed in chapter one). Skinner claims that Hobbes knew Donne, at least "as a fellow member of the Virginia Company," and in having opportunities to hear his preaching (234). Even so, Hobbes's "twins" make a more original combination than Donne's, which were "old" not only in his own experience but also in that of Suckling and countless others, as "common passions" making a rote pair, which explains why I did not argue for any verbal likeness between Suckling's phrasing and Hobbes's, urging affinities in thought instead. But whereas Donne's possible impact on Suckling and Hobbes remains no less uncertain in the following example, this draws on imagery establishing one of several connections between Suckling's vocabulary and Hobbes's.

XI: "nothing else but"

In his *Obsequies to the Lord Harrington, Brother to the Lady Lucy, Countess of Bedford* (ca. 1614), Donne writes of

> small pocket-clocks, whose every wheel
> Doth each mismotion and distemper feel,
> Whose hand gets shaking palsies, and whose string
> (His sinews) slackens, and whose soul, the spring,
> Expires, or languishes, whose pulse, the fly,
> Either beats not, or beats unevenly,
> Whose voice the bell, doth rattle, or grow dumb,
> Or idle. (131–38)

Reversing the flow of comparison, *Leviathan* begins with these rhetorical questions:

> seeing life is but a motion of Limbs, the beginning whereof is in some principall part within; why may we not say, that all *Automata* (Engines that move themselves by springs and wheeles as doth a watch) have an artificiall life? For what is the *Heart*, but a *Spring*; and the *Nerves*, but so many *Strings*; and the *Joynts*, but so many *Wheeles*, giving motion to the whole Body, such as was intended by the Artificer? (81)

Such chronometric imagery for Suckling constituted "a favourite conceit," as Clayton notes (*Cavalier Poets*, 235). In his poem "[Love's Clock]" (1646), Suckling demonstrates that "Lovers have in their hearts a clock still going" with an analysis centering on this stanza:

> Hope is the main spring on which moves desire,
> And these do the lesse wheels, fear, joy, inspire;
> > The ballance is thought, evermore
> > > clicking
> > > and striking
> > and ne're giving ore. (2, 7–12)

Similarly, *Aglaura*'s title character remarks that "When once the maine-spring, *Hope*, is falne into / Disorder; no wonder, if the lesser wheeles, / *Desire*, and *Joy*, stand still" (IV.iv, 26–28). Lovers again prove mechanical beings in Suckling's verses "To His Rival [II]" (1646): "thou and I, like Clocks, are wound / Up to the height, and must move round" (11–12). Suckling's "Sonnet II" (1646) likewise maintains that

> What in our watches, that in us is found,
> So to the height and nick
>   We be up wound,
> No matter by what hand or trick. (21–24)

"Lest someone jump to stigmatize Suckling as proto-Hobbesian mechanist for his conceit, let it be said that it is no more original with him than was Donne's compass conceit with him," cautions Earl Miner regarding these lines.[37] But the point that Suckling's chronometric imagery lacks originality need not preclude his sharing both it and a "mechanist" outlook with Hobbes. Indeed, the stanza just quoted begins with a commonplace dictum nonetheless suggesting that a psychology akin to Hobbes's account of human nature informs its explanation of how people tick: " 'Tis not the meat, but 'tis the appetite / makes eating a delight" (17–18).[38]

Moreover, Suckling sometimes defines his terms in a manner equivalent to Hobbes's, in both form and content. According to *Leviathan*, "When a man *Reasoneth*, hee does nothing else but conceive a summe totall, from *Addition* of parcels; or conceive a Remainder, from *Subtraction* of one summe from another," for "he can Reason, or reckon, not onely in number; but in all other things, whereof one may be added unto, or subtracted from another" (110, 113). Suckling defines by subtraction in a letter (fall 1633): "Joy (the thing we all so Court) is but our hopes stript of our fears" (129). Whether adding or subtracting, Hobbes's definitions have often been thought reductive. Certainly they incorporate reductionism in their wording: such phrases as "nothing else but" recur constantly. Suckling likewise boils things down: "Joy . . . is but." He nonetheless proves more optimistic here than in his "common passions" prologue, where "hopes" and "feares" are inseparable, "Joy" is out of the question, and he alone can attain a careless equanimity.

In their different ways, however, both letter and prologue eschew the despair articulated in Rochester's poem "*The Fall*," with its vision of the postlapsarian drudgery of "poor slaves to hope and fear" who "Are never of . . . Joyes secure," knowing only "dull delights."[39] Focusing on "our hopes" and "our fears," Suckling accepts himself as a Hobbesian everyman: he does not here exemplify how "a man . . . gives a different judgement of an action when he does it than when someone else does the very same thing." In contrast, the cavalier persona developed in his "common passions" prologue and elsewhere expresses a unique freedom from Hobbesian norms regulating the conduct even of other gentlemen, thus taking aristocratic exceptionalism to the furthest extreme imaginable.

Chapter Seven

"Sufficiently Disposed": Hobbes and Godolphin

I: "&c."

Whereas no evidence of this kind has survived in Suckling's case, Waller and Hobbes were "acquainted at Paris—I believe before," according to Aubrey, who also reports that Davenant met Hobbes under one or both of the same sets of circumstances: "at Paris (e.g. epistle)" or "perhaps before."[1] Such double recollection invites the suspicion that a single free-floating half-memory has been wrongly assigned at least once. Davenant's entitlement to "before" status thus remains uncertain and appears in any case the more vulnerable supposition: Aubrey relates that Waller "told me he was not acquainted with Ben. Johnson (who dyed about 1638), but familiarly with Lucius, lord Falkland; Sydney Godolphin; Mr. Hobbes; &c." (2: 275). Moreover, that unspecified remnant possibly needed no spelling out because Waller's circle overlapped so substantially with Great Tew's as to be indistinguishable from it. But the problems associated with reconstructing the celebrated group hosted by Falkland I have already noted in connection with Suckling's *Wits*, where Davenant, Waller, Godolphin, and Falkland himself all feature. Such considerations ensure that little advantage can be had from speculating whether Waller met Hobbes in that setting during the later 1630s. If they were certainly aware of each other then and there, some value might attach to reading their work against such a shared backdrop. Even in that scenario, however, Hobbes's ideas would need to be imported from *Elements*, on the conceivably unwarranted assumption that his thinking was already far advanced toward the form it takes in that manuscript, or from *Eight Books* (a translation, however much remade in its translator's image), or from one or more of the discourses *Upon the Beginning*, *Of Laws*, and *Of Rome* (anonymous, however convincing their modern editors' attribution). These caveats likewise apply to Davenant's possible friendship with Hobbes prior to their shared exile, except that Great Tew disappears from the equation, unless *The Wits* declares otherwise.

Nonetheless, I cautiously invert Christopher Hill's point that during the post-Restoration period "Hobbes's ideas were in the air," stressing their currency in an earlier era, accessible in a less diffuse form, though possibly not as his primary or exclusive property: the Hobbesian approach of the three discourses mentioned, of Davenant's contempt for parliamentary praters, of Waller's rationalistic treatment of myth, and of Suckling's laws of human nature and recourse to chronometric imagery, expressed in most if not all instances before the circulation of *Elements*, cannot certainly be referred to a direct or recoverable influence exerted by Hobbes, but must reflect a common cultural environment that shaped him too, if he did not shape it.[2] Such reflections underscore Godolphin's unique significance as a figure known to have encountered Hobbes during the 1630s in circumstances that undeniably sealed their mutual admiration. Moreover, their friendship apparently occurred in the framework of the Great Tew circle and helps substantiate the received impression of that setting as one where people met fruitfully whose paths might otherwise have crossed to trivial effect, if at all. Despite these promising indicators, or rather because of them, Godolphin features here as the third of Hobbes's illegitimate heirs. But if the following pages stress that Hobbes's importance for Godolphin has been overstated, they also show how Godolphin's importance for Hobbes has been underestimated. In this matter, the differing concerns of literary critics and specialists in Hobbes prove especially divergent.

II: "redress"

Godolphin was just thirteen when he contributed to the volume *Carolus Redux* (1623), celebrating the future Charles I's safe return from his unsuccessful courtship of the Spanish Infanta. One episode from this journey occasioned Waller's *Of the Danger*. But whereas Godolphin's literary debut consists of a chronogram with an appended couplet, both in Latin, Waller's English poem encompasses 170 lines and did not appear in print before his first collection. Though these works therefore share nothing besides an overlap in subject, writing about the same or comparable themes became a staple for Waller and Godolphin, in a context where the two men's literary practices increasingly coincided. In 1638, both penned encomiums for George Sandys's metrical translation of the Psalms, as well as memorial poems for Jonson and Lady Anne Rich. Some doubt, however, lingers over

Godolphin's authorship of the excellent elegy in *Jonsonus Virbius* that has been attributed to him ("The *Muses* fairest *light* in no darke time"). Because Falkland supervised the volume commemorating Jonson and also wrote praising Sandys's rendering of the Psalms, and because the circle he hosted probably formed the setting in which Waller and Godolphin became friends, those poets today most frequently associated with Great Tew showed some solidarity. Drawing on his own research, as well as that of Mary Frear Keeler, David Norbrook nonetheless emphasizes the especially close links between Waller and Godolphin, who bonded more strongly as men of letters than either did in the same capacity with Falkland or Sandys.[3]

In format, Godolphin's poem "To the King and Queene" (1906) anticipates Waller's folio *Panegyric*; but just as Waller's intentions are not certainly captured by that text's couplet-quatrains, so the earlier work's stanzas possibly lack authorial sanction. Perhaps Godolphin, who wrote an uncontested elegy for Donne, knew his *Lamentations of Jeremy, for the Most Part According to Tremellius* (1633), in quatrains rhyming AABB; but here constant enjambment swamps the couplets. George Saintsbury insists that "To the King and Queene" "was evidently intended to be in the continuous couplet"; preserving the text he found, for "a first edition," he stresses that its wooden lines represent an emergent form (the neoclassical distich) handled "with a firmness which neither Waller nor Sandys had surpassed by anticipation."[4] Similarly, Saintsbury judges that Godolphin's contribution to an English rendering of the *Aeneid*'s fourth book, *The Passion of Dido for Aeneas* (1658), "ought to take much higher rank than it has yet usually done, as a document in the history of the regular heroic couplet," for "It must be earlier than 1642, and may be considerably so, while, as is well known, there is some doubt about the date of the earliest exercises in the kind of its continuator—Waller" (235). But William Dighton, Saintsbury's own "continuator" in editing Godolphin, argues that "To the King and Queene" belongs in quatrains and concludes of the joint translation, whose genesis and chronology remain uncertain, that "Godolphin's ability to handle the couplet was very nearly equal to that of Waller or . . . Waller's reworking of the whole poem was considerable."[5]

Whereas both poets presumably drew some stimulus from translating Virgil, or, if those efforts were not coordinated, from the amicable rivalry suggested by their recourse to identical subjects, Godolphin borrowed from Waller when answering his poem "Of Love" with a "Replye" (1813) that dates both texts' composition as prior to 1643.

Though Saintsbury observes of Godolphin's response that "It seems to answer something" (244n), its rebuke addressed "Unhappy East" (1) reverses Waller's "Unwisely we the wiser East / Pity," as Dighton recognized (74).[6] Possibly "Of Love" in its witty-worm perspective as a poem essentially of fear prompted or owed its own inspiration to Godolphin's "Song" (1906), a pastoral dialogue where Damon admonishes an unnamed shepherd for his lack of confidence in approaching his likewise anonymous mistress, "you leave the Image of yor feare / In her fayre Breast"; "I hope noe happinesse / but what already I possesse / Receivd thus neere," he answers, "Yet I confesse, though not soe vaine / as one poore hope to entertaine / I still have feare" (17–24). More certainly, "Of Love" informs Godolphin's poem "Chorus" (1906) or derives from it: the two poets disagree in a context where either might have started the debate and they differ by drawing on the same vocabulary. Whereas Waller's poem claims that "every passion, but fond love, / Unto its own redress does move" (1: 5–6), Godolphin's insists that "Love to itt selfe is recompence / besides the pleasure of the sence," and that

> they who love truly through the clyme
> of freesing North and scalding lyne,
> Sayle to their joyes, and have deep sence,
> both of the losse, and recompense. (31–32, 45–48)

Though capable of sometimes slapdash writing, Waller typically avoids the maladroit level of Godolphin's phrasing here, where the identical rhymes "recompence" or "recompense" and "sence" occur in close proximity, and where he has twice beforehand paired the second of these end-words with "indigence" (7–8, 19–20). Moreover, both "redress" and "recompense" figure prominently in Waller's diction, partly reflecting his propensity for quarrying the silver lining in any cloud. ("Of Love" exempts only its primary subject when generalizing that "every passion" tends "Unto its own redress.") By contrast, "recompense" features only once more among the poems attributed to Godolphin, when *The Passion* depicts Iarbus, the Libyan king jilted by Dido, angrily asking Jupiter after the beginning of her rumored affair with Aeneas, "is this our pay, our recompense, whilst wee / consume our flocks in sacrifice to thee" (225–26). These words cannot be distinguished as certainly Godolphin's rather than Waller's. But then again, Waller's habits of thought and expression are far easier to assess because he wrote so much more than Godolphin did, the vast majority of it unambiguously his own.

III: "testimonies of . . . good opinion"

On the other hand, Bruce King underscores the distinctiveness of Godolphin's "Chorus," as well as its range. Whereas Saintsbury styles it "Senecan," remarking that it "has some curious expressions in it" (238n), King terms it "a surprising mixture of late Elizabethan Senecanism and what appears to be the sensationalist psychology of Godolphin's friend Thomas Hobbes." Godolphin's "Vaine man, borne to noe happinesse" (1), according to King, "is dissatisfied because he either desires what he lacks or is satiated by what he has."[7] Hobbes would not have recognized this dilemma as a reflection of his thought: he considered humans incapable of being "satiated." He therefore did not make the distinction between literal and figurative lack of vitality that Godolphin both draws and collapses in his question about "desire": "is it not deadnesse to have none, / and satisfied, are wee not stone?" (9, 11–12). The case for viewing "Chorus" as Hobbesian rests on essentially the same evidence marshaled for the equivalent claim made about Rochester's lyrics. King acknowledges as much when he describes Rochester's "*Love* and *Life*" and "Song" as representing "a Hobbesian view of the mind," without clarifying how (197). He can only have been thinking that his prior argument concerning Godolphin's indebtedness to Hobbes's "sensationalist psychology" rendered that same thinker's influence on Rochester self-evident. Furthermore, "Chorus" typifies a genre popular in seventeenth-century England: debates over the merits of sexual consummation, such as "Against Fruition [I]" (1646) and Waller's reply, "In Answer of Sir John Suckling's Verses" (1645).

Even so, Hobbes remembered Godolphin in *Leviathan* as one who, "when he lived, was pleas'd to think my studies something, and otherwise to oblige me . . . with reall testimonies of his good opinion, great in themselves, and the greater for the worthinesse of his person"; these included a bequest of £200.[8] Though "studies" receive no further specification, their evaluation as "something" must date from before the end of 1640 if this compliment was delivered in person rather than by letter, and they presumably encompassed *Elements* or the equivalent material expressed in conversation. But a nagging question arises if such evidence underwrites Godolphin's familiarity with Hobbes's "sensationalist psychology" and perhaps justifies considering the fear in "Song" a likely reflection of his influence (as well as, or instead of, interaction with Waller's corpus): should "studies" deemed "something" not have exerted a greater impact than this, if having any at all?

Saintsbury appears to answer this question when he confidently anatomizes Godolphin's poetic style as a fairly typical early-Caroline "Spenser–Jonson–Donne compound . . . with a special inclination towards the Donne-strain," except that "Hobbes has rather replaced the great Dean" (235). The sole support for this alleged mutation proves to be Godolphin's poem "Constancy" (1906), where "in point of thought he shows us more than a glimpse of the subtlety and depth which must have attracted Hobbes" (232). That Hobbes liked Godolphin for writing like a philosopher does not establish the specific likemindedness that Saintsbury needs to buttress his claim: many lyrics written in England between the end of the sixteenth century and that of the following exhibit deep and subtle thought. As H. M. Richmond suggests, "the word 'experimental' is . . . no less applicable to the lyricism of Stuart England than to the contemporary advance of the physical sciences. It is tempting to see in lyricism a miniature war of hypotheses analogous to the larger and frequently less urbane rivalries of scientists."[9]

Moreover, a very different view of Godolphin's mind emerges from his poem beginning "Lord when the wise men came from Farr" (1906). Explicating its couplet "To know, can only wonder breede, / And not to know, is wonders seede" (17–18), but giving the second line as "And not to know is wisdom's seed," Hugh Maclean comments that

> The outlook informing these lines is perhaps most explicitly phrased by Cornelius Agrippa von Nettesheim (c. 1486–1535), whose work Godolphin very probably knew: "How can one perceive truth? Is it by scientific speculations, by the pressing witness of sensation, by the artificial arguments of logic, by evident proofs, by demonstrative syllogisms, by the light and efforts of human reason? Bah! Get rid of all that: the only means of discerning truth is faith."[10]

Because Godolphin's lines could not be any more "explicitly phrased," such annotation scarcely needs to clarify a theological position far removed from the Socinianism typical of the Great Tew circle and alien to Hobbes's thinking about religion. Hitching Godolphin's pietism to an intellectual source, Maclean reduces the distance by making him seem more bookish in his faith (and thus less different from most of Falkland's friends), but renders him slightly absurd: a scholar investigating how "not to know." In addition, dressing Godolphin in borrowed robes only accentuates the slightness of his oeuvre, as Saintsbury's comment about Hobbes's impact further attests. Like Falkland, Godolphin was a diminutive person looming large in the eyes of contemporaries, but one who cannot now be esteemed a giant on the basis of any surviving work. Though both men died young—victims of the same conflict, at the same age, in the same year, while fighting for the same side—they did not lack time to develop their potential, which must be considered modest, unless realized only in productions since lost.

IV: "distant vertues reconcil'd"

There are nonetheless other grounds for considering Godolphin a Hobbesian figure, based on his life rather than his work. *Leviathan* portrays him as an ideal synthesis for simultaneously embodying such divergent traits as "cleernesse of Judgment, and largenesse of Fancy; strength of Reason, and gracefull Elocution; a Courage for the Warre, and a Fear for the Laws" (718). As Hobbes perhaps knew, Godolphin had exploited the same trope in "An Epitaph upon the Lady *Rich*" (1658), styling its subject (née Cavendish), one "Who best all distant vertues reconcil'd, / Strict, cheerful, humble, great, severe, and mild" (15–16). But the specific terms of Hobbes's *concordia discors* differ; and he had only introduced his admiring portrait of Godolphin because he found no other way to forestall objections that the rigor and comprehensiveness of his political philosophy entailed "an impossibility that any one man should be sufficiently disposed to all sorts of Civill duty" (717). Though a unique instance, by then dead, let Hobbes reject such criticism, it did not justify his concomitant shortening of the odds from "Impossibilities" to "great difficulties" (718). Furthermore, Hugh Trevor-Roper argues that Clarendon's assault on *Leviathan* chiefly reflected his eagerness to defend Godolphin from the implicit calumny of association with such a work, as betraying both a royalist hero and by extension the entire Great Tew circle.[11] Clarendon maintained that "of all men living, there were no two more unlike then Mr. *Godolphin* and Mr. *Hobbes*, in the modesty of nature, or integrity of manners."[12] These words reject a comparison that Hobbes had not directly attempted (leaving tacit his own status as an exemplar of "Civill duty") and cannot gainsay his recollected rapport with Godolphin or the resultant bequest, whose payment Clarendon had to arrange, as he stressed several times when attacking *Leviathan*, as proof of his impartiality. "To be praised by Clarendon *and* Hobbes is indeed to have your name struck in double bronze," Saintsbury notes of Godolphin (232); but whereas such twofold admiration enhances his stature, it also reduces him to a permanently voiceless bone of contention.

Though the five other virtuous extremes that Hobbes attributes to Godolphin might have been dyed-in-the-wool characteristics, his "Courage for the Warre" certainly was not. Prior to 1642, he had no known military experience; and Clarendon paints him as an unlikely soldier: "inclined somewhat to melancholy, and retirement amongst his books," and "of so nice and tender a composition, that a little rain or wind would disorder him, and divert him from any short journey."[13] Such details nonetheless support Hobbes's claims: Godolphin had a pronounced sense of "Civill duty" when "sufficiently disposed" to endure as a soldier a level of discomfort far exceeding that produced by inclement weather. But that he heeded his obligations does not explain how he assessed them. If he reluctantly bore arms out of a quasi-feudal sense of obligation to Charles I, he epitomized not Hobbes's conception of obedience but a more traditional one. An unapt soldier, however, is not the same as an unready one: Saintsbury classifies Godolphin as "A fervent royalist and a strong partisan of Strafford" (231); Dighton likewise comments that "Throughout his parliamentary career he was a staunch Royalist and adherent of Strafford" (xix). But neither commentator substantiates Godolphin's ultra-royalism or devotion to Strafford. Moreover, the span of his "parliamentary career" was too short for "Throughout" to mean much. Dighton quotes just one comment by Godolphin regarding the constitutional crisis of 1640–42: it merely warns that "by a war the Parliament would expose itself to unknown dangers; for when the cards are once shuffled no man knows what the game will be" (xix).

Another asymmetry in Hobbes's praise reflects the passage in time between Godolphin's death and *Leviathan*'s publication. In 1642, "Civill duty" arguably entailed fighting for a monarch whose inability to protect his own subjects from each other had become obvious, but who might once again rule over all of them if still commanding the allegiance of some; a year or so later, the terms remained the same. Eight years after Godolphin's death, however, too much had changed for "Civill duty" to be as before. *That every man is bound by Nature, as much as in him lieth, to protect in Warre, the Authority, by which he is himself protected in time of Peace,*" *Leviathan* stipulates (718–19). These words commend Godolphin for how he died and advise a different course of action for anyone alive to heed their message in upholding the fragile peace brokered by England's post-regicide government. Following the Restoration, Hobbes liked to profess that *Leviathan* embodied orthodox royalism; but in making Godolphin that work's paragon, he falsified it or him.

V: "a way to learn civility"

In this connection, I see as significant one of two poems by Collop where Conrad Hilberry judges that he "seems to be trying to accommodate himself to Cromwell's rule."[14] Both derive from Collop's collection *Poesis Rediviva* (1656) and reflect his experience of the Interregnum. Hilberry's description of "To the Son of the Late King," indicates why he does not claim in this case that Collop "follows Hobbes": on this view, the poet

> tells Charles that he raises his hand daily in prayer for him but he will not raise it in blood. And he goes on to console the pretender by describing at some length the hardships and uncertainties of rule and urging him to rejoice, with Christ, that his kingdom is not here. This was doubtless cold comfort for Charles, but it evidently served Collop as a rationale for accepting Cromwell's government against his real convictions. (10, 11)

Though I doubt that Collop "follows Hobbes" in the other poem either, "Summum Jus Summa Injuria in Jure Regni" sheds light on Hobbes's thought pertaining to Cromwell's rise to power and Godolphin's status as *Leviathan*'s paragon.

"Gold Crowns are Coyn'd by steel, and stamp'd by might," "Summum" begins, citing examples from British history: "Thus th' Saxons, Danish, Normans, Tudors right" (1–2). This point parallels *Leviathan*'s admission that "there is scarce a Common-wealth in the world, whose beginnings can in conscience be justified" (722), except that Collop does not shrink from specifying examples, including two not comfortably remote: "Tudors right" encompassed fairly recent history; and Charles I's opponents sometimes conceived their resistance as a belated liberation from the Norman yoke. But Collop also supports his view of political power by instancing how "The Roman Eagles ceased on their prey; / Their talons swords were carv'd the Empires way" (3–4). Hilberry's notes clarify that "ceased" should be understood as "seized," but err in proposing "curv'd" as an emendation of "carv'd" (201). Collop often over-compresses his syntax: the Roman eagles had swords for talons that carved their empire's way.

Whereas one of Hobbes's infrequent comments on the benefits of imperialism stresses that Rome's legions brought civilization with their dominion (see chapter two), Collop explains how

> 'Twas steel that gave the Spaniard all his gold:
> By's *Bilbo* blades he doth his Indies hold.

To edge blunt tools the Priest talks of the word.
'Tis steel that conquers, not the two-edg'd sword.
The Ottoman Moon had else bin in the wane;
Refulgent steel doth it new lustre gain.
The greatest injury is the greatest right:
Yet out of darknesse God creates a light. (5–12)

Few of Collop's compatriots would have reflected so soberly on Spanish and Ottoman power. Though Waller was unusual in repeatedly urging Christian nations to unite in a new crusade against Islam to recover the biblical holy lands, his Western coreligionists anxiously monitored any changes in the Ottoman Empire's status, and most of his readers shared his devotion to the cliché of Spanish cruelty. Moreover, Collop's initial audience might have been struck by his contradictory treatment of scripture: in the beginning was "the word" he dismisses, as was the "light" brought "out of darknesse" whose fiat he endorses.

Only with that act of creation in mind does he turn to the benefits of imperialism, with an emphasis akin to Hobbes's:

While *Greece* did make a Conquest of the world,
She with her arms her arts about it hurl'd.
Civility did with Roman Eagles fly;
To *Tame's* a way to learn civility.
Who Conquers bodies, may he Conquer Minds;
And leave us men whom he like wild beasts finds. (13–18)

Though Collop does not explain the circumstances under which the hypothetical "Who" in the last of these couplets should encounter "men" resembling "wild beasts," the recent Civil Wars would fit, producing a less explicit version of the argument in Waller's *Panegyric* against those who "own no liberty but where they may / Without control upon their fellows prey" (2: 7–8). But whereas these lines feasibly reflect Waller's knowledge of *De Cive*, no record survives of Collop's acquaintance with Hobbes's work. Though Collop openly relied on a handful of favorite authors (Donne, Grotius, Henry Hammond), Hilberry notes that he "prided himself on the independence of his thought" and deems him "never a blind follower of any sect," for "his opinions are never meekly orthodox" (8). Collop was thus capable of reaching his own conclusions in the aftermath of the Engagement controversy, but might have been attracted to Hobbes's work as likewise "never meekly orthodox." Regardless of whether he found his own way in speculating about "Who . . . may . . . Conquer Minds," however, Collop no more resolved how this could happen than Davenant and Hobbes did.

Hilberry interprets *"Tame's"* as "italicized because the printer mistook it for *Thames"* (201): the physical appearance of "Summum" offers no sure guide to Collop's own choices in such matters as punctuation. Possibly revealing, however, is his sudden deviation from the heavily end-stopped lines and couplets characterizing the rest of the poem and most of his verse:

> Though he a Kingdom gains, she shall lose none;
> When every man doth in himself gain one,
> Who is no prop to a declining throne,
> Sins 'gainst his Kings in Earth, in Heav'n his own,
> He's traitor helps a traitor to a Throne,
> Yet who resists him on it may be one. (19–24)

From the confidence of the first of these couplets, plausibly Hobbesian (gained security outweighs liberty lost), Collop's verses slide through another four lines, as if he could not maintain the percussive Clevelandisms normative for his secular poetry, running through all conflicting possibilities encompassed by "Civill duty" at this juncture, experiencing them as antithetical pairs in a free-fall of insoluble contradictions. Possibly a byproduct of profound moral agitation, the lines sufficiently typify Collop's phrasing to obscure a simple meaning: Hilberry unravels "in Heav'n his own" as "against God as well" (201).

The concluding lines of "Summum" bring no closure, explaining how

> *Martlets* and *Capets* treasons thrones acquir'd:
> Yet both so well rul'd, *France* thought both inspir'd.
> A petty notary rul'd so well in *Rome*
> The time of th' golden Age, did th' name assume.
> *Otho* may sacrifice't all for publick good;
> Good with ten thousands losse's no right of blood. (25–30)

Hilberry identifies the "petty notary" as Cicero (201): Collop ignores that figure's superb oratory in an apparent bid to associate him with the commoner Cromwell. To the best of my understanding (Hilberry offers no help here), Collop's French examples offer a corollary to his earlier equivalent of Hobbes's point about the paucity of regimes "whose beginnings can in conscience be justified," though one implicit in "Tudors right": for better or for worse, some dynasties with questionable origins end up being remembered fondly. Collop likewise sees history as a lottery in the case of Otho.

Defeated by Vitellius at Betriarcum, Otho committed suicide instead of regrouping his forces, alleging that he wished to prevent further conflict. But civil war among the Romans did not cease until Vitellius had been ousted in turn by Vespasian. Moreover, Otho himself had instigated such strife by killing Galba, only the first of four emperors to reign in A.D. 69. Nonetheless, Otho for many came to embody a supreme altruism. Collop takes this view in his poem "To the Son," which exhorts its subject "See *Otho* fall, Fift *Charls* resign a Throne, / That Eagle-like he may mount heav'n for one" (35–36). That Otho features in both poems further justifies Hilberry's taking them as a pair. But they are complementary in offering quite different views of Otho, just as Collop explicitly addresses the one poem to the future Charles II and implicitly focuses the other on Cromwell. The last line of "Summum" gives a sardonic account of the "good" accomplished by Otho: the "ten thousands" whose "losse" accompanied his ambitions could hardly be salvaged through his ensuing self-sacrifice.

"Summum" therefore invokes not the noble Otho of Collop's "To the Son" but the fraudulent and falsely celebrated figure depicted by Suetonius, who notes of his "defeat" that "Otho at once resolved to take his own life, rather from a feeling of shame, as many have thought with good reason, and an unwillingness to persist in a struggle for imperial power at the expense of such danger to life and property, than from any despair of success or distrust of his troops." Suetonius also quotes his father's verdict: "Otho, even when he was a private citizen, so loathed civil strife, that at the mere mention of the fate of Brutus and Cassius at a banquet he shuddered." Suetonius's concluding words turn from Otho's own hypocrisy to that of his posthumous admirers: "In short the greater part of those who had hated him most bitterly while he lived lauded him to the stars when he was dead; and it was even commonly declared that he had put an end to Galba, not so much for the sake of ruling, as of restoring the republic and liberty."[15]

Thus, "To the Son" urges the future Charles II to imitate the noble Otho in resigning a throne, whereas "Summum" doubts that any "publick good" can accompany "ten thousands losse," but hints that Cromwell should make the Civil Wars' sacrifices meaningful by continuing to rule, and in such a way as to "Conquer Minds," rather than repeat the fraudulent Otho's failure to be true to his own ambition.[16]

Hoping to convince his compatriots that the evils of such conflict left no reasonable grounds for disrupting the status quo, Hobbes "so loathed civil strife" that he would probably have regarded Otho as insane for acting as he did. He nonetheless expected individuals to judge when an extant regime could no longer uphold its end of the contract obliging subjects to "Civill duty." He felt unsafe enough to leave England at a relatively early date, but safe enough to return when the future Protector had yet to consolidate his power with that title, plus control over a government as well as an army. Free to exercise his own interpretation of Charles I's collapsing rule, Godolphin stayed in England to fight on that king's behalf. Hobbes's doctrine in turn permitted him to acclaim this course of action as highly honorable for any citizen young enough to bear arms. But Godolphin left too little evidence of his own political views to indicate how he might have construed his obligations if he had survived to face the acute dilemmas that "Summum" well conveys, despite or because of its clumsy organization and phrasing. Moreover, Collop's poem makes a point as applicable to Hobbes as to Godolphin, albeit in different ways: whereas powerful figures can change regimes, no single subject can significantly control how such disruptions of the status quo will be viewed in hindsight or at the time by those whose opinions carry most weight. Hobbes could feasibly enfold Godolphin's "Civill duty" within his own to convert "one man" into an entire theory of political obligation, but was unable (except rhetorically) to carry even that single person with him as endorsing his "studies" in relation to Interregnum England, much less to "Conquer Minds" on a sufficiently large scale that a critical mass of contemporaries would agree with his definitions of such key concepts as loyalty. In portraying history as a lottery, Collop does not express his own version of Hobbes's nominalism; but his sardonic and possibly anxious remarks illustrate how readily the label "traitor" could attach to the same individual choosing either of two opposed models of "Civill duty."

VI: *"every man"*

As Deborah Baumgold notes, Hobbes's "law of nature regarding the duty to fight for the state" was a late addition; not explicitly formulated before the advent of *Leviathan*, it did not feature even there until that work's "Review, and Conclusion."[17] For Baumgold, this apparent afterthought assumes great significance: she argues that most Hobbes scholars have been mistaken in their "assumption that everyman (the abstract individual) is the principal subject of his political analysis," insisting that "He is preoccupied not so much with the *incivisme* of ordinary subjects as with the danger posed by ambitious elites" (2). In her view, Hobbes's political philosophy "manifests a structural, as opposed to individualistic, way of thinking about the performance of civic duties." "Rather than discuss the duties of an abstract individual," according to her, Hobbes "ties obligations to roles, drawing a distinction between the obligations of ordinary subjects and those of soldiers who have enlisted in some more or less voluntary fashion" (5). As she stresses, Hobbes typically "excuses cowardly subjects from the obligation to fight for the state, as well as those who furnish a substitute soldier" (89). Nonetheless, the law of nature belatedly appended to *Leviathan*'s "Review, and Conclusion" incorporates the caveat *"as much as in him lieth,"* reserving *"every man"* apparently unlimited discretion when determining his own aptitude for warfare, which accents his individuality over his abstract universality, but also subordinates "roles" to subjective interpretation of circumstances. Godolphin either exceeded Hobbes's expectations of "ordinary subjects" and should not have served as *Leviathan*'s epitome of "Civill duty" or undermines Baumgold's case that Hobbes consistently distinguished between the war-time "roles" of citizen and soldier. She never addresses, however, where Godolphin fits in the picture: too exceptional a figure to serve as a representative everyman or the occupant of any shared role, he remains an obstinately singular and equivocal paragon.

The number of Hobbes's real-life exemplars soars, though, if *Behemoth* dramatizes the theoretical framework established by *Leviathan*, as Stephen Holmes claims in his introduction to the later work. For Holmes, Hobbes's history of the Civil Wars represents a "fine-grained account of human motivation" contradicting the standard perception that he shows people "propelled exclusively by a desire for self-preservation."[18] In Holmes's view, "the notion that human beings are, by nature, relentless pursuers of their own advantage conflicts wildly with *Behemoth*'s fabulous chronicle of human folly," whereby "Impulsiveness and compulsions, hysterical frenzy and aimless drifting, are more characteristic of man's history than eye on the ball purposiveness, thoughtful self-preservation, or the sober cultivation of material interests" (xv). Holmes further maintains that *Behemoth* "consistently" distinguishes "between the calculating and the noncalculating, between the players and the played-with," so that "Broadly speaking, there are two types of human being: the cynic and the dupe" (xxv). But this distinction proves malleable when Holmes acknowledges that "After first denouncing the common people as one of the 'seducers' of the commonwealth (2, 4), Hobbes shifts to accusing them of being one of the commonwealth's 'distempers' (20). This is a switch from active to passive, from craft to disease, from player to played-with" (xxv n.33). Some shifting also occurs when Holmes explains why "Hobbes exaggerates the relative importance of self-interest," claiming that "Political theorists traditionally divided humanity into two groups: a vast majority, motivated by lowly self-interest, and elites, propelled by higher ideals such as glory or the common good." According to this line of thought, "When Hobbes writes of universal self-interest, he means the stress to fall on *universal*. He is universalizing, so to speak, the morality of the common man" (xiii n.16). But even if Holmes correctly assesses Hobbes's emphasis, this does not convert "self-interest" into something else. Holmes nonetheless assumes that *Behemoth*'s "psychological assumptions . . . are ultimately indistinguishable from those expounded almost two decades earlier, in *Leviathan*," though "illustrated with greater concreteness and color" (xlix), scornfully rejecting the view that Hobbes's political philosophy chiefly concerns "the utility bundle of a rational maximizer" (xxix). On the one hand, contrasting degrees of "concreteness and color" demand different readings; on the other, Holmes raises a legitimate point by attempting to close the gulf between a "fabulous chronicle of human folly" and a political philosophy whose declared paragon no more exemplifies "the cynic" or "the dupe" than he does "eye on the ball purposiveness."

David Johnston offers one version ("essentially rational, egoistic, self-possessed") of the abstract Hobbesian everyman that Baumgold and Holmes differently reject.[19] Acknowledging and seeking to resolve a dissonance central to Hobbes's thinking, Johnston discerns in *Leviathan* alone a counterpart to the contrast between a less and a more graphic approach that Holmes frames in terms of the overall difference between that work and *Behemoth*. "The discrepancy between the theoretical model of man upon which Hobbes had drawn to build the initial version of his political philosophy and the descriptive portrait of man developed in *Leviathan* opened up a problem of fundamental importance," according to Johnston: "If men are ignorant, superstitious, and irrational, none of the basic mechanisms upon which his political argument relies will be likely to work" (120). Accepting the presence of rival everymen in Hobbes's thought, Johnston proposes this "answer" to the question of why Hobbes "continued to cling to his initial model of man as an egoistic, rational actor": that he

> believed actual human behavior might, in time, come to resemble the pattern described by his model. In the present, men were ignorant, superstitious, and irrational. Their behavior was poles apart from the pattern described by his model and required by his political theory. But Hobbes did not think that men were essentially and permanently irrational beings. (121–22)

On this account, whether such a paragon as Godolphin had ever existed mattered little, provided that persons like him might eventually be educated into being. But I have already noted Hobbes's unrealistic expectations for *Leviathan*'s dissemination (see chapter two). Moreover, Godolphin again fits readily into none of the available categories: unlikely as an example of "essentially rational, egoistic, self-possessed" humanity, he hardly qualifies as "ignorant, superstitious, and irrational," any more than he takes sides in a clash of "cynics" and "dupes" or maintains Hobbes's allegedly tidy conception of differing "roles" for soldiers and "ordinary subjects."

Whereas Holmes in finding no room for Godolphin neglects a portion of *Leviathan* featuring the "concreteness" he finds more typical of *Behemoth*, Baumgold in likewise slighting the same figure spurns the opportunity presented by a test case pertinent to her claims regarding the significance of "roles," and Johnston failed even to mention the "one man" whom Hobbes felt that he needed as an embodiment of his "theoretical model" for that paradigm not to seem too remote from reality to have much practical relevance.

VII: "Impossibilities"

Stephen Collins likewise ignores Godolphin's status as *Leviathan*'s paragon, despite making bold claims for Hobbes's ideas about individuals. Flying to the opposite extreme from Derek Hughes (see chapter five), though no less wildly, Collins links Hobbes's work not with the Davenant–Dryden *Tempest* but with Shakespeare's original (1611). Remarking that "the isolation of the state is analogous to the dramatic isolation of the self in Shakespeare's great tragedies from *Hamlet* to *Coriolanus* [1607–08]," Collins explains how "As Prospero overcame this isolation (he conquered his island imagination) so too Hobbes reunited the individual and social nature in the sovereign state."[20] This interpretation does not mean that Hobbes and Shakespeare thought alike; rather, the first "rejected the traditional and the radical Christian perceptions of one order only. And he denied the Shakespearean vision of complementarity. In their place, Hobbes substituted a new perceived order by deifying the self-reflective and self-consciously definitive one choice" (164). Nor does Collins claim that his authors saw themselves or each other in such terms: "Perhaps only now can we self-consciously and ironically reflect upon that magical, cultural product, which the great conjurers Shakespeare, Bacon, and Hobbes textually created to be the responsible authority for social reality—individual man" (167–68). Even allowing for Newton's interest in alchemy, the gap dividing such wand-waving from Bacon's and Hobbes's concern with scientific method seems too wide for these ruminations to carry much weight. Moreover, Collins's thesis looks equally strained when he switches from conjuring to philosophy: he sheds "light" on "Hobbes' relationship to Shakespeare" by echoing Northrop Frye: "while tragedy is existential, existentialism is post-tragic" (187 n.40). Collins's most straightforward expression of the nature of this "relationship" betrays a revealing awkwardness: "I offer Hobbes as a focal point (as I do Shakespeare) because I believe that he most particularly crystallizes, in his works, theoretical positions argued by a range of contemporary political thinkers. Rather than anomalous, Hobbes' work is arguably paradigmatic in its impact" (175–76 n.54). The pronoun "he" forms part of an absolute claim about Hobbes, who as "a focal point" nonetheless occupies the same space (and role?) as Shakespeare.

Though Hobbes is much more "anomalous" than Collins supposes, which explains why drawing him into the orbit of other authors requires comparisons more often that not forced, I myself hazard the claim that the author of *Leviathan* resembled a satirist when struggling to find even one good man to extol. I do not therefore retract chapter five's contrast between Hobbes's rhetoric and Rochester's in *A Satyre against Reason and Mankind*: the poem's ironic recantation has a tone and serves a function quite different from Hobbes's attempt to exclude "Impossibilities." Quentin Skinner nonetheless installs Hobbes "in a tradition running from Erasmus and More to Rabelais, Montaigne and other Renaissance satirists who dealt with their intellectual adversaries less by arguing with them than by ridiculing their absurdities."[21] This indirect attempt to corral Hobbes into the mainstream of Renaissance humanism ignores his methodological concerns as a science-minded system-builder, but points in a valuable direction. As Skinner's equivocal "less by . . . than by" concedes, the question is not whether Hobbes could wax satirical but how often he did so and where. Chapter eight focuses on Jonson, not because he sometimes wrote as a formal verse-satirist, but because in addition he produced plays featuring satire and had an often vexed relationship with readers and theatergoers that sometimes led him to assess in satirical terms their reception of his entire enterprise. Here again, however, I trace affinities, not attempting to certify an influence exerted by or on Hobbes.

Chapter Eight

"Ordinary Artifice": Hobbes and Jonson

I: "copie of words"

Whereas Mulgrave praised him as a stylist for his philosophy (see chapter three), Hobbes's literary credentials during his own lifetime and a little beyond chiefly rested on his topographical poem *De Mirabilibus Pecci* (ca. 1626–28): according to A. P. Martinich, who gives its approximate date of composition, it was published in 1636, reprinted in 1666 and 1675, and anonymously translated into English in 1678; it inspired Cotton to write *The Wonders of the Peake* (1681), a poem praising Hobbes as "He who is in *Nature* the best read, / Who the best hand has to the wisest head, / Who best can think, and best his thoughts express," albeit with the caveat that he "Does but, perhaps, more rationally guess, / When he his sense delivers of these things," and that "To seek investigable *Causes* out, / Serves not to clear, but to increase a doubt."[1] Active throughout his life as a translator of verse and prose, and a frequent composer of Latin poetry, however, Hobbes wrote just one poem in English, "not long before his death," according to Aubrey, who prints it:

> Tho' I am now past ninety, and too old
> T' expect preferment in the court of Cupid,
> And many winters made mee ev'n so cold
> I am become almost all over stupid,
>
> Yet I can love and have a mistresse too,
> As fair as can be and as wise as fair;
> And yet not proud, nor anything will doe
> To make me of her favour to despair.
>
> To tell you who she is were very bold;
> But if i' th' character your selfe you find
> Thinke not the man a fool thô he be old
> Who loves in body fair a fairer mind.[2]

Even if this were not a distant cousin of Jonson's *Celebration of CHARIS in Ten Lyrick Peeces* (the first ca. 1623, the remainder ca. 1612–16), Hobbes would still qualify as an overlooked Son of Ben, especially compared with some of the twelve thousand other authors routinely classified thus.

Hobbes apparently showed Jonson a letter (dated May 14, 1621) helping him write the portrait of Bacon in his commonplace book *Timber, or Discoveries* (ca. 1623–35).[3] Requesting a favor in return from "his loving and familiar friend and acquaintance," Hobbes presented both Jonson and their mutual friend Sir Robert Ayton with a copy of *Eight Books* so that they could "give their judgement" as to its "style," according to Aubrey (1: 365). Regarding Hobbes's last visit to their native Wiltshire (July or August 1634), Aubrey notes that "His conversation about those times was much about Ben: Jonson, Mr. Ayton, etc." (1: 332). Maddeningly typical of Aubrey's casual approach, that "etc." presumably means that Hobbes's fund of Jonson-lore extended beyond Ayton into territory that only a close associate of Jonson's might know. That Hobbes's recollections from the earlier 1630s seem to have centered on Jonson has an additional significance, given the overall bleakness of that figure's last decade.

Having never enjoyed the same favor at Charles I's court that he had enjoyed at James I's, Jonson suffered a stroke in 1628 that left him grossly overweight, partially paralyzed, and confined to one room; he was then widely written off as over the hill or prematurely senile, often by former friends. Richard Burt offers a more complex view of Jonson's decline, stressing that his final decade did not feature reversals exclusively and that other authors during these years suffered commercial failures and setbacks at court.[4] But Jonson never thought of himself as just one writer among many, subject to the same vagaries affecting all; conversely, the great eminence from which he fell reflected not only his own self-importance. During this mainly dismal period, however, he also found a Maecenas in Hobbes's primary employer, Newcastle, whom Dale Randall terms "One of the most thoroughly Jonsonized of the Sons of Ben."[5]

Though unhelpfully offering no more precise date than "Before Thucydides," Aubrey records that Hobbes "spent two yeares in reading romances and playes, which he haz often repented and sayd that these two yeares were lost of him" (1: 361). Hobbes also regretted the costs associated with serving William Cavendish, second earl of Devonshire, when the miscellaneous duties he performed in addition to tutoring began reversing his own intellectual development: Aubrey explains, "By this way of life, he had almost forgot his Latin. . . . He therefore bought him bookes of an Amsterdam print that he might carry in his pocket (particularly Caesar's Commentarys), which he did read in the lobbey, or ante-chamber, whilest his lord was making his visits" (1: 331). Such foresight could not shield him from other occupational hazards: according to Aubrey, "he tooke colds, being wett in his feet," when Devonshire, "a waster, sent him up and downe to borrow money, and to gett gentlemen to be bound for him, being ashamed to speake him selfe" (1: 347). But if Hobbes had little choice but to accept this way of life, he also derived advantages from his employment as a savant-servant to sundry Cavendishes. By contrast, he was free to embrace or reject on any terms both "romances" (which most men of the time derided as fit only for women and children) and "playes" (which for many readers had to date from classical antiquity to be taken seriously). Ridiculed by Suckling and others, Jonson in publishing *Workes* boldly declared not only his own stature but also that of his plays. As Jonas Barish has shown, however, even that self-consciously serious dramatist harbored a profound ambivalence: "it is precisely the uneasy synthesis between a formal antitheatricalism, which condemns the arts of show and illusion on the one hand, and a subversive hankering after them on the other, that lends to Jonson's comic masterpieces much of their unique high tension and precarious equilibrium."[6] Though Hobbes on this point was content to adopt a merely commonplace position, Aubrey dared question it: "perhaps he was mistaken too. For [such reading] might furnish him with copie of words" (1: 361).

II: "Safe"

Charles Cantalupo finds Aubrey's dissent so persuasive that he makes "copie of words" a recurrent theme in presenting *Leviathan* as an omnium gatherum whose teeming plenitude encompasses many different kinds of literature. He observes that

> In his more philosophical middle age Hobbes might have regretted his overweening attraction to Elizabethan plays and prose romances; but Aubrey, attributing "copie of words" to Hobbes's writing, means that that writing has a copiousness, richness, and variety of language comparable to that found in fiction and drama.[7]

Though Cantalupo plausibly interprets Aubrey's drift, "Elizabethan" lacks sanction: "Before Thucydides" might refer to some point in the Jacobean period and concerns a period of his life when Hobbes possibly read literary works of different vintages.

But Cantalupo's study has a further value in linking Hobbes's and Jonson's embattled views of themselves. In *Leviathan*, Hobbes explains his procedure when citing numerous passages from scripture to support his ideas:

> I have endeavoured to avoid such texts as are of obscure, or controverted Interpretation; and to alledge none, but in such sense as is most plain, and agreeable to the harmony and scope of the whole Bible; which was written for the re-establishment of the Kingdome of God in Christ. For it is not the bare Words, but the Scope of the writer that giveth the true light, by which any writing is to bee interpreted; and they that insist upon single Texts, without considering the main Designe, can derive no thing from them cleerly; but rather by casting atomes of Scripture, as dust before mens eyes, make every thing more obscure than it is; an ordinary artifice of those that seek not the truth, but their own advantage.[8]

Cantalupo comments of this "dramatic epilogue" that it

> shows Hobbes bitterly criticizing but only gesturing toward an unspecified "they." For a reader "they" are "those" persons or factions with whom he or she is least sympathetic. Such general obloquy gives Hobbes's attack a rhetorical advantage that it would not have if it were aimed only at certain Royalists, Parliamentarians, or Roman theologians. Nevertheless, there is no one who could read *Leviathan* and not be offended by at least some part of it. Thus Hobbes appears as an isolated figure, as every great writer must be at moments, imprecating an entire world ruining itself with the most self-seeking and "ordinary artifice." His attitude resembles that often struck by Jonson, caught between "the wolve's black jaw, and the dull ass's hoof." (189–90)

Cantalupo does not specify whether he connects Hobbes's views about biblical exegesis with Jonson's words as figuring in the "Apologeticall Dialogue" included with his comedy *The Poetaster* (1601) or as concluding his defiant "Ode" addressed "To Himselfe" (1640), where he aspires to be "Safe from the wolves black jaw, and the dull Asses hoofe" (8: 35); nor is the occasion for the posthumously published outburst now known; but the repetition and the early expression of the dateable version reveal considerable frustration. Moreover, Cantalupo offers a comparison more illuminating than he realizes.

Not "every great writer" is doomed to be sometimes "isolated"; conversely, authors of all levels spend their working lives with no company besides a wastepaper basket. The dimension on which Jonson and Hobbes resembled each other, too, was not intrinsic to literary greatness or any other trait conceivably shared with their peers. Though the abuse greeting Milton's divorce-tracts of the 1640s moved him to reflect that "this is got by casting Pearl to Hoggs," he proved willing to meet readers half-way, as when explaining (albeit grumpily) his choice of blank verse for *Paradise Lost*, supplying arguments summarizing its ten books, and even restructuring his epic to satisfy expectations that it include two more.[9] By contrast, Barish judges that "Jonson, despite a lifetime of writing for the stage, never arrived at a comfortable *modus vivendi* with his audiences" (133). Though Cantalupo stresses Hobbes's rhetorical guile in directing his anger toward an unspecified "they," the further point that "no one . . . could read *Leviathan* and not be offended by at least some part of it" so undermines the value of "general obloquy" as to epitomize the history of that text's reception. Furthermore, Hobbes's assumption that he could avoid "texts" of an "obscure" or "controverted" nature when discussing scripture strikes an odd note for an author of his time and place: his stance looks staggeringly naïve or breathtakingly disingenuous. Overall, too, this "dramatic epilogue" in its defensive aggressiveness or aggressive defensiveness betrays the viewpoint of a combative author prone to satire.

How closely Hobbes's embattled perspective resembles Jonson's emerges from a passage in *Discoveries*. "I have beene accus'd to the Lords, to the *King*; and by great ones," Jonson acknowledges, responding because

> I durst not leave my selfe undefended, having a paire of eares unskilfull to heare lyes; or have those things said of me, which I could truly prove of them. They objected, making of verses to me, when I could object to most of them, their not being able to reade them, but as worthy of scorne. Nay, they would offer to urge mine owne Writings against me; but by pieces, (which was an excellent way of malice) as if any mans Context, might not seeme dangerous, and offensive, if that which was knit, to what went before, were defrauded of his beginning; or that things, by themselves utter'd, might not seeme subject to Calumnie, which read entire, would appeare most free. (8: 604, 605)

The commentary to the edition quoted parallels this passage with these words of Donne's: "That sentences in Authors like haires in an horse-taile, concurre in one root of beauty, and strength, but being pluckt out one by one, serve onely for springes and snares" (11: 253–54). The greater intensity of concern for "Context" that unites Hobbes and Jonson stems from their grim awareness of just whom those "springes and snares" will then be deployed to entrap.

III: "twin rocks"

Giving Hobbes's nearest equivalent to the Scylla-and-Charybdis trope that Cantalupo quotes from Jonson, *Leviathan* explains how "in a way beset with those that contend on one side for too great Liberty, and on the other side for too much Authority, 'tis hard to passe between the points of both unwounded" (75). Hobbes was not the only controversialist in the time of the Civil Wars to adopt the extreme position of representing one of very few moderates. But though many readers have wondered with Stephen Holmes how there can possibly be "too much Authority" for Hobbes, Holmes answers his own question in his introduction to *Behemoth*: "when it is self-defeating, when it undermines itself by alienating potential cooperators."[10] Inhibited from criticizing Charles I with any but the subtlest of hints, however, Hobbes made "too much Authority" a paper tiger, whereas he always felt free to paint in lurid colors the dangers of "too great Liberty." Perhaps only *Behemoth*'s equivocal verdict on William Laud, archbishop of Canterbury, qualifies as an incipiently clear picture of such "self-defeating" rule: he was "a very honest man for his morals, and a very zealous promoter of the Church-government by bishops, and that desired to have the service of God performed, and the house of God adorned, as suitable as was possible to the honour we ought to do to the Divine Majesty"; but "his squabblings . . . about free-will, and his standing upon punctilios . . . was not . . . an argument of his sufficiency in affairs of State" (73). Had he been less "zealous," he would not have been so inclined toward "squabblings" and "punctilios," and vice versa.

Leviathan evokes another kind of double jeopardy in explaining how

> There wants onely, for the entire knowledge of Civill duty, to know what are . . . Lawes of God. For without that, a man knows not, when he is commanded any thing by the Civill Power, whether it be contrary to the Law of God, or not: and so, either by too much civill obedience, offends the Divine Majesty, or through feare of offending God, transgresses the commandements of the Common-wealth. To avoyd both these Rocks, it is necessary to know what are the Lawes Divine. (395)

Hobbes supposes that radical uncertainty rather than ideological conflict makes any attempt "to passe . . . unwounded" a difficult course, and for all equally rather than for him alone, or him and very few others. But "too much civill obedience" as a hazard faced by his English contemporaries rings no more true than does "too much

Authority" as a pitfall his political philosophy resists. Moreover, the Civil Wars came about partly because so many of Charles I's subjects, whether or not they had "too great Liberty," faced no dilemma in cases when they were entirely sure "commandements of the Common-wealth" clashed with "the Law of God": they knew in which direction they would rather err and were not awaiting Hobbes's instruction about either.

In another Scylla-and-Charybdis trope, *De Cive* remarks how most Christians at most times have found it "almost impossible to avoid the twin rocks of *Atheism* and *superstition*," unless receiving "special assistance from God."[11] As neither sharper nor more salient than its "twin," "*Atheism*" in this provocatively bland formulation proves no more of a peril than "*superstition*"; and "to passe between the points of both unwounded" proves a routine challenge. To Hobbes's many later critics, the picture looked different: in what he saw as attacks on "*superstition*" that did not lapse into "*Atheism*," they saw lapsing in abundance; and insofar as he assailed "*superstition*," he did not redeem himself: his efforts seemed to ridicule orthodox believers such as they took themselves to be, for whom "special assistance from God" could valuably assume almost any function but the one he assigned it. As with "too much Authority" and "too much civill obedience," so with "*Atheism*," Hobbes's spectrum of possibilities looked highly idio-syncratic to other interpreters ("they" were indeed legion), suggesting that he risked being shot by any number of sides while occupying an otherwise empty foxhole in a no-man's-land of his own.

IV: "only as *people*"

"The same should probably be said of Hobbes," comments Martinich (227) concerning *Eight Books*' account "Of the Life and History of Thucydides" when it judges that "in his writings our author appeareth to be, on the one side not superstitious, on the other side not an atheist."[12] But whereas Jonson's cultivation of a Horatian persona served to embroil in the War of the Theaters a genial, non-combative, and not exclusively satirical figure, Hobbes's possible identification with the embattled Thucydides would have coincided with a point when his own career was too young to have occasioned any kind of controversy.[13] "Of the Life and History" serves in many cases as a vindication of Thucydides and a counterattack mounted against his contemporary detractors, such that his declared status as neither "superstitious" nor "an atheist" is not the merely innocuous claim it appears quoted out of that context: Hobbes's insistence on his author's blameless orthodoxy redraws the battle-lines by imputing superstitiousness to those accusing him of atheism. In defending Thucydides, too, Hobbes most notably forecast his own future when explaining how the Greek historian had not been "malevolent" in his remarks about his fellow citizens: there is nothing "written of them that tendeth to their dishonour as Athenians, but only as *people*; and that by the necessity of the narration, not by any sought digression. So that no word of his, but their own actions do sometimes reproach them" (17). Such a protestation of Thucydides's innocence reiterates the "reproach" for which he had been reproached; it encourages the citizens of Athens to salve their wounded civic pride by recognizing that they had brought the criticism on themselves, and merely as poor specimens of humanity. But perhaps the most striking feature of the passage just quoted is its claim that "the necessity of the narration" tied Thucydides's hands. Whereas historians (and their translators) seldom address such issues, controversies over the "malevolent" inspiration or earned nature of "reproach" are a staple corollary of satirical writing: wielders of the lash answer the call of a melancholy duty imposed by whole societies of knaves and fools; for those receiving the stripes, the one vice on display belongs to self-appointed floggers.

Leviathan shows how people's "own actions do sometimes reproach them" in acknowledging how

> It may seem strange to some man, that has not well weighed these things; that Nature should . . . dissociate, and render men apt to invade, and destroy one another: and he may therefore, not trusting to this Inference, made from the Passions, desire perhaps to have the same confirmed by Experience. Let him therefore consider with himselfe, when taking a journey, he armes himself, and seeks to go well accompanied; when going to sleep, he locks his dores; when even in his house he locks his chests; and this when he knows there bee Lawes, and publike Officers, armed, to revenge all injuries shall bee done him; what opinion he has of his fellow subjects, when he rides armed; of his fellow Citizens, when he locks his dores; and of his children, and servants, when he locks his chests. Does he not there as much accuse mankind by his actions, as I do by my words? (186–87)

Martinich faults these reflections for their illogic, even linking Hobbes with "the radical paranoid" because of them:

> His implication that the ordinary cautious behaviour of people verifies that everyone suspects everyone else of aggressive feelings is not correct.

The cautious person does not think that everyone is intent on taking his belongings, nor that everyone has an inclination to harm him. Rather, the cautious person believes (1) that some people are intent on harming him and that (2) he does not know which ones these people are.[14]

Such objections to Hobbes's triumphant *tu quoque* fail to explain why "ordinary cautious behaviour" can take the relatively extreme form of ensuring that "chests" be off limits to "children" and "servants" (together with wives?), a phenomenon whose actuality Martinich does not attempt to dispute (though it could be explained in other ways). More importantly, too, Martinich makes no allowance for the fact that Hobbes illustrates a point about life in the state of nature by invoking very different circumstances, where "there bee Lawes and publike Officers." If people feel sufficiently insecure to engage in "ordinary cautious behaviour" when they have safeguards in place, then they would feel vastly more threatened in a world bereft even of Dogberries.

This point also eludes Warren Chernaik, who quotes the passage from "Let him therefore consider" to "by my words" in substantiating this claim about post-Restoration libertines: "Hobbes to some extent anticipates them . . . by treating the state of nature sometimes as a theoretical construct . . . and sometimes as a psychological or sociological truth verifiable by observation."[15] Nonetheless, the terms of Hobbes's formulations are significant when they come down to a question of whether he has presumed to "accuse mankind" or has merely documented ways in which "mankind" does this to itself: they show how much he occupies a satirist's contested position. Moreover, Hobbes himself so far deviated from "ordinary cautious behavior" as to regard venturing into print with the trepidation he attributes to a person "taking a journey." Like Jonson, he held an unrealistic view of his audience, expecting at times too little, at times too much; both authors wrote in the near certainty of being mugged by willful incomprehension.

V: "the few and better sort"

Though many factors might have accounted for the hefty interval between the conclusion of Hobbes's formal education and the appearance of his first major publication, that work hints at the leading role played by authorial anxiety. *Eight Books'* preface offers two reasons for the "long" delay before its publication (8). Much the smaller obstacle admitted a simple solution: Hobbes's readers would not be so baffled by the sheer number of locations peppering Thucydides's narrative if he furnished maps—one of them drawn by himself (8–9). This stumbling block should never have slowed an author whose verse-memoir recollects his university years as a period in which "My Phancie and my Mind divert I do, / With Maps Celestial and Terrestrial too."[16] Perhaps he exaggerated the extent of his lesser impediment so that the greater would not seem so insuperable. There nonetheless remains a comic disparity between his reader-friendly concern that even minor inconveniences in his narrative might hinder understanding and his reader-hostile doubt that his audience had any competence. He fretted that

> for the greatest part, men came to the reading of history with an affection much like that of the people in Rome: who came to the spectacle of the gladiators with more delight to behold their blood, than their skill in fencing. For they be far more in number, that love to read of great armies, bloody battles, and many thousands slain at once, than that mind the art by which the affairs both of armies and cities be conducted to their ends. (8)

However "long" he had brooded on this problem, Hobbes eventually exercised rhetorical legerdemain to conclude that such foreboding "ought not to be of any weight at all, to him that can content himself with the few and better sort of readers: who, as they only judge, so is their approbation only considerable" (9).

Ultimately "content" with a fit audience, however "few," Hobbes thus relaxed into a form of snobbery upheld by many authors in seventeenth-century England, but uncharacteristic of his own outlook. Milton probably had different considerations in mind when *Paradise Lost* recorded his hope that his muse might "fit audience find, though few" (2.1: 31). Context suggests that, "fall'n on evil dayes," he regarded post-Restoration England as an unpropitious environment for his work, so that he and his ideal readers would remain a minority (25). Even under such defeating circumstances, however, he retained sufficient optimism to imagine reaching some "fit" company. By contrast, Hobbes's "few" are aristoi; but he also embraces them as a last resort, after beginning with a more pessimistic assessment of his prospective audience. Social bias figures only in the vehicle of his analogy between most readers of history and "the people in Rome." Plebeians in seventeenth-century England were unlikely to show much enthusiasm for a translation of Thucydides, having never received enough education to appreciate it on any terms. Conversely, "skill in fencing" and its analogous counterpart should have been of immediate interest to the members of a social and intellectual elite constituting Hobbes's probable audience. Though David Underdown reports that Eliot's comparison between Sejanus and Buckingham "led to a run on Roman histories at the booksellers," the audience for such works must generally have been quite small.[17] Thus, Hobbes's career as a published author (at least under his own name) nearly ended before it began; but it would continue with the production of works addressing on the highest plane of abstraction "the art by which . . . affairs . . . be conducted to their ends" and making "bloody battles" still less conspicuous than they are in Thucydides's pages, even with *Behemoth*'s narrative of the Civil Wars.

Davenant's preface to *Gondibert* also takes a dim view of "those horrid spectacles (when the latter race of *Gladiators* made up the excesses of Roman feasts)," because they "did more induce the Guests to detest the cruelty of mankinde, then increase their courage by beholding such an impudent scorne of Life." The odd logic of these words condemns "excesses" while supposing them to have had a beneficial outcome; perhaps "the Guests" hoped to enjoy "horrid spectacles" rather more than they did in thus learning "to detest . . . cruelty." Davenant here sought to justify the value of a heroic poem such as *Gondibert* for its approach toward the depiction of vice: "I never meant to prostitute Wickednesse in the Images of low and contemptible people, as if I expected the meanest of the multitude for my Readers (since only the Rabble is seen at common executions)."[18] Measured against this perspective, Davenant's Roman example looks like a clumsy attempt to explain why "horrid spectacles" neither express nor foster depraved tastes, even in the context of "excesses." "Guests" at "feasts" sound like no "Rabble," but view on a fairly routine basis "common executions" in the shape of *"Gladiators"* butchering each other. Both Davenant and Hobbes thus ignore the mixed social composition of audiences for "horrid spectacles," the one distinguishing "Guests" at "feasts" from "the Rabble," the other assimilating most readers to "the people." In contrast, however, Davenant never even contemplates having "the meanest of the multitude for my Readers," whereas Hobbes's Roman example condemns not the depraved tastes of "the Rabble" but those shown "for the greatest part" in "the reading of history" by "men" in general—or rather, within the narrow category of literate males disposed toward consuming that type of material.

VI: "from people to tumult"

I therefore disagree with T. W. Harrison's claim that Dryden's rendition of the same epic simile from the *Aeneid*'s first book echoed in Waller's *Panegyric* should be considered not only "significant . . . of the fears of the seventeenth century, and its conservative celebration of order, the order of monarchy," but also "almost Hobbesian," because this translation attributes to "th' ignoble Crowd" an "innate Desire of Blood" not found in Virgil's original.[19] Hobbes made more effort than most of his contemporaries to move beyond received stereotypes about the supposed bloodlust of the masses. To be sure, his initial illustration of free association ended on a jaundiced note, just as *Leviathan*'s later and more famous counterpart originated in a "malicious question" (95):

> The cause of the coherence or consequence of one conception to another, is their first coherence, or consequence at that time when they were produced by sense. As for example: from St. Andrew the mind runneth to St. Peter, because their names are read together; from St. Peter to a stone, for the same cause; from stone to foundation, because we see them together; and for the same cause, from foundation to church, from church to people, and from people to tumult. And according to this example, the mind may run almost from any thing to any thing. (*Elements*, 31)

But Hobbes was playing on his readers' prejudices here, as in his barb at the expense of Scots' "treason" in *Leviathan*'s equivalent passage, where the sentiment similarly is and is not his own (95). In either case, he clarifies how easily the links follow by invoking a chain of association that he thought his original audience could most readily accept. Moreover, even if he was partly venting his own spleen in making "people" and "tumult" immediately adjacent concepts, this is a far cry from attributing an "innate Desire of Blood" to "th' Ignoble Crowd," and does not closely correspond with the leveling tendencies of his philosophy, constructed on a logically more rigorous basis than that of free association. In its gloomy remarks about the jaded appetites of most readers of histories, *Eight Books*' preface addresses a vicarious bloodlust, but also confirms that the egalitarian dimensions of his thinking entailed sometimes leveling down as well as up.

In yet another instance of the extent to which Hobbes scholars have agreed that *Eight Books* marks an important stage in the development of its translator's own thought, Quentin Skinner stresses that the "iconography" of this work's frontispiece, though not certainly a feature of the volume about which Hobbes had any say, "is no less suggestive than in the more famous cases of *De Cive* and *Leviathan*," and serves "to associate Thucydides with one of the central tenets of English Renaissance humanism: that wise and virtuous noblemen represent the best and most natural 'governors' in any well-ordered state."[20] Skinner sees this visual material as underscoring the degree to which, in Hobbes's own phrase from *Eight Books*, Thucydides "least of all liked the democracy" (13). But Skinner buttresses his argument with the ultimately ambiguous evidence that "the earl of Devonshire's dictation-book" bears the inscription "that vertue is the true nobilitie" (242 n.225). This clincher would convince if it did not depend on assuming that Hobbes and the Cavendishes thought as one (instead of just exhibiting a high level of agreement), and focused on a motto reversing the emphasis. Though Hobbes's remarks about "the . . . better sort" could be taken as the viewpoint of a person who thought that nobility is the true virtue, his first thoughts had taken the different form of condemning the crude tastes of most readers of history. Whereas the humbly born Jonson achieved prominence at James I's court as poet laureate and author of masques, but strove to maintain his independence, consciously distinguishing from effusions of flattery his considered praise of select members of the Jacobean aristocracy, the likewise plebeian Hobbes attained his most exalted rank when appointed as mathematics tutor to the future Charles II, but chiefly experienced this brief episode as a troublesome interruption to the essentially even tenor of his service to the Cavendishes, in which more modest capacity he could be highly productive, as when developing a philosophy that by the standards of its time and place seems remarkably free of rote genuflections toward aristocratic exceptionalism.

In focusing on everyman, Hobbes generalized for the most part discreetly, avoiding open war against aristocratic self-regard. But his unconventionally mild view of so-called tyrants as disliked rulers rested on the conviction, also unconventional, that only the powerful suffer when despots reign. "One may be able to excuse Hobbes's inability to imagine the likes of Hitler, Stalin, or Pol Pot, but he should have remembered Caligula," according to Martinich (*Dictionary*, 5). Hobbes did not forget that particular psychopath, however, and invoked another one too: *De Cive* explains that

> when a *Nero* or a *Caligula* is in power, no one can suffer undeservedly, except those who are known to him, namely Courtiers, or those who hold some conspicuous position; and not all of them, but only those

who have something that he covets; for those who are troublesome or insolent towards him deserve their punishment. In a *Monarchy* therefore anyone who is prepared to live quietly is free of danger, whatever the character of the ruler. Only the ambitious suffer, the rest are protected from being wronged by the powerful. (120)

Hobbes explicitly draws the fangs of "too much Authority"; but he also shows a total lack of sympathy for any among "the powerful" who do not put themselves on a par with "the rest" by their obedience and resolution "to live quietly." Possibly callous, his perspective expresses no awe for nobility as such.

VII: "readinesse in replies"

Invoking a comparison so startling that it connects his own employers' amusements with the "excesses" of imperial Rome, Hobbes acknowledged in his sole surviving letter to Waller how

> I serve when I can be matched as a gladiator; My odde opinions are bayted. but I am contented wth it, as beleeving I have still the better, when a new man is sett upon me; that knowes not my paradoxes, but is full of his owne doctrine, there is something in the disputation not unpleasant. He thinkes he has driven me upon an absurdity when t'is upon some other of my tenets and so from one to another, till he wonder and exclayme and at last finds I am of the Antipodes to ye schooles.[21]

In debates of this kind, Hobbes did not fear that Newcastle and other listeners would be too preoccupied with "spectacle" to appreciate "skill in fencing." His participation in blood sports of the intellect continued after the Restoration, according to Aubrey's recollection of how "The witts at Court were wont to bayte him" (1: 340), much as those in the reign of Charles I had made Suckling "the bull that was bayted" (2: 240). Aubrey further explains that Hobbes

> was marvellous happy and ready in his replies, and that without rancor (except provoked)—but now I speake of his readinesse in replies as to witt and drollery. He would say that he did not care to give, neither was he adroit at, a present answer to a serious quaere: he had as lieve they should have expected an extemporary solution to an arithmeticall probleme, for he turned and winded and compounded in philosophy, politiques, etc., as if he had been at analyticall worke. He always avoided, as much as he could, to conclude hastily. (1: 340–41)

Aubrey seems to suggest that Hobbes excelled at witty repartee, like Suckling, but wished to distinguish such exchanges from "serious" disputations and "analyticall worke," which required more ample reflection and could not be so spontaneous. Presumably, the debates in which he participated "as a gladiator" gave him opportunities to prepare sufficiently well that he did not need "to conclude hastily."

But whether he faced baiting or was more formally "matched as a gladiator," his audience in both cases consisted of listeners and disputants with whom he enjoyed direct contact and over whose responses he could exert some control. In contrast, he could most fully meditate the words that he eventually published, but at that point lost touch with the expression of ideas now privately consumed by strangers. Perhaps he therefore felt more comfortable debating or being baited than when committing his printed work to a faceless void. To the extent that he ended his days alienated from his own words, as chapter one and my treatment of Hobbists suggest, his concerns were partly justified. But his anxiety about his audience still assumed a form so extreme as to exceed even Jonson's.

Lacking any obvious equivalent for Jonson's mutually bruising encounters with theater audiences, Hobbes likewise had no point of comparison from which to view publishing in a more favorable light. Rather, he approached the medium of print exactly as if he were an already rebuffed Jonson once more writing for the stage, and without the consolations Barish supposes were available to that dramatist: "Readers, simply by virtue of literacy, possess a certain irreducible minimum of knowledge and discipline. In addition, they are removed from the passions of the playhouse. They can ponder, instead of reacting blindly" (139). Hobbes's preface to *Eight Books* ventures that "there is something, I know not what, in the censure of a multitude, more terrible than any single judgment, how severe or exact soever" (6). That feeble "I know not what" registers a Pandora's box he did not care to open. As the contrast with "single" conveys, he fears no Hydra-headed mob (unlikely to be reading Thucydides in any version), but worries about submitting his work to a public that he neither knows nor trusts. Thus, he did not shy away from showing his translation to Jonson and Ayton, but rather sought their input. Even so, the feedback of handpicked reviewers did not always satisfy him.

VIII: "rem suam agunt"

In his preface to the revised *De Cive*, Hobbes explains how, prior to publication, he "took the trouble to distribute to friends a few privately printed copies, so that after testing other people's reactions, I might correct, soften and explain anything that seemed erroneous, harsh or obscure" (14). "I found my book very sharply criticized," he adds, identifying his reviewers' concerns and in the same breath dismissing them:

> on the ground that I have immoderately enhanced the civil power, but by Churchmen; on the ground that I have taken away liberty of conscience, but by Sectarians; on the ground that I have exempted Sovereigns from the civil laws, but by lawyers. I was not moved by their criticisms to do more than tie those knots more tightly, as each one was simply defending his own position. (15)

De Cive apparently benefited from the feedback it received in this way from at least two "friends" in each of the three categories mentioned: Richard Tuck remarks that "Hobbes added to the second edition a number of lengthy explanatory footnotes which often illuminate puzzling areas of his argument better than anything else he ever wrote."[22] But Hobbes himself defined his own reaction as essentially stubborn: a reinforced conviction that he must be right. His willingness to make changes therefore involved not correcting or softening but only explaining with added rigor, in a determination to "tie . . . knots more tightly." As a consequence, both author and book became more tensely upwound.

Hobbes recalls the author of *Catiline* (1611), as described by Barish:

> One of his authentic masterpieces, *Sejanus* [1605], was hissed from the stage for the excess of its verbiage, yet when Jonson sat down to write a second tragedy for the same troupe a few years later, far from conceding anything to the preferences of his audiences he defiantly administered a double dose of what they had already once spat out. (136)

But as with Jonson's ability to find in publication a salve to the various indignities he suffered when writing for the stage, so here: Hobbes's predicament was fundamentally worse and entailed fewer constructive alternatives. Whereas Jonson could have cut the "verbiage" that made some of his most self-consciously serious plays indigestible for theater audiences, but adamantly refused to do so, Hobbes had a track record of seeking approval for his "style" and being willing to change it, but faced the rather daunting problem that the content of his work, however phrased and presented, was being rejected. Either his labors had been in vain or his handpicked reviewers lacked competence.

Where the translation of *De Cive* just quoted offers "defending his own position" for the original "rem suam agunt," *Philosophical Rudiments* had supplied the possibly more accurate "do their own business."[23] Ambiguous, "position" fails to clarify whether Hobbes, in objecting to his reviewers' essentially closed minds, blames their ideological stances or their standings in life. The second seems more likely: individual "Churchmen," "Sectarians," and "lawyers" might entertain various ideological stances, but had in each case a "business" of paramount concern. If *Philosophical Rudiments* gives the better guide to Hobbes's meaning at this juncture, then his response to his reviewers' feedback looks less petulant than it otherwise would, again featuring that mixture of defensiveness and aggression typifying a satirical outlook.[24] But even if Hobbes inveighs here against "ordinary artifice," questions remain. How did he expect "to passe . . . unwounded" in this particular scenario, with three sets of "points" arrayed about him? Given his own emphasis on the prominence of self-interest in human affairs, did he imagine that his "friends" could all see past the "business" peculiar to each for a more enlightened and dispassionate response? Disappointed on that score, did he still hope that other readers, complete strangers, would respond in a less hostile way, as having no cherished turf to protect? Though some such questions seem unavoidable in light of his own assessment of the difficulties involved in securing a fair hearing, he still entertained the pipe dream that *Leviathan* would become official doctrine spoonfed to the masses by preachers and lecturers whom he persistently excoriated as asses and wolves.

IX: "Impostures wrought by Confederacy"

Another parallel that Cantalupo draws between Hobbes and Jonson further complicates any understanding of what "the Scope of the writer" means for either, broaching an issue often addressed in literary criticism from a variety of angles: the fraught relationship between a satirical outlook and the world it purports to describe with unvarnished fidelity. Cantalupo's point of departure is *Leviathan*'s discussion of how *"men are apt to be deceived by false Miracles,"* which observes that "A Juggler by the handling of his goblets, and other trinkets, if it were not now ordinarily practised, would be thought to do his wonders by the power at least of the Devil" (475). Having noted this instance of "ordinary artifice," Hobbes then demystifies the seeming miracles accomplished by *"Ventriloqui,"* who can "make very many men beleeve" that theirs "is a voice from Heaven," and by "those men, which the Greeks called *Thaumaturgi*, that is to say, workers of things wonderfull," who merely "do all they do, by their own single dexterity" (475, 476). But he concedes that "there be many," using transparently fraudulent methods, who nonetheless "obtain the reputation of being Conjurers"; and he concludes that

> if we looke upon the Impostures wrought by Confederacy, there is nothing how impossible soever to be done, that is impossible to bee beleeved. For two men conspiring, one to seem lame, the other to cure him with a charme, will deceive many: but many conspiring, one to seem lame, another so to cure him, and all the rest to bear witnesse; will deceive many more. (476)

Cantalupo judges that in this analysis "the supernatural yet historical events of Exodus are replaced by a Jonsonian London carnival where miracles are performed by characters like Subtle or Volpone" (165–66).

Unlike the London-based Subtle (*The Alchemist*, 1610), Volpone is the title character of a play set in Venice (1606); but this does not disqualify Cantalupo's verdict, for the earlier play includes satirical passages meant to carry home. Volpone's sycophantic servant Mosca praises him for running an extortion racket morally superior to some of the more predatory financial practices current in Jacobean society: he will not "devoure / Soft prodigalls," or "swallow / A melting heire, as glibly, as your *Dutch* / Will pills of butter," or "Teare forth the fathers of poore families / Out of their beds, and coffin them, alive, / In some kind, clasping prison," as one whose "sweet nature doth abhorre these courses" (5: I.i, 40–46, 48). Though a high level of social realism is often seen as a hallmark of Jonson's comedies, this distinguishing feature is still one of degree. Hobbbes's phrase "ordinary artifice" points up the double perspective involved here: if the behavior condemned were rare, it would not justify the outrage expressed; but because readers need no help recognizing the truly commonplace, they actually receive help in detecting a level of "artifice" so extraordinary that its ubiquity eludes the casual gaze. Moreover, giving equal weight to the twin halves of the quotidian bizarre permits a twofold disparagement, belittling the merely typical, while magnifying monstrosity.

Hobbes's tirade against Roman Catholicism as the most elaborately sustained fraud of all time occupies the entire fourth part of *Leviathan*. Though scholars disagree whether this treatment "Of the

Kingdome of Darknesse" represents a structurally essential part of his political philosophy (never before included) or a self-contained tour de force (a "carnival" excursion or Roman holiday), no one disputes the rhetorical effectiveness of its concluding *"Comparison of the Papacy with the Kingdome of Fayries"* (712) or such palpable hits as this: "The *Fairies* marry not; but there be amongst them *Incubi*, that have copulation with flesh and bloud. The *Priests* also marry not" (714). As Skinner notes, Hobbes exploits the malicious trope aposiopesis, letting the other shoe drop (419). The inspired level of Hobbes's writing here makes "Of the Kindome of Darknesse" a fitting climax to his masterpiece. Ahead still lies "A Review, and Conclusion," however, where among other bits of unfinished business Godolphin makes his tardy appearance as *Leviathan*'s paragon.

But neither Godolphin's lack of prominence as an apparent afterthought nor the contrastingly vast bulk of a possibly digressive diatribe against Catholicism has given Hobbes scholars much pause for thought. For most, the chief stumbling block and bone of contention is his pervasively skeptical treatment of religion—more than half of *Leviathan*'s total volume of pages and the chief way in which its content differs from its precursors'. Whereas one school of interpreters takes at face value the minimalistic Christianity that Hobbes overtly professed, another sees him as a thinker whose conviction that "there is nothing . . . impossible to be beleeved" had the corrosive effect, if not perhaps the intention, of rendering all belief suspect. With the exception of its fourth book's self-contained polemic against Catholicism, therefore, *Leviathan* is a text whose handling of religious issues has fostered diametrically opposed readings, and overall a much wider range of disagreement than characterizes debates about the meanings of Jonson's plays.

X: "mysteries"

One example will suffice to show how unstable or malleable *Leviathan* can be on this dimension: "it is with the mysteries of our Religion, as with wholesome pills for the sick, which swallowed whole, have the vertue to cure; but chewed, are for the most part cast up again without effect" (410). Paul Cooke accuses Hobbes of not practicing what he preaches: his entire approach to scripture murders to dissect.[25] Most responses to the passage just quoted take a different line, however, attempting to gauge Hobbes's tone. Paul Johnson wonders whether such writing "with its epigrammatic compression and crude simile" represents "the sarcasm of a disbeliever" or "with its positive message of wholesome cures" serves as "an assertion of the legitimacy of faith."[26] Citing two commentators answering the question the first way and another two answering the second, Johnson breaks the tie by arguing for a non-sarcastic reading, instancing comparably gross imagery deployed by authors whose piety has never been doubted (103–05). Similarly, Martinich concedes the general point that Hobbes's words "were often barbed and harsh, and sometimes vulgar," but maintains that in this case a commonplace observation is being made in commonplace language with no satirical bite.[27] By contrast, J. C. A. Gaskin in his introduction to *Elements* supposes that Hobbes's words "come from the heart," even though he also identifies them as typical of their author's "exceptionally waspish comments about religion," leaving readers to ponder for themselves what such stinging sincerity must entail (xli). More extremely, Skinner unhesitatingly identifies Hobbes's language as equivalent to that of "a Jonsonian . . . carnival," with Christian doctrine comparable to the quack cures peddled by Volpone when he moonlights as the mountebank Scoto of Mantua: according to this interpretation, "swallowed whole" must trigger thoughts about gullibility, even though the idiom can hardly be avoided as a necessary component of the analogy that *Leviathan* presents (412). But my concern here is not to break the new tie (now doubled, with four voices on each side) or to attempt with Cooke a fresh angle on the evidence; though I am a Son of Johnson in this issue, my larger point is the sheer number of "single Texts," at least where *Leviathan*'s focus on religion is concerned, that have similarly generated hugely different estimates of Hobbes's "main Designe."

Rejecting this or that analysis as strained cannot alter how *Leviathan*'s own treatment of scripture precludes any attempt by Hobbes's readers "to avoid . . . texts . . . of obscure, or controveted Interpretation": there is almost no other kind on display. Moreover, even the consensus that his language does take a satirical turn in being sometimes "barbed" or "waspish" encompasses a startling diversity of opinion about where such cruxes reside and to what mutually reinforcing effect. Martinich argues that in this case scholars preoccupied with contested issues have forgotten about their many agreements; as a consequence, "the commonly held beliefs disappear into the background" (*Thomas Hobbes*, 129). Opposing this optical illusion, however, is the question of what constitutes "background" or its reverse in *Leviathan* itself. Many readers have experienced its treatment of religion as sufficiently subversive to displace Hobbes's overt professions of faith. Despite its plethora of explicit directives as to how it should be taken, the radical indeterminacy of *Leviathan*'s collectively perceived meaning exceeds even that of Jonson's most open-ended and disorientating play.

XI: "the part of a right godly man"

In its anarchic foreground, *Bartholomew Fair* (1614) features so many bit-players that its fair field full of folk seems to be viewed through both ends of a telescope, or filmed by Robert Altman. Though the play includes instructions on how to receive it, these also represent a locus classicus of carnivalesque ambivalence: the concinnity between *Bartholomew Fair* and Bartholomew Fair means that the play constantly draws attention to a spectacle—itself—for whose sordid nature it also apologizes. Ironically, Jonson thereby expresses an attitude similar to that of the arch-Puritan Zeal-of-the-Land Busy, whom he mocks for advising his brethren at the fair to "turne neyther to the right hand, not to the left: let not your eyes be drawne aside with vanity, nor your eare with noyses" (6: III.ii, 30–32).

When Busy disputes not only with a puppet-master but also with his puppets, he reveals how far a stereotypical Puritan surpasses Hobbes's dismissive attitude toward contemporary drama, expressing a strident animus against *"Stage-players, Rimers*, and *Morrise-dancers"* (V.v, 10–11). Treating the puppets as real, Busy also reduces himself to their level. But ideological opposition did close the theaters in 1642. Hobbes's Catholics in *Leviathan*'s fourth part likewise both threaten and amuse as representatives of the quotidian bizarre. On the one hand, *"Fairies"* belong in the same category as puppets; on the other, creatures exactly resembling them constitute and perpetuate "the Kingdome of Darknesse."

Busy nonetheless poses an especially acute problem of interpretation because the ontological status of any Puritan in seventeenth-century England remains so open to question. Aubrey explains Jonson's commitment to satirizing Busy and his kind by relating that "King James made him write against the Puritans, who began to be troublesome in his time" (2: 14). But Patrick Collinson conjectures that "it may have been the stage-Puritan who invented, or re-invented, the Puritan, and not the other way round."[28] Though the stage Puritan in his view did not originate with Jonson, he classifies *Bartholomew Fair* as "this most powerful and memorable of all theatrical attacks on Puritanism" (163). Thus, Jonson did strike a blow "against the Puritans," either by bringing them on the stage in definitive form or by sealing the illusion that in this matter life imitated art. Compounding the apparent chicken-and-egg conundrum of the relationship between Puritans on and off the stage is the debate over Puritanism as such.

Michael Finlayson has queried the very existence of this form of Protestantism, at least as conventionally understood.[29] He observes that, with some notable exceptions, individual Puritans are hard to identify with absolute confidence, which ought to moderate the significance often attached to their collective impact. In his view, those historians who invoke Puritanism as a reified agent of revolutionary change write too loosely and explain away at least as much as they explain. He also notes that the godly movers and shakers who created such turbulence during the Civil Wars reemerge in studies of post-Restoration England with a new and rather tepid identity as Nonconformists having negligible impact on the political culture of their day. One obvious objection to Finlayson's skepticism is the stage Puritan, presented as mirroring a real-life nuisance with an identifiable dialect and certain bugbears that had undeniable consequences so far as the stage itself was concerned. Moreover, when Finlayson stresses that the essentially negative character of much heated rhetoric in seventeenth-century England has been underestimated, so that many historians discern swarms of Puritans where he sees a high percentage of anti-Papists, the complex issues of nomenclature that he raises do not themselves go far toward explaining why Busy buzzes onto the stage when he does, as a figure audiences could comprehend immediately: he would still be what he was and is if standard usage had developed a term other than (stage) Puritan to describe him.

As J. P. Kenyon points out, " 'Presbyterian' is almost as difficult a word to construe as 'Puritan.' "[30] Though *Behemoth* nowhere names Puritans, it shows Presbyterians exerting so malevolent an impact that Hobbes's interpretation of the Civil Wars offers unexpectedly strong support for historians grinding the opposite ax when they approvingly assess the years 1640–60 as a Puritan Revolution, even though he used the latter term only because those two decades had featured "a circular motion of the sovereign power through two usurpers . . . from the late King to . . . his son" (204). *Behemoth* stresses that "The mischief" in question "proceeded wholly from the Presbyterian preachers, who, by a long practised histrionic faculty, preached up the rebellion powerfully" (159). Because Hobbes identifies seven factors precipitating the Civil Wars and influencing their course (2–4), his statement is hyperbolic; but it is neither an isolated outburst nor an exceptional aspect of his overall interpretation: pride of place goes to "ministers . . . pretending to have a right from God to govern every one his parish and their assembly the whole nation" (2).

Moreover, *Behemoth* gives this more detailed account of the Presbyterians' "histrionic faculty," which proves not a passing slur but a perceived trait so important that it primarily explains how a sufficient number of Charles I's subjects became disaffected enough for internecine conflict even to occur:

> first, for the manner of their preaching; they so framed their countenance and gesture at their entrance into the pulpit, and their pronunciation both in their prayer and sermon, and used the Scripture phrase (whether understood by the people or not), as that no tragedian in the world could have acted the part of a right godly man better than these did; insomuch as a man unacquainted with such art, could never suspect any ambitious plot in them to raise sedition against the state, as they then had designed; or doubt that the vehemence of their voice (for the same words with the usual pronunciation had been of little force) and forced-ness of their gesture and looks, could arise from anything else but zeal to the service of God. And by this art they came into such credit, that numbers of men used to go forth of their own parishes and towns on working-days, leaving their calling, and on Sundays leaving their own churches, to hear them preach in other places, and to despise their own and all other preachers that acted not so well as they. And as for those ministers that did not usually preach, but instead of sermons did read to the people such homilies as the Church had appointed, they esteemed and called them *dumb dogs*. (24)

These Presbyterian actors prove more real and sensationally fraudulent than any stage-Puritans.

Hobbes's actors nonetheless resemble Busy in self-servingly main-taining a self-righteous pose with an extensive repertoire of narcissistic mannerisms. But Busy fools no one: he is, as Michael Cordner notes, "a total, though largely self-deceiving, fraud," and "remains a censorious outsider in the world of the fair, where the comedy's real initiates in the craft of cheating industriously practise their skills."[31] By contrast, Hobbes's actors possess an ever-expanding world for their stage and fool so many as to be chiefly (if not "wholly") responsible for the "mischief" of the Civil Wars. Moreover, by so ostentatiously calling attention to his own godliness, Busy reveals that he merely lives by the word: all talk, he is, except for his rhetoric, no less worldly than others in the play. Hobbes's actors are hypocrites on such a grand scale, however, that their mummery serves all too well to disguise their "ambitious plot . . . to raise sedition against the state."

Their only competition stems from those whom their own wiliness as foxes demotes to the condition of *"dumb dogs."* Arrestingly, Hobbes supposes that these rival ministers "acted not so well"; ambiguity aside, he might have insisted that they did not act at all. Their mere reading of "homilies . . . appointed" would seem to rule out much need or room for theatrical flair, as would the assumption that their piety was straightforwardly sincere. But then perhaps they should have "acted" better than they did if their audience's expectations and developing tastes were such that their best efforts in effect reduced them to silence in being heard as *"dumb,"* or no longer within earshot of parishioners gone elsewhere. As Barish points out, "Puritan hostility" toward the stage had an "economic aspect" in "the charge that the theater encourages, or is thought to encourage, idleness, perverting youth from its business of learning a trade, hindering thrift and diligence, and (coincidentally) competing with the pulpit for the leisure of its parishioners" (235). Hobbes's actors so successfully counter this alleged tendency that they perpetuate it in reverse, drawing people away from "their own parishes and towns," even "on working-days," at the expense of "their calling," but when offering the apparently legitimate satisfaction of "preaching" that just happens to be indistinguishable from a theatrical performance, except for its higher level of skill.

Hobbes's analysis lends a retrospective validation to Aubrey's claim that James I commissioned Jonson to "write against the Puritans": what wise king would not have wished to nip in the bud a "troublesome" influence having the ultimately ruinous effects that *Behemoth* traces? But then again the supposed recruitment of Jonson suggests that drama was perceived as a potentially more powerful vehicle for the expression of crown-approved ideology than the "homilies . . . appointed" that Hobbes describes as seeming merely tepid to many hearing them. Notwithstanding his disdain for contemporary plays, Hobbes himself concedes in *Elements* that "a tragedy affecteth no less than a murder if well acted" (76). This emphasis on quality of performance accords with *Behemoth*'s verdict on the Presbyterian preachers: "no tragedian in the world could have acted the part of a right godly man better than these did." Their "zeal," however, is no less phony than that of stage Puritans, mere "vehemence" and "forcedness."

That Hobbes held contemporary plays in low esteem does not mean that he was shielded from the theater's broad cultural impact during his lifetime or that he retained nothing from his "reading" during "two yeares," even though he classified that time as simply "lost of him." Whereas he betrays no awareness of how his words compound the ironies already embedded in the relations of stage Puritans, Puritans perceived as mannered performers, and Puritans hostile to theater, his earliest readers could not have failed to sense some of this rich context. Randall instances the case of one George Ridpath who in 1698 recollected having "heard some preachers call their Text . . . a Play or Spectacle, dividing their Texts into Actors, Spectators, Scenes, &c as if they had been Acting a Play" (54). In the verdict of Jonson's epigram "On Lippe, the Teacher" (1616),

> I cannot thinke there's that antipathy
> 'Twixt *puritanes*, and *players*, as some cry;
> Though LIPPE, at PAULS, ranne from his text away,
> T<o>' inveigh 'gainst playes: what did he then but play? (8: 1–4)

If Hobbes feigned obliviousness of these connections, but counted on his earliest readers to register them unaided, he could exploit the credibility established by so well-founded a tradition of acting and enacted Puritans, without seeming merely to add to it. Either way, however, his actors are real, despite their utter inauthenticity; their actions constitute a "plot" that is no mere story; and this "affecteth" more "than a murder," as resulting in much actual bloodshed.

But anyone equally conversant with Presbyterian preachers and Jonson's stage Puritans should have been ideally placed to detect and guard against the hypocrisy common to both. Perhaps Hobbes's actors attracted to their theater an audience indifferent or hostile to any other type of performing art; perhaps they were preaching to the converted, so that their particular playhouse encompassed only stage Puritans, greeting each other from either side of the same mirror. If the audience was thus enthralled, however, the authorities vetting plays should surely have intervened before this other type of drama grew completely out of hand. Hobbes proves the sole "man" not "unacquainted with such art" as he discovers, one concealing itself so entirely that he alone can appreciate the greatest actors of all. He uniquely can see past the "forcedness" to the machinations of actors disguising themselves as non-actors as they advance the action in accordance with their seditious agenda. As with his Presbyterian actors, so with *"Thaumaturgi," "Ventriloqui,"* and fairy-Papists from the "Kingdome of Darknesse," unmasking the whole "Jonsonian . . . carnival" of "ordinary artifice" falls to him.

XII: "t' have pleas'd the *King*"

Whereas Charles II refused Hobbes permission to publish *Behemoth*, Jonson could write this epilogue for the court performance of *Bartholomew Fair*:

> Your *Majesty* hath seene the *Play*, and you
>   can best allow it from your eare, and view.
> You know the scope of *Writers*, and what store
>   of *leave* is given them, if they take not more,
> And turne it into *licence*: you can tell
>   if we have us'd that *leave* you gave us, well:
> Or whether wee to *rage*, or *licence* breake,
>   or be *prophane*, or make *prophane* men speake?
> This is your power to judge (great Sir) and not
>   the envy of a few. Which if wee have got,
> Wee value lesse what their dislike can bring,
>   if it so happy be, t' have pleas'd the *King*. (1–12)

I do not deny the validity of Burt's response:

> Jonson's appeal to James's authority is itself problematic. For the very invitation to judge the play evinces a tension between the king and the actors, who may, in fact have exceeded the king's leave by admitting licentiousness and profanity into the play. That there is no record of a subsequent performance at court suggests that James, who made no secret of his aesthetic likes and dislikes, did not especially enjoy the privilege of judging Jonson's play. (102)

Nor do I deny that Burt has a case when he comments of Jonson's comic induction for public performances of *Batholomew Fair* that it "does not constitute . . . an easy resolution to the problem of license dramatized within the play itself. Like the license and warrants in the play, the contract and Jonson's play are themselves alienable commodities, hence open to misjudgment" (108). But I also agree with Richard Dutton's claim: "Jonson's most lasting achievement was his whole career, with its tensions and internal contradictions, a unique 'document' which transcends all the individual documents that record it, and absolutely central to the development of the profession of letters in England."[32] As these words imply, "problematic" features of literary texts need not be interpreted in a wholly negative light and may even form part of their enduring value. Moreover, we should not simply assume that works of art can be free of all tensions or that any such freedom automatically confers excellence.

When Leah Marcus rules that "Jonson's hedges against free interpretation are desperately futile attempts at containing his own ludic impulses along with the popular energies he purported to despise," she gives the author of *Bartholomew Fair* no credit, even for his own ambivalence, treating contested terrain as wholly lost ground, as if these conflicting elements did not reengage to variable effect with each fresh experience of the play.[33] As Marcus herself acknowledges, her stance partly reflects her determination to put as much distance as possible between a newly adopted approach and an older one, also her own, that in retrospect she deems culpable because "Readings of the play have traditionally divided between vitalist admiration for its energy and moralist condemnations of its vice: my reading allowed me to have Jonson's Fair both ways and at the same time avoid the feminist interpretive issues that I found most troubling." Those "issues" play no salient role in her revised estimate, however, which is subtle enough to register how "There is much of Jonson himself in the Puritan at *Bartholomew Fair*," but apparently oblivious of the punitive severity informing her conviction that having something "both ways" is simply unacceptable and not a fairly typical way of inducing or enjoying a complex aesthetic response (176, italics in the original).

In thus puritanically viewing the author of *Bartholomew Fair* as "irrevocably mired in the 'low' popular anarchic vitalism he purported to despise, a Jonson whose control over his materials was tenuous rather than masterful" (177), Marcus positions herself as working the same line of interpretation promoted by Peter Stallybrass and Allon White, whose discussion of the play also supplies the focus for a book-length study by Kevin Dunn: "The moment," as he terms it, "where the writer attempts an ideological separation of himself and his work from the market that created both in order to establish the work as inimitable artifact rather than commodity and himself as an author rather than craftsman or chapman."[34] Dunn's discussion of this historical juncture takes an unexpected direction, leading to the claim that

> One can . . . see in Hobbes a new theory of prefatory rhetoric emerging, a theory more answerable to a new sense that audience is a constitutive part of authority. In Hobbes's view, rhetoric must be *representative* as well as *ethical*—that is, it must demonstrate the author's adherence to common sense rather than merely dramatize his personal quest to enter into canons of textual authority. (15–16)

According to this way of thinking, "The primary 'textual' implication of Hobbes's theory is a configuration in which the author tends to be assimilated not to his material, not to the master text, but to his audience, with whom he shares a common bond" (131). Unless it pinpoints a final attainment whose immense difficulty explains why Hobbes was delayed many times beforehand, however, such a reading seems to ignore much evidence of friction between him and his audience, as well as the crucially "constitutive" role played by sovereign power in establishing his doctrines' ultimate "authority," even if, as Dunn claims (following Margery Corbett and Ronald Lightbown), in *Leviathan*'s pictorial frontispiece "the face of the 'king' whose body represents and is represented by the people is actually a portrait of Hobbes himself" (129).

By contrast, Nancy Armstrong and Leonard Tennenhouse see Hobbes as a belated figure, not inaugurating "a new sense" but being left behind by it:

> In part 1 of *Leviathan*, Hobbes puts forward a creationist definition of human nature; in doing so, he reveals his affiliation with the cultural moment that was passing away rather than with one that was emerging. According to Hobbes's epistemology, the mind neither constitutes a territory unto itself nor acquires knowledge in the same way that men acquire property. He lacks a semiotic, then, that would account for the production of interior (personal) and exterior (political) discursive worlds.[35]

Armstrong and Tennenhouse virtually admit their half-hearted treatment of Hobbes by omitting this material from the main body of their narrative and introducing it thus: "The framework of a single chapter will not allow us to explain why Hobbes has been excluded from our account of the discursive take-off that allowed words to produce a whole new set of origins both for themselves and for the English 'people' " (257 n.35). Amusingly, these authors deny some of their own agency, even though authorial agency and its frequent denial furnish one of their main concerns: their own chapter ties their hands. Their depiction of Hobbes as a belated figure looks belated too. Though they do scant justice to the scope of Hobbes's writing about authority and authorization, however, he did give strikingly little detailed attention to the way in which his "words" could secure their own "origins," except in theory.

Whereas in Dutton's words "Jonson repeatedly invokes the concept of the *reader par excellence*," variously "embodied," and yet "essentially an abstract principle, the potential 'understander', discrimination itself" (101), Hobbes formally restricted his options to two versions of Jonson's bid to secure James I's imprimatur. The future Charles II received a copy of *Leviathan* when a throneless exile's sanction meant nothing, though he thereby acquired a means of braining Cromwell at Worcester. But *Leviathan* itself defines Hobbes's ideal reader thus:

> I recover some hope, that one time or other, this writing of mine, may fall into the hands of a Sovereign, who will consider it himselfe, (for it is short, and I think clear,) without the help of any interested, or envious Interpreter; and by the exercise of entire Soveraignty, in protecting the Publique teaching of it, convert the Truth of Speculation, into the Utility of Practice. (408)

Lodging in one pair of "hands" at a particular "time" that text he hoped might some day "fall into" another, Hobbes shows how he could have embraced Cromwell as such a patron, but still seeks a mode of dissemination for his work in terms guaranteeing the frustration of his aims. As G. A. J. Rogers observes, "We still await such a reader."[36]

XIII: "a working head"

Those readers Hobbes did find have often judged him the opposite of open-minded. Comparing him with another libertine hero not on that account but because of their shared propensity for "perpetual Dictatorship," Dryden elaborates in his preface to *Sylvæ* (1685) how

> the distinguishing Character of *Lucretius*; (I mean of his Soul and Genius) is a certain kind of noble pride, and positive assertion of his own Opinions. He is every where confident of his own reason, and assuming an absolute command not only over his vulgar Reader, but even his Patron *Memmius*. For he is always bidding him attend, as if he had the Rod over him; and using a Magisterial authority, while he instructs him. From his time to ours, I know none so like him, as our Poet and Philosopher of *Malmsbury*.[37]

Moreover, Hobbes's quest for certainty reflected not his own uncertainty but rather his determination to achieve a method capable of making his readers as "confident of his own reason" as he already was himself. On the other hand, his willingness to switch from *Elements*, the most self-consciously scientific version of his political philosophy, to *Leviathan*, the most self-consciously literary, illustrates his readiness to rethink how best to convince his audience. Given that Hobbes laid out his doctrine not only in those works but also in his two editions of the transitional *De Cive*, he might be supposed a dogmatist so in love with his own views as to keep reiterating them. In fact, however, he seldom repeated himself. Even though Aubrey rather exaggerates in reporting that "His Latin *Leviathan* is altered in many particulars . . . and enlarged with many considerable particulars," that Hobbes included any changes when he was eighty reveals the evolving fluidity of his political philosophy (1: 361). Had he achieved an even greater longevity than he did, and not been subject to publishing restrictions, he conceivably might have reformulated his characteristic views yet again.

Hobbes's working life proved finite in still another way: he could not make the choices that his flexibility permitted except at the expense of different choices. Unable to clone himself, he lacked the ability to undertake multiple projects simultaneously. Dryden himself drew attention to this important truth about "our Poet and Philosopher of *Malmsbury*," though perhaps harboring no higher ambition than to kill two birds with one stone: his preface to *Fables* attributes Hobbes's "bald Translation of the *Ilias*" to his "studying Poetry as he did Mathematicks, when it was too late."[38] Aubrey likewise stressed Hobbes's belated entrance into the second of these studies: "I have heard Sir Jonas Moore (and others) say that 'twas a great pity he had not begun the study of the mathematics sooner, for such a working head would have made great advancement in it. So had he donne, he would not have layn so open to his learned mathematicall antagonists" (1: 332–33). Though primarily concerned to place Hobbes the mathematician in the best possible light, Aubrey also makes this point:

> After he began to reflect on the interest of the king of England as touching his affaires between him and the parliament, for ten yeares together his thoughts were much, or almost altogether, unhinged from the mathematiques; but chiefly intent on his *De Cive*, and after that on his *Leviathan*: which was a great putt-back to his mathematicall improvement—quod N.B.—for ten yeares' (or better) discontinuance of that study (especially) one's mathematiques will become very rusty. (1: 333)

Aubrey thus regretted how Hobbes's activities as a political philosopher had interrupted a promising career in mathematics already compromised by its belated commencement. By contrast, later commentators see those activities as the heart of his achievement, deplore the ill-advised tenacity with which he advanced his claims as a mathematician, and sometimes wonder whether his engagement with geometry contributed anything to his political philosophy, other than to "putt-back" the appearance of *Leviathan*. But Aubrey's perspective should not be dismissed as overly indulgent or merely idiosyncratic: one of my chief aims in this study has been to re-contextualize Hobbes's work in the culture he sought to transform, in relation to contemporaries who could not know in advance how his story would end or be read in later generations.

How far was Hobbes himself conscious of the limitations under which he labored in having nine decades at his disposal, not nine lives? Aubrey reports his verdict on Descartes: "He would say that had he kept himself to Geometry he had been the best geometer in the world but that his head did not lye for philosophy." Though Aubrey interprets an alternative formulation of these words as evidence of Hobbes's "high respect" for Descartes, they seem to rob Peter in paying Paul. (1: 367) Hobbes disposes of an intellectual rival by reserving greatness in "philosophy" for himself while conferring merely virtual laurels on Descartes for what he might have done in "Geometry." Had Descartes in fact "been the best geometer in the world," Hobbes might have been altogether less willing to yield him that precedence. But he does not commit himself to the modern view that significant achievements in any field of study require a willingness to specialize: his comment probably means only that Descartes misinterpreted the nature of his own gifts and consequently misdirected his efforts.

"It is to be remembered that about these times, Mr. T. H. was much sddicted to musique, and practised on the base-violl," Aubrey reports, further adding to the range of Hobbes's interests in apparently referring to his period of service as Bacon's secretary and confirming his own stature as an often indispensable source (1: 331). My hunch is that Aubrey does not contradict himself, calling the accuracy of his testimony into question, but brings out the extent of the addiction at issue, by also maintaining that Hobbes "When young . . . loved musique and practised on the lute" (1: 347). Though this devotion by the end of Hobbes's life had dwindled, no more than a pragmatic recourse to nightly singing as part of the regimen described in chapter five, he was then suffering from Parkinson's disease. He would not have been an exceptional figure in a great age of amateur music-making if such activities had featured more prominently in his existence when he was no longer "young" but still enjoying good health. His priorities lay elsewhere at that point, however, which precisely explains why his original level of investment tends not "to be remembered."

Even so, the same era was also one in which every Sir Somethyngge Orotherre seemed capable of dashing off at least one imperishable lyric between tasks. By contrast, neither Hobbes's "bald Translation" nor his original lyric warrants inclusion in any anthology of the best English poetry: he lacked a feel for the cadences of such writing, whatever his competence as a versifier in Latin. But this point only underscores the extent to which he would have needed to work on his English poetry if he had aspired to a higher level of accomplishment in that area. Though the apprenticeship he did not serve as an English poet he did serve as a budding mathematician, he started "too late," not only for the reasons given by Aubrey but also because most mathematicians peak early. An authentically Renaissance man for the range of his gifts and interests, Hobbes proved a pioneering early modern for his enthusiastic embrace of the possibilities that mathematics and science had to offer, but lived long enough to see his competence in the first of these fields sharply challenged and his conception of the second beginning to be outmoded, in both cases by younger contemporaries showing more of a disposition towards specialization, though not at anything like the level typifying most intellectual endeavors today. I certainly do not mean to cast Hobbes as a failure, however, or to imply that his contemporaries, poetic and otherwise, yield the only valid perspective from which to assess his efforts on a variety of fronts: my aim throughout this study has been to bring a sense of proportion to the complex process of cultural transmission issuing in and from his life's work.

Notes

Preface

1. Strier, *Resistant Structures*, 66, 2.
2. Parkin, "Liberty Transpros'd," 269.

Chapter One "How He Did Grow": Hobbes, Hobbes, and Hobbes

1. Martinich, *A Hobbes Dictionary*, ix.
2. Sorell, *Hobbes*, 1.
3. Hobbes, *On the Citizen*, ed. and trans. Richard Tuck and Michael Silverthorne, 13.
4. *The English Works of Thomas Hobbes*, ed. Sir William Molesworth, 4: 414 (square brackets added).
5. Skinner, *Reason and Rhetoric in the Philosophy of Hobbes*, 229.
6. Tuck, *Hobbes*, 26.
7. Malcolm, *Aspects of Hobbes*, includes a chapter on "Hobbes and the European Republic of Letters" responding to a problem outlined on its opening page: "Anglophone scholars still tend to discuss not only the intellectual context of Hobbes's work, but also its influence and the responses it aroused, in a largely Anglocentric way" (457).
8. Hobbes, *The Elements of Law*, ed. J. C. A. Gaskin, 247. I quote both forms of Hobbes's Latin memoirs from this edition. The prose version is as translated by Mary Lyons, the verse anonymous.
9. Malcolm, "A Summary Biography of Hobbes," 24.
10. On the factionalism rife at the exiled English court and Hobbes's awkward position because of it, see Hobbes, *The Correspondence*, ed. Malcolm, 2: 818–19. Martinich, *Hobbes*, adds that his subject "had at least as much reason to fear the French Roman Catholic clergy" (214).
11. Quoted by Sommerville, *Thomas Hobbes*, 66. Sommerville notes that "The Engagement did not invoke God and so was no oath, though modern commentators on Hobbes invariably describe it as one" (67). For a useful summary of the Engagement controversy, see Baumgold, *Hobbes's Political Theory*, 124–33.

12. Johnston, *The Rhetoric of "Leviathan."*
13. A useful guide to Hobbes's strained relations with leading figures in the Royal Society is Reik, *The Golden Lands of Thomas Hobbes*, 165–88. For a sympathetic assessment of Hobbes's over-confident ventures as a mathematician, see Grant, "Hobbes and Mathematics."
14. *The English Works of Thomas Hobbes*, ed. Molesworth, 10: x.
15. Quoted in Borgman, *Thomas Shadwell*, 90.
16. Novak, "Libertinism and Sexuality," 62.
17. See for instance Hinnant, *Thomas Hobbes*, 146–47.
18. Turner, "The Properties of Libertinism."
19. Miner, *The Restoration Mode from Milton to Dryden*, 182. Miner refers to the seventeenth-century Samuel Butler, not the nineteenth-century one.
20. Chernaik, *Sexual Freedom in Restoration Literature*, 223 n.1 (square brackets added).
21. Hampton, *Hobbes and the Social Contract Tradition*, 5.
22. Martinich, *The Two Gods of "Leviathan,"* 335.
23. Tuck, "Hobbes's Moral Philosophy," 175.
24. Stephen, *Hobbes*, 3.
25. Aubrey, *Brief Lives*, ed. Andrew Clark, 1: 353.
26. Introduction to *Hobbes's Thucydides*, ed. Richard Schlatter, xi; Strauss, *The Political Philosophy of Thomas Hobbes*, 44.
27. Norbrook, *Writing the English Republic*, 5, 34.
28. Curtis, "The Alienated Intellectuals of Early Stuart England," 312–13.
29. Kenyon, *The Stuarts*, 70.
30. Charles I's view of Eliot has been explained in these terms by many historians, including Carlton, *Charles I*, 122.
31. Hobbes, *Three Discourses*, ed. Reynolds and Saxonhouse, 126.
32. Dryden, *Poems*, ed. William Frost and Vinton Dearing, 278, 281. For a subtle investigation of the translation's politics, see Cameron, "John Dryden's Jacobitism."
33. Mendelsohn, "Theatres of War."
34. Wallerstein, "The Development of the Rhetoric and Metre of the Heroic Couplet, Especially in 1625–1645," 181.
35. Trevor-Roper, *Catholics, Anglicans and Puritans*, 210.
36. The sentiment quoted introduces a "seven point comparison" that Reynolds and Saxonhouse claim "reappears in a slightly expanded and rearranged form near the end of *Leviathan*, chapter 26" (117 n.34).

Chapter Two   "To Governe the Reader": Hobbes and Davenant

1. Tuck, *Hobbes*, 2, 27.
2. *Sir William Davenant's "Gondibert,"* ed. David Gladish, 3. I also quote from this edition Hobbes's reply and verses satirizing both authors.

3. Hobbes, *On the Citizen*, ed. and trans. Tuck and Michael Silverthorne, 22, 48.

4. Thorpe, *The Aesthetic Theory of Thomas Hobbes*, 170–88.

5. Winn, *John Dryden and His World*, 72–77.

6. Thomas, "The Social Origins of Hobbes's Political Thought," 214.

7. A useful guide to its subject is Tuck, "Hobbes and Descartes." For a case that Thomas's now classic essay has garnered a reputation exceeding its deserts, see my "Keith Thomas's 'Definitive Refutation' of C. B. Macpherson."

8. Quoted in Edmond, *Rare Sir William Davenant*, with emphasis on how Davenant's "contribution to the royalist cause . . . has been much undervalued" (96).

9. Hobbes, *Behemoth*, ed. Ferdinand Tönnies, 61.

10. For a definitive account, see Russell, "The First Army Plot of 1641."

11. Davenant, *The Shorter Poems, and Songs from the Plays and Masques*, ed. A. M. Gibbs, 19–20. Gibbs credits C. V. Wedgwood with establishing the Strafford allusion and gives the historical context (359–60).

12. Butler, "Politics and the Masque," 70.

13. In "A Troubled Arcadia," 49, Graham Parry discerns various political tensions straining Davenant's ode.

14. Hobbes, *Leviathan*, ed. Macpherson, 362.

15. Rivers, *The Poetry of Conservatism 1600–1745*, 34.

16. Lockyer, *The Early Stuarts*, 133.

17. Smith, *The Stuart Parliaments 1603–1689*, 121.

18. Macpherson is the scholar attaching most significance to Hobbes's recourse to language of the marketplace: see his "Hobbes's Bourgeois Man," reprinted with Thomas's "Social Origins" as a rebuttal.

19. Aubrey, *Brief Lives*, ed. Andrew Clark, 1: 205.

20. Nethercot, *Sir William D'avenant*, 43.

21. Stephen, *Hobbes*, 85 n.1

22. Lumpers include Strauss, *The Political Philosophy of Hobbes*, 135 n.3; Peters, *Hobbes*, 15–19; Rogow, *Thomas Hobbes*, 64–68; and Tuck, 10. Splitters include Laird, *Hobbes*, 43–48; Reik, *The Golden Lands of Thomas Hobbes*, 15–16, 139, 158; Martinich, *Hobbes*, 66–69; and Malcolm, "A Summary Biography of Hobbes," 17–19. Thorpe sees Hobbes's theory of imagination as building upon and extending Bacon's (77–78).

23. Skinner, *Reason and Rhetoric in the Philosophy of Hobbes*, 305–06.

24. Ross, "Some Puzzles in Hobbes," 56.

25. Gauthier, *The Logic of "Leviathan*," 207.

26. Among many commentators remarking Hobbes's metaphors and ambiguity about ambiguity and metaphors is Cantalupo, *A Literary "Leviathan*," 59.

27. Condren, *Thomas Hobbes*, recognizes Hobbes's incoherence about eloquence but minimizes its significance with a facile repair-job (148).

28. *The English Works of Thomas Hobbes*, ed. Sir William Molesworth, 1: ix.

29. Dewey, "The Motivation of Hobbes's Political Philosophy," 23.

30. Introduction to Hobbes, *A Dialogue between a Philosopher and a Student of the Common Laws of England*, ed. Cropsey, 18.
31. Martinich, *A Hobbes Dictionary*, 67, 66.
32. For some astute remarks about the relationship between geometry and politics in Hobbes's thought, see Barker, "In the Wars of Truth," especially 104, 106. But I am puzzled by this essay's claim that "with [the sovereign] in Hobbes it is axiomatically impossible to make a contract" (though there are clearly difficulties in this area of Hobbes's argument); and I do not see how it can be objected to Hobbes that in his thought "the sovereign remains in a state of nature in respect of other sovereigns and their commonwealths," for he freely conceded this point and explained why he considered it no problem (106).
33. Dent, *Foundations of English Opera*, 62. This page includes a brief overview of the resemblances between *The Siege* and *Gondibert*—itself modeled on a five-act play. On the paradoxical phenomenon of Davenant's flourishing career as an Interregnum dramatist, see Wiseman, " 'History Digested.' "
34. Kroll, "William Davenant and John Dryden," 312.
35. Hobbes, *The Elements of Law*, ed. J. C. A. Gaskin, 35.
36. Barbeau, *The Intellectual Design of John Dryden's Heroic Plays*, 38–39.
37. Hume, *The Development of English Drama in the Late Seventeenth Century*, 199.
38. Hughes, *English Drama 1660–1700*, 12.

Chapter Three   "Plain Magick": Hobbes and Cowley

1. *Sir William Davenant's "Gondibert,"* ed. David Gladish, 54. I also quote Davenant himself from this edition.
2. *The Poems of Edmund Waller*, ed. G. Thorn Drury, 2: 27–30.
3. Cowley, *Poems*, ed. A. R. Waller, 42.
4. Vaughan, *The Complete Poems*, ed. Alan Rudrum, 13–20.
5. Introduction to Davenant, *The Shorter Poems, and Songs from the Plays and Masques*, ed. A. M. Gibbs, xlvii.
6. Trotter, *The Poetry of Abraham Cowley*, 5.
7. Trotter quotes Hobbes, *Leviathan*, ed. C. B. Macpherson, 133, but modernizes the spelling. I also cite this edition, keeping the original spelling.
8. Nethercot, *Abraham Cowley*, 96.
9. Aubrey, *Brief Lives*, ed. Andrew Clark, 1: 368.
10. Laird, *Hobbes*, v.
11. Bobbio, *Thomas Hobbes and the Natural Law Tradition*, 218.
12. Mintz, *The Hunting of "Leviathan,"* viii.
13. Skinner, *Reason and Rhetoric in the Philosophy of Hobbes*, 234–35.

14. Mulgrave, *The Poems of John Sheffield*, 97.

15. *The Poems of Alexander Pope*, ed. John Butt, 360–61.

16. Denham, *The Poetical Works*, 151.

17. *Carmina*, 4.2 (25–26), as rendered in *The Complete Works of Horace*, trans. Charles Passage; like the ode itself, the phrase quoted offers an admiring portrait of Pindar.

18. *The Poems and Fables of John Dryden*, ed. James Kinsley, 528.

19. Griffin, ed., *Selected Poems of Abraham Cowley, Edmund Waller and John Oldham*, 144.

20. Chambers, *Andrew Marvell and Edmund Waller*, 76.

21. Ashton, *The English Civil War*, 160.

22. The introduction to Cowley, *The Civil War*, ed. Allan Pritchard, gives a comprehensive overview of the poem's genesis and character. The conclusion of Jonathan Sawday, " 'Mysteriously Divided,' " also offers some astute comments about Cowley's aborted epic. Pritchard's introduction locates an earlier version of the ode's Etna conceit in a passage from *The Civil War* (54).

23. Anselment, *Loyalist Resolve*, 175.

24. See Pitchard's introduction, *The Civil War*, 52–55.

25. Locke, *Two Treatises of Government*, ed. Peter Laslett, 328.

26. Margaret Anne Doody, *The Daring Muse*, 63, sees not the confining notes to *Davideis* but the poem's own open-endedness as problematic: "The project ramifies so much under the poet's treatment that it is little wonder he never completed his great work."

27. Butler, "The Stagirite and the Scarecrow."

28. Cowley, *The Complete Works in Verse and Prose*, ed. Alexander Grosart, 2: 340. Butler justifies his substitution of "immediately" for "irremediably" but thinks the latter "seems to make better sense" (12 n.8).

29. Butler quotes Sprat's *Account of the Life and Writings of Mr. Abraham Cowley* (1668).

30. Butler quotes Hinman's *Abraham Cowley's World of Order*, 159, which, instead of specifying links, vaguely references "Hobbes's spirit."

31. Reik, *The Golden Lands of Thomas Hobbes*, 188.

Chapter Four   "Joynt Innterest": Hobbes and Waller

1. Aubrey, *Brief Lives*, ed. Andrew Clark, 1: 205.

2. *The Poems of Edmund Waller*, ed. G. Thorn Drury, 1: vii–viii. I have inserted grave accents where Waller's scansion seems to require them.

3. *Sir William Davenant's "Gondibert,"* ed. David Gladish, 51.

4. Griffin, ed., *Selected Poems of Abraham Cowley, Edmund Waller and John Oldham*, 158; Maclean, ed., *Ben Jonson and the Cavalier Poets*, 244 n.8.

5. I follow the introduction to Robert Durling, ed. and trans., *Petrarch's Lyric Poems*.

6. Hammond, *Fleeting Things*, 33; Butler, "Politics and the Masque," 59, 60.

7. Allison, *Toward an Augustan Poetic*, 52.

8. *The Aeneid*, trans. Robert Fitzgerald, 1.201–12.

9. Langley, *Image Government*, 31, 54.

10. Bateson, *English Poetry*, 169, 170, 170, 169.

11. Wallerstein, "The Development of the Rhetoric and Metre of the Heroic Couplet, Especially in 1625–1645," 181.

12. Hobbes, *On the Citizen*, ed. and trans. Richard Tuck and Michael Silverthorne, 48, 22.

13. For a fuller account, see my "Better Read than Dead," where I mistakenly give the poem's year of first publication as 1686.

14. Hobbes, *Leviathan*, ed. C. B. Macpherson, 197.

15. Garrison, *Dryden and the Tradition of Panegyric*, 123.

16. Chernaik, *The Poetry of Limitation*, 154.

17. Gilbert, *Edmund Waller*, 83.

18. Norbrook, *Writing the English Republic*, 307, 383.

19. Chernaik, " 'Every Conqueror Creates a Muse,' " 211 n.3.

20. Wallerstein, *Studies in Seventeenth-Century Poetic*, 278–79.

21. See for instance Martinich, *A Hobbes Dictionary*, 196, and Malcolm, "A Summary Biography of Hobbes," 32.

22. Hobbes, *Behemoth*, ed. Ferdinand Tönnies, 163–64.

23. Sommerville, *Thomas Hobbes*, 70, 38.

24. See the bibliographical discussions of Martinich, *Thomas Hobbes*, 147–48, and Sommerville, *Thomas Hobbes*, 187 n.20.

25. Hobbes, *The Correspondence*, ed. Malcolm, 1: 124. I also quote Waller's letter to Hobbes from this edition.

26. Wikelund, " 'Thus I Passe My Time in This Place,' " 268 and 268 n.17.

27. Preface to Milton, *"Poems 1645," "Lycidas 1638,"* sig. A4.

28. *The Life of Edward, Earl of Clarendon*, 1: 45.

29. Kishlansky, *A Monarchy Transformed*, 60.

30. *Bishop Burnet's History of His Own Time*, 1: 388.

31. "Mr. Wallers Speech in Parliament, at a Conference of Both Houses in the Painted Chamber," 10, 8, in Waller, *"Poems 1645," together with Poems from Bodleian MS Don D 55*.

32. Ashton, *The English Civil War*, 209.

33. Introduction to *De Cive: The English Version*, ed. Warrender, 7–8, 8 n.1.

34. Malcolm, *Aspects of Hobbes*, 239, 235.

35. Tuck, *Hobbes*, 27.

36. *Poems of Charles Cotton, 1630–1687*, ed. John Beresford, 277.

37. *The English Works of Thomas Hobbes*, ed. Sir William Molesworth, 4: 415.

38. Clarendon, *A Brief View and Survey* (1676), 7–8.

39. Peters, *Hobbes*, 36.

40. Hobbes, *A Dialogue*, ed. Joseph Cropsey, 64.
41. Hampton, *Hobbes and the Social Contract Tradition*, 200, 201.
42. Patterson, "The Very Name of the Game," 24.
43. Hirst, *Authority and Conflict*, 298.
44. Martinich, *The Two Gods of "Leviathan,"* 339–53.
45. Introduction to Hobbes, *De Cive: The Latin Version*, ed. Warrender, 22.
46. See my "Edmund Waller's Sacred Poems."

Chapter Five *"Absurd and Foolish Philosophy":* Hobbes and Rochester

1. *The Works of John Wilmot, Earl of Rochester*, ed. Harold Love, 56. I quote only a portion of Rochester's praise, which Gilbert, *Edmund Waller*, analyzes in its entirety as astute criticism shedding light on Waller's whole oeuvre (127–28).
2. The sources for Dorimant's quotations from Waller appear in the notes to Salgādo, ed., *Three Restoration Comedies*, 49, 50, 72, 93, 96, 102, 125, 134.
3. *The Critical Works of John Dennis*, ed. Edward Niles Hooker, 2: 248.
4. Burnet, *Some Passages of the Life and Death of Rochester* (1680), 49; Aubrey, *Brief Lives*, ed. Andrew Clark, 2: 279.
5. Parsons, *A Sermon Preached at the Funeral of the Rt Honourable John Earl of Rochester*, 7, 9.
6. Carver, "Rascal before the Lord," 112 n.23.
7. Bramhall, *The Catching of "Leviathan," or the Great Whale* (1658), 569–70.
8. Hobbes, *On the Citizen*, ed. and trans. Richard Tuck and Michael Silverthorne, 64.
9. Stephen, *Hobbes*, 65.
10. Hobbes, *Leviathan*, ed. C. B. Macpherson, 141–42.
11. Farley-Hills, *Rochester's Poetry*, 1.
12. Wood, *Athenae Oxonienses* (1692), 170.
13. Turner, "The Properties of Libertinism," 81.
14. Donne, *An Anatomy of the World* (1611), 205, in *The Complete English Poems*, ed. A. J. Smith.
15. Introduction to Adlard, ed., *The Debt to Pleasure*, 17.
16. Introduction to *The Letters of John Wilmot, Earl of Rochester*, ed. Treglown, 36; Lamb, *So Idle a Rogue*, 87–88.
17. Walker, ed., *The Poems of John Wilmot, Earl of Rochester*, x.
18. Turner, *Libertines and Radicals in Early Modern London*, x.
19. *The Critical Works of Thomas Rymer*, ed. Curt Zimansky, 81.
20. Pinto, *Enthusiast in Wit*, 22.
21. Griffin, *Satires against Man*, 8.

22. Vieth, ed., *The Complete Poems of John Wilmot, Earl of Rochester*, xli, 94. Though Vieth supplies conjectural dates of composition, I follow him only for years of first publication.
23. Creech, preface (unpaginated) to *T. Lucretius Carus the Epicurean Philosopher*.
24. Mintz, *The Hunting of "Leviathan,"* 142.
25. Fujimara, "Rochester's 'Satyr against Mankind,' " 209.
26. Ross, "Some Puzzles in Hobbes," 57.
27. *Hobbes and Bramhall on Liberty and Necessity*, ed. Vere Chappell, 64.
28. Sherman, ed., *The Restoration and the 18th Century*, 2283 n.1.
29. *The Poems of Edmund Waller*, ed. G. Thorn Drury, 2: 4.7–12.
30. Thormählen, *Rochester*, 220, 221.
31. Chernaik, *Sexual Freedom in Restoration Literature*, 24.
32. Laird, *Hobbes*, 173.
33. Sorell, *Hobbes*, 125.
34. Brinton, *The Anatomy of Revolution*, 15, 69.
35. Novak, "Libertinism and Sexuality," 59.
36. Munns, *Restoration Politics and Drama*, 148; *Poem to the Kings Most Sacred Majesty*, 88, in Davenant, *The Shorter Poems, and Songs from the Plays and Masques*, ed. A. M. Gibbs. I quote this portion of the poem more fully and discuss it in my second chapter.
37. Turner, *The Politics of Landscape*, 91.
38. Hughes, "Heroic Drama and Tragicomedy," 202.
39. Parsons, "Restoration Tragedy as Total Theatre," 49.
40. Hughes, *English Drama 1660–1700*, 52.
41. *The Riverside Shakespeare*, ed. G. Blakemore Evans et al., I.ii, 1.
42. Strier, *Resistant Structures*, 220 n.54.
43. Radzinowicz, "The Politics of *Paradise Lost*," 227.
44. Spragens, *The Politics of Motions*, 193.
45. Tricaud, "Hobbes's Conception of the State of Nature from 1640 to 1651," 122.
46. Though Love credits Treglown's edition of Rochester's letters for making the connection between "*Love and Life*" and *Leviathan* (358), Thormählen notes that the link was first suggested by Treglown in an essay published in 1973 (69).
47. Mulgrave, *The Poems of John Sheffield*, 97.
48. See Humphreys, "The Social Setting," 39; Greene, *Lord Rochester's Monkey*, 206; and Rogers, "Introduction," 5. Humphreys states that the lines come from another poem by Mulgrave; Rogers attributes them to the Duke of Buckingham. In recounting how Mulgrave's tribute featured at the Malmesbury commemoration of the tercentenary of Hobbes's death, Rogow, *Thomas Hobbes*, notes its misattribution on that occasion to Buckingham and either quotes the standard two couplets or follows "the printed program for the dinner" in doing so (233).
49. Hill, *Writing and Revolution in 17th Century England*, 304.

Chapter Six "Common Passions": Hobbes and Suckling

1. Wedgwood, *Seventeenth-Century English Literature*, 62.
2. See Salgādo, ed., *Three Restoration Comedies*, 97 n.1.
3. Aubrey, *Brief Lives*, ed. Andrew Clark, 1: 151.
4. *The Life of Edward, Earl of Clarendon*, 1: 40.
5. Malcolm, "A Summary Biography of Hobbes," 23.
6. Trevor-Roper, *Catholics, Anglicans and Puritans*, 170.
7. Occupying the middle ground between Malcolm and Trevor-Roper is the approach to defining the Great Tew circle taken by Weber, *Lucius Cary, Second Viscount Falkland*.
8. On the identities of the contestants, see *The Works of Sir John Suckling: The Non-Dramatic Works*, ed. Thomas Clayton, 268–69. This is the edition from which I quote Suckling's letters and poems of his not linked with his plays. I have omitted the square brackets establishing *The Wits* as an editorial title.
9. Tuck, *Natural Rights Theories*, 101 n.1 and 101.
10. For Falkland's enthusiasm as a Son of Ben, see the poems of his reprinted in *Ben Jonson*, ed. C. H. Herford and Percy and Evelyn Simpson, 11: 399–404, 430–37. Clayton notes "Suckling's long-standing hostility to Jonson and his attacks upon him during his declining years of theatrical failure and illness" (267). See also the foreword to *The Works of Sir John Suckling: The Plays*, ed. L. A. Beaurline, ix, together with the associated commentaries to which it points. This is the edition from which I quote Suckling's drama and verse relating to it.
11. Sommerville, *Thomas Hobbes*, 159; see also 135–37.
12. On Socinianism in its various senses, see Trevor-Roper, *Catholics, Anglicans and Puritans*, 186–92, and Sommerville, *Thomas Hobbes*, 142, 198 n.11.
13. Hobbes, *Leviathan*, ed. C. B. Macpherson, 161.
14. Hobbes, *The Elements of Law*, ed. J. C. A. Gaskin, 59–60, 59.
15. Spragens, *The Politics of Motion*, 190.
16. Martinich, *Hobbes*, 133, 137.
17. *The Poetical Works of Tennyson*, ed. G. Robert Strange, 70.
18. Clarendon, *A Brief View and Survey*, 8.
19. Goldsmith, *Hobbes's Science of Politics*, 56–57.
20. Elias, *Power and Civility*, 274.
21. Clayton, " 'At Bottom a Criticism of Life,' " 222.
22. Introduction to Clayton, ed., *Cavalier Poets*, xx.
23. Hobbes, *On the Citizen*, ed. and trans. Tuck and Michael Silverthorne, 5.
24. *The Complete Plays of William Congreve*, ed. Herbert Davis, IV.i, 106.
25. Rogers, "The Meaning of Van Dyck's Portrait of Sir John Suckling," 742. On Suckling's affection for Shakespeare's plays, see Beaurline's editorial apparatus, vii–viii and 274–75.

26. Whigham, *Ambition and Privilege*, 95.
27. *The Riverside Shakespeare*, ed. G. Blakemore Evans et al., III.i, 55.
28. *The Poems of Alexander Pope*, ed. John Butt, 347.
29. Carew's death dates the poem as no later than ca. 1639; Clayton assigns it to ca. 1626–32.
30. The definitive treatment of the plain style remains Trimpi, *Ben Jonson's Poems*.
31. Donne, *The Complete English Poems*, ed. A. J. Smith, 1–3.
32. *The Poems of Sir Philip Sidney*, ed. William Ringler, sonnet 1 (14); "Jordan (I)," 11, in *The Works of George Herbert*, ed. F. E. Hutchinson.
33. *Sir William Davenant's "Gondibert,"* ed. David Gladish, 51.
34. Sprat, *History of the Royal Society*, ed. Jackson Cope and Harold Whitmore Jones, 113.
35. Skinner, *Reason and Rhetoric in the Philosophy of Hobbes*, 304.
36. Winn, *John Dryden and His World*, 74.
37. Miner, *The Cavalier Mode from Jonson to Cotton*, 225–26 n.32.
38. On the prevalence and significance of chronometric imagery in seventeenth-century England, see Shapin, *The Scientific Revolution*, 32–37.
39. *The Works of John Wilmot, Earl of Rochester*, ed. Harold Love, 9, 10, 12.

Chapter Seven   "Sufficiently Disposed": Hobbes and Godolphin

1. Aubrey, *Brief Lives*, ed. Andrew Clark, 1: 369, 370.
2. Hill, *Writing and Revolution in 17th Century England*, 304.
3. Norbrook, *Writing the English Republic*, 102 n.33.
4. Introduction to Saintsbury, ed., *The Poems of Sidney Godolphin*, 233.
5. Introduction to *The Poems of Sidney Godolphin*, ed. Dighton, xli; see also 73. This is the edition I follow when quoting Godolphin's work.
6. *The Poems of Edmund Waller*, ed. G. Thorn Drury, 1: 21–22.
7. King, *Seventeenth-Century English Literature*, 114.
8. Hobbes, *Leviathan*, ed. C. B. Macpherson, 75.
9. Richmond, *The School of Love*, 218.
10. Maclean, ed., *Ben Jonson and the Cavalier Poets*, 278 n.4, also diverging on this point from Saintsbury's text.
11. Trevor-Roper, *Catholics, Anglicans and Puritans*, 185–86.
12. Clarendon, *A Brief View and Survey*, 320.
13. *The Life of Edward, Earl of Clarendon*, 1: 43.
14. Introduction to *The Poems of John Collop*, ed. Hilberry, 10.
15. *Suetonius*, trans. J. C. Rolfe, 2: 243, 247.

16. Sir Richard Fanshawe wrote a poem about Strafford comparing him with Otho; I discuss it in relation to three other poems about Strafford (including one by Collop) in the second chapter of my "Royalist Verse of the English Civil War."
17. Baumgold, *Hobbes's Political Theory*, 88.
18. Introduction to Hobbes, *Behemoth*, ed. Ferdinand Tönnies, xlix, x.
19. Johnston, *The Rhetoric of "Leviathan,"* 110.
20. Collins, *From Divine Cosmos to Sovereign State*, 213 n.92.
21. Skinner, *Reason and Rhetoric in the Philosophy of Hobbes*, 13.

Chapter Eight   "Ordinary Artifice": Hobbes and Jonson

1. Martinich, *A Hobbes Dictionary*, 318; *Poems of Charles Cotton*, ed. John Buxton, 452–54, 455–56, 444–45. Buxton in his notes doubts that Cotton produced the English *De Mirabilibus* (265–66); Malcolm, *Aspects of Hobbes*, takes the same view (258 n.91). According to Rogow, *Thomas Hobbes*, "the one book by Hobbes in the library of Isaac Newton was *De Mirabilibus Pecci*" (70n.).
2. Aubrey, *Brief Lives*, ed. Andrew Clark, 1: 364–65.
3. Commentary in *Ben Jonson*, ed. C. H. Herford and Percy and Evelyn Simpson, 11: 244. This is the edition I follow when quoting Jonson.
4. Burt, *Licensed by Authority*, 115–23.
5. Randall, *Winter Fruit*, 314.
6. Barish, *The Antitheatrical Prejudice*, 154.
7. Cantalupo, *A Literary "Leviathan,"* 18.
8. Hobbes, *Leviathan*, ed. C. B. Macpherson, 626.
9. Sonnet XII (1.1: 8), in *The Works of John Milton*, ed. Frank Allen Patterson.
10. Introduction to Hobbes, *Behemoth*, ed. Ferdinand Tönnies, xlii.
11. Hobbes, *On the Citizen*, ed. and trans. Richard Tuck and Michael Silverhorne, 187.
12. *Hobbes's Thucydides*, ed. Richard Schlatter, 12.
13. On Horace's profound importance for Jonson, see my "In More than Name Only," especially 1–2.
14. Martinich, *Thomas Hobbes*, 31.
15. Chernaik, *Sexual Freedom in Restoration Literature*, 24.
16. Hobbes, *The Elements of Law*, ed. J. C. A. Gaskin, 255. I quote an anonymous translation. I also follow this edition for *Elements* itself.
17. Underdown, *A Freeborn People*, 19.
18. *Sir William Davenant's "Gondibert,"* ed. David Gladish, 15.
19. Harrison, "Dryden's *Aeneid*," 167; Dryden, *Poems*, ed. William Frost and Vinton Dearing, 213, 220.

20. Skinner, *Reason and Rhetoric in the Philosophy of Hobbes*, 242.
21. Hobbes, *The Correspondence*, ed. Malcolm, 1: 124.
22. Tuck, *Hobbes*, 26.
23. *De Cive: The Latin Version*, 84, and *De Cive: The English Version*, 37, ed. Howard Warrender.
24. For another example of how *Philosophical Rudiments* might be more accurate than the Tuck-Silverthorne version of *De Cive*, see my "Hobbes's Explicated Fables and the Legacy of the Ancients," 279–81.
25. Cooke, *Hobbes and Christianity*, 117.
26. Johnson, "Hobbes's Anglican Doctrine of Salvation," 103.
27. Martinich, *The Two Gods of "Leviathan,"* 16, 215.
28. Collinson, "The Theatre Constructs Puritanism," 164.
29. Finlayson, *Historians, Puritanism, and the English Revolution.*
30. Kenyon, *The Civil Wars of England*, 226n.
31. Cordner, "Zeal-of-the-Land Busy Restored," 182.
32. Dutton, *Ben Jonson*, 19.
33. Marcus, "Of Mire and Authorship," 177.
34. Dunn, *Pretexts of Authority*, 10–11.
35. Armstrong and Tennenhouse, *The Imaginary Puritan*, 258 n.35 (continued from 257).
36. Rogers, "Hobbes's Hidden Influence," 205.
37. Dryden, *Poems 1685–1692*, ed. Earl Miner and Vinton Dearing, 10.
38. *The Poems and Fables of John Dryden*, ed. James Kinsley, 524. Martinich, *Hobbes*, makes an unconvincing case for the merits of Hobbes's renderings of Homer's epics (338–43). For a more judicious estimate, see Jerry Ball, "The Despised Version."

Works Cited

Adlard, John. Ed. *The Debt to Pleasure: John Wilmot, Earl of Rochester, in the Eyes of His Contemporaries and in His Own Poetry and Prose.* Cheadle, Cheshire: Carcanet, 1974.

Allison, Alexander Ward. *Toward an Augustan Poetic: Edmund Waller's "Reform" of English Poetry.* Lexington: University of Kentucky Press, 1962.

Anselment, Raymond A. *Loyalist Resolve: Patient Fortitude in the English Civil War.* Newark: University of Delaware Press, 1988.

Armstrong, Nancy and Leonard Tennenhouse. *The Imaginary Puritan: Literature, Intellectual Labor, and the Origins of Personal Life.* The New Historicism: Studies in Cultural Poetics 21. Berkeley: University of California Press, 1992.

Ashton, Robert. *The English Civil War: Conservatism and Revolution, 1603–1649.* 1978. New York: Norton, 1979.

Aubrey, John. *"Brief Lives," Chiefly of Contemporaries, Set Down by John Aubrey, between the Years 1669 & 1696.* Ed. Andrew Clark. 2 vols. Oxford: Clarendon, 1898.

Ball, Jerry L. "The Despised Version: Hobbes's Translation of Homer." *Restoration* 20.1 (1996): 1–17.

Barbeau, Anne T. *The Intellectual Design of John Dryden's Heroic Plays.* New Haven: Yale University Press, 1970.

Barish, Jonas. *The Antitheatrical Prejudice.* Berkeley: University of California Press, 1981.

Barker, Francis. "In the Wars of Truth: Violence, True Knowledge and Power in Milton and Hobbes." 91–109. Healy and Sawday.

Bateson, F. W. *English Poetry: A Critical Introduction.* London: Longmans, Green, and Co., 1950.

Baumgold, Deborah. *Hobbes's Political Theory.* Cambridge: Cambridge University Press, 1988.

Bobbio, Norberto. *Thomas Hobbes and the Natural Law Tradition.* Trans. Daniela Gobetti. Chicago: University of Chicago Press, 1993.

Borgman, Albert S. *Thomas Shadwell: His Life and Comedies.* 1928. New York: Blom, 1969.

Bramhall, John (Bishop of Derry). *The Catching of "Leviathan," or the Great Whale.* 449–574. *Castigations of Mr. Hobbes 1658.* New York: Garland, 1977.

———. *A Defence of True Liberty.* 43–68. *Hobbes and Bramhall on Liberty and Necessity.* Ed. Vere Chappell. Cambridge: Cambridge University Press, 1999.

Brinton, Crane. *The Anatomy of Revolution*. 2nd rev. ed. New York: Vintage, 1965.

Brown, K. C., ed. *Hobbes Studies*. Oxford: Blackwell, 1965.

Burnet, Gilbert (Bishop of Salisbury). *Some Passages of the Life and Death of Rochester*. 47–92. Farley-Hills.

———. Vol. 1 of *Bishop Burnet's History of His Own Time*. 2 vols. London: Ward, 1724.

Burt, Richard. *Licensed by Authority: Ben Jonson and the Discourses of Censorship*. Ithaca: Cornell University Press, 1993.

Butler, Charles. "The Stagirite and the Scarecrow: Stanza 3 of Cowley's 'Ode to the Royal Society.' " *Restoration* 21.1 (1997): 1–14.

Butler, Martin. "Politics and the Masque: *Salmacida Spolia*." 59–74. Healy and Sawday.

Cameron, William J. "John Dryden's Jacobitism." 277–308. Love.

Cantalupo, Charles. *A Literary "Leviathan": Thomas Hobbes's Masterpiece of Language*. Lewisburg, PA: Bucknell University Press, 1991.

Carlton, Charles. *Charles I: The Personal Monarch*. 1983. London: Ark, 1984.

Carver, Larry. "Rascal before the Lord: Rochester's Religious Rhetoric." 89–112. Vieth. First printed in 1982.

Chambers, A. B. *Andrew Marvell and Edmund Waller: Seventeenth-Century Praise and Restoration Satire*. University Park: Pennsylvania State University Press, 1991.

Chernaik, Warren L. *The Poetry of Limitation: A Study of Edmund Waller*. New Haven: Yale University Press, 1968.

———. *Sexual Freedom in Restoration Literature*. Cambridge: Cambridge University Press, 1995.

———. " 'Every Conqueror Creates a Muse': Conquest and Constitutions in Marvell and Waller." 195–216. Chernaik and Dzelzainis.

Chernaik, Warren L. and Martin Dzelzainis, eds. *Marvell and Liberty*. London: Macmillan, 1999.

Clarendon, Earl of (Edward Hyde). *A Brief View and Survey of the Dangerous and Pernicious Errors to Church and State, in Mr. Hobbes's Book, Entitled "Leviathan."* Oxford: at the Theater, 1676.

———. Vol. 1 of *The Life of Edward, Earl of Clarendon*. 2 vols. Oxford: Oxford University Press, 1857.

Clayton, Thomas, ed. *The Cavalier Poets: Selected Poems*. Oxford: Oxford University Press, 1978.

———. " 'At Bottom a Criticism of Life': Suckling and the Poetry of Low Seriousness." 217–41. *Classic and Cavalier: Essays on Jonson and the Sons of Ben*. Ed. Claude J. Summers and Ted-Larry Pebworth. Pittsburgh: Pittsburgh University Press, 1982.

Collins, Stephen L. *From Divine Cosmos to Sovereign State: An Intellectual History of Consciousness and the Idea of Order in Renaissance England*. Oxford: Oxford University Press, 1989.

Collinson, Patrick. "The Theatre Constructs Puritanism." 157–69. Smith, Strier, and Bevington.

Collop, John. *The Poems of John Collop.* Ed. Conrad Hilberry. Madison: University of Wisconsin Press, 1962.

Condren, Conal. *Thomas Hobbes.* Twayne's English Authors Series 559. New York: Twayne, 2000.

Congreve, William. *The Complete Plays of William Congreve.* Ed. Herbert Davis. Chicago: University of Chicago Press, 1967.

Cooke, Paul D. *Hobbes and Christianity: Reassessing the Bible in "Leviathan."* New York: Rowman and Littlefield, 1996.

Cordner, Michael. "Zeal-of-the-Land Busy Restored." 174–92. *Re-Presenting Ben Jonson: Text, History, Performance.* Ed. Martin Butler. London: Macmillan, 1999.

Cotton, Charles. *Poems of Charles Cotton, 1630–1687.* Ed. John Beresford. London: Cobden-Sanderson, 1923.

———. *Poems of Charles Cotton.* Ed. John Buxton. London: Routledge and Kegan Paul, 1958.

Cowley, Abraham. *Poems: "Miscellanies," "The Mistress," "Pindarique Odes," "Davideis," "Verses Written on Several Occasions."* Ed. A. R. Waller. Cambridge: Cambridge University Press, 1905.

———. Vol. 2 of *The Complete Works in Verse and Prose.* Ed. Alexander Grosart. 2 vols. New York: Ams, 1967.

Creech, Thomas. *T. Lucretius Carus the Epicurean Philosopher, His Six Books "De Natura Rerum" Done into English Verse, with Notes.* [Trans. Creech] Oxford: Stephens, 1681.

Curtis, Mark H. "The Alienated Intellectuals of Early Stuart England." 309–31. *Crisis in Europe 1550–1660.* Ed. Trevor Aston. 1965. New York: Anchor, 1967.

Davenant, Sir William. *The Shorter Poems, and Songs from the Plays and Masques.* Ed. A. M. Gibbs. Oxford: Clarendon, 1971.

———. *Sir William Davenant's "Gondibert."* Ed. David F. Gladish. Oxford: Clarendon, 1971.

Denham, Sir John. *The Poetical Works of Sir John Denham.* Ed. Theodore Howard Banks. 2nd ed. Hamden, CT: Archon, 1969.

Dennis, John. Vol. 2 of *The Critical Works of John Dennis.* Ed. Edward Niles Hooker. 2 vols. Baltimore: Johns Hopkins, 1943.

Dent, Edward J. *Foundations of English Opera: A Study of Musical Drama in England during the Seventeenth Century.* Cambridge: Cambridge University Press, 1928. 2nd reprint New York: Da Capo, 1967. With an introduction by Michael M. Winesanker.

Dewey, John. "The Motivation of Hobbes's Political Philosophy." 8–30. Ross, Schneider, and Waldman.

Donne, John. *The Complete English Poems.* Ed. A. J. Smith. 1971. Harmondsworth: Penguin, 1980.

Doody, Margaret Anne. *The Daring Muse: Augustan Poetry Reconsidered.* Cambridge: Cambridge University Press, 1985.

Dryden, John. *Poems 1685–1692.* Ed. Earl Miner and Vinton A. Dearing. Vol. 3 (1969) of *The Works of John Dryden.* 20 vols. Berkeley: University of California Press, 1956–.

Dryden, John. *The Poems and Fables of John Dryden*. Ed. James Kinsley. Oxford: Oxford University Press, 1970.

———. *Poems: The Works of Virgil in English, 1697*. Ed. William Frost and Vinton A. Dearing. Vol. 5 (1987) of *The Works of John Dryden*.

Dunn, Kevin. *Pretexts of Authority: The Rhetoric of Authorship in the Renaissance Preface*. Stanford: Stanford University Press, 1994.

Durling, Robert M., ed. and trans. *Petrarch's Lyric Poems: The "Rime Sparse" and OtherLyrics*. Cambridge, MA: Harvard University Press, 1976.

Dutton, Richard. *Ben Jonson: Authority: Criticism*. London: Macmillan, 1996.

Edmond, Mary. *Rare Sir William Davenant: Poet Laureate, Playwright, Civil War General, Restoration Theatre Manager*. Manchester: Manchester University Press, 1987.

Elias, Norbert. *Power and Civility, The Civilizing Process: Volume 2*. Trans. Edmund Jephson. New York: Pantheon, 1982.

Farley-Hills, David, ed. *Rochester: The Critical Heritage*. London: Routledge and Kegan Paul, 1972.

———. *Rochester's Poetry*. Totowa, NJ: Rowman and Littlefield, 1978.

Finlayson, Michael G. *Historians, Puritanism, and the English Revolution: The Religious Factor in English Politics before and after the Interregnum*. Toronto: University of Toronto Press, 1983.

Fujimara, Thomas H. "Rochester's 'Satyr against Mankind': An Analysis." 203–21. Vieth. First printed in 1958.

Garrison, James D. *Dryden and the Tradition of Panegyric*. Berkeley: University of California Press, 1975.

Gauthier, David P. *The Logic of "Leviathan": The Moral and Political Theory of Thomas Hobbes*. Oxford: Clarendon, 1969.

Gilbert, Jack G. *Edmund Waller*. Twayne's English Authors Series 266. Boston: Twayne, 1979.

Godolphin, Sidney. *The Poems of Sidney Godolphin*. Ed. William Dighton. Oxford: Clarendon, 1931.

Goldsmith, M. M. *Hobbes's Science of Politics*. 1966. New York: Columbia University Press, 1968.

Grant, Hardy. "Hobbes and Mathematics." 108–28. Sorell.

Greene, Graham. *Lord Rochester's Monkey: Being the Life of John Wilmot, Second Earl of Rochester*. New York: Viking, 1974.

Griffin, Dustin H. *Satires against Man: The Poems of Rochester*. Berkeley: University of California Press, 1973.

Griffin, Julia, ed. *Selected Poems of Abraham Cowley, Edmund Waller and John Oldham*. Harmondsworth: Penguin, 1998.

Hammond, Gerald. *Fleeting Things: English Poets and Poems, 1616–1660*. Cambridge, MA: Harvard University Press, 1990.

Hampton, Jean. *Hobbes and the Social Contract Tradition*. 1986. Cambridge: Cambridge University Press, 1995.

Harrison, T. W. "Dryden's *Aeneid*." 143–67. *Dryden's Mind and Art*. Ed. Bruce King. Edinburgh: Oliver and Boyd, 1969.

Healy, Thomas and Jonathan Sawday, eds. *Literature and the English Civil War*. Cambridge: Cambridge University Press, 1990.

Herbert, George. *The Works of George Herbert*. Ed. F. E. Hutchinson. 1941. Oxford: Clarendon, 1953.

Hill, Christopher. *Writing and Revolution in 17th Century England*. Vol. 1 of *The Collected Essays of Christopher Hill*. 3 vols. Amherst: University of Massachusetts Press, 1985.

Hillyer, Richard. "Better Read than Dead: Waller's 'Of English Verse.' " *Restoration* 14.1 (1990): 33–43.

———. "In More than Name Only: Jonson's 'To Sir Horace Vere.' " *The Modern Language Review* 85.1 (1990): 1–11.

———. "Royalist Verse of the English Civil War." Ph.D. diss., University of Michigan, 1990.

———. "Edmund Waller's Sacred Poems." *SEL* 39.1 (1999): 155–69.

———. "Keith Thomas's 'Definitive Refutation' of C. B. Macpherson: Revisiting 'The Social Origins of Hobbes's Political Thought.' " *Hobbes Studies* 15 (2002): 32–44.

———. "Hobbes's Explicated Fables and the Legacy of the Ancients." *Philosophy and Literature* 28.2 (2004): 269–83.

Hinman, Robert B. *Abraham Cowley's World of Order*. Cambridge, MA: Harvard University Press, 1960.

Hinnant, Charles H. *Thomas Hobbes*. Twayne's English Authors Series 215. Boston: Twayne, 1977.

Hirst, Derek. *Authority and Conflict: England, 1603–1658*. Cambridge, MA: Harvard University Press, 1986.

Hobbes, Thomas. Vols. 1, 4, and 10 of *The English Works of Thomas Hobbes of Malmesbury*. Ed. Sir William Molesworth. 11 vols. London: Bohn, 1839–45. 2nd reprint Darmstadt: Aalen, 1966.

———. *Behemoth, or the Long Parliament*. Ed. Ferdinand Tönnies. London: Simpkin, Marshall, 1889. Chicago: University of Chicago Press, 1990. With an introduction by Stephen Holmes.

———. *Leviathan*. Ed. C. B. Macpherson. 1968. Harmondsworth: Penguin, 1975.

———. *The Answer of Mr. Hobbes to Sir Will. D'Avenant's Preface before "Gondibert."* 44–55. Davenant (1971, ed. Gladish).

———. *A Dialogue between a Philosopher and a Student of the Common Laws of England*. Ed. Joseph Cropsey. Chicago: University of Chicago Press, 1971.

———. *Hobbes's Thucydides*. Ed. Richard Schlatter. New Brunswick, NJ: Rutgers University Press, 1975.

———. *De Cive: The Latin Version*. Ed. Howard Warrender. Vol. 2 of *The Clarendon Edition of the Philosophical Works of Thomas Hobbes*. Oxford: Clarendon, 1983.

Hobbes, Thomas. *De Cive: The English Version*. Ed. Warrender. Vol. 3 (1983) of *The Clarendon Edition of the Philosophical Works of Thomas Hobbes*.

———. *The Correspondence*. Ed. Noel Malcolm. 2 vols. Vols. 6 and 7 of *The Clarendon Edition of the Works of Thomas Hobbes*. 1994. Oxford: Clarendon, 1997.

———. *The Elements of Law, Natural and Politic: Part I, Human Nature; Part II, De Corpore Politico; with Three Lives*. Ed. J. C. A. Gaskin. Oxford: Oxford University Press, 1994.

———. *Three Discourses: A Critical Modern Edition of Newly Identified Work of the Young Hobbes*. Ed. Noel B. Reynolds and Arlene W. Saxonhouse. Chicago: University of Chicago Press, 1995.

———. *On the Citizen*. Ed. Trans. Richard Tuck and Michael Silverthorne. Cambridge: Cambridge University Press, 1998.

Horace. *The Complete Works of Horace (Quintus Horatius Flaccus) Translated in the Meters of the Originals, with Notes*. Trans. Charles E. Passage. New York: Ungar, 1983.

Hughes, Derek. *English Drama 1660–1700*. Oxford: Oxford University Press, 1996.

———. "Heroic Drama and Tragicomedy." 195–210. Owen.

Hume, Robert D. *The Development of English Drama in the Late Seventeenth Century*. 1976. Oxford: Clarendon, 1977.

Humphreys, A. R. "The Social Setting." 15–48. *From Dryden to Johnson*. Vol. 4 of *The Pelican Guide to English Literature*. Ed. Boris Ford. 3rd rev. ed. 1968. Harmondsworth: Penguin, 1977.

Johnson, Paul J. "Hobbes's Anglican Doctrine of Salvation." 102–25. Ross, Schneider, and Waldman.

Johnston, David. *The Rhetoric of "Leviathan": Thomas Hobbes and the Politics of Cultural Transformation*. Princeton: Princeton University Press, 1986.

Jonson, Ben. *Ben Jonson*. Ed. C. H. Herford and Percy and Evelyn Simpson. 11 vols. Oxford: Clarendon, 1925–54.

Kenyon, J. P. *The Stuarts: A Study in Kingship*. 1958. London: Fontana, 1974.

———. *The Civil Wars of England*. New York: Knopf, 1988.

King, Bruce. *Seventeenth-Century English Literature*. New York: Schocken, 1982.

Kishlansky, Mark. *A Monarchy Transformed: Britain 1603–1714*. London: Penguin, 1996.

Kroll, Richard. "William Davenant and John Dryden." 311–25. Owen.

Laird, John. *Hobbes*. 1934. New York: Russell and Russell, 1968.

Lamb, Jeremy. *So Idle a Rogue: The Life and Death of Lord Rochester*. London: Allison and Busby, 1993.

Langley, T. R. *Image Government: Monarchical Metamorphoses in English Literature and Art, 1649–1702*. Pittsburgh: Duquesne University Press, 2001.

Locke, John. *Two Treatises of Government: Student Edition*. Ed. Peter Laslett. 1988. Cambridge: Cambridge University Press, 2003.

Lockyer, Roger. *The Early Stuarts: A Political History of England 1603–1642*. London: Longman, 1989.

Love, Harold. Ed. *Restoration Literature: Critical Approaches*. London: Methuen, 1972.

Maclean, Hugh. Ed. *Ben Jonson and the Cavalier Poets*. New York: Norton, 1974.

Macpherson, C. B. "Hobbes's Bourgeois Man." 169–83. Brown. First printed in 1945.

Malcolm, Noel. "A Summary Biography of Hobbes." 13–44. Sorell.

———. *Aspects of Hobbes*. Oxford: Clarendon, 2002.

Marcus, Leah. "Of Mire and Authorship." 170–81. Smith, Strier, and Bevington.

Martinich, A. P. *The Two Gods of "Leviathan": Thomas Hobbes on Religion and Politics*. 1992. Cambridge: Cambridge University Press, 2002.

———. *A Hobbes Dictionary*. Cambridge, MA: Blackwell, 1995.

———. *Thomas Hobbes*. New York: St. Martin's, 1997.

———. *Hobbes: A Biography*. Cambridge: Cambridge University Press, 1999.

Mendelsohn, Daniel. "Theatres of War." *The New Yorker* (January 12, 2004): 79–84.

Milton, John. Vols. 1.1 and 2.1 of *The Works of John Milton*. Ed. Frank Allen Patterson. 18 vols. New York: Columbia University Press, 1931.

———. *"Poems 1645," "Lycidas 1638."* Menston: Scolar, 1970.

Miner, Earl. *The Cavalier Mode from Jonson to Cotton*. Princeton: Princeton University Press, 1971.

———. *The Restoration Mode from Milton to Dryden*. Princeton: Princeton University Press, 1974.

Mintz, Samuel I. *The Hunting of "Leviathan": Seventeenth-Century Reactions to the Materialism and Moral Philosophy of Thomas Hobbes*. 1962. Cambridge: Cambridge University Press, 1969.

Mulgrave, third Earl of (John Sheffield, Duke of Buckinghamshire). *The Poems of John Sheffield, Duke of Buckinghamshire*. 69–102. Vol. 10 of *The Works of the English Poets, from Chaucer to Cowper*. 21 vols. London: Whittingham, 1810. New York: Greenwood, 1969.

Munns, Jessica. *Restoration Politics and Drama: The Plays of Thomas Otway, 1675–1683*. Newark: University of Delaware Press, 1995.

Nethercot, Arthur H. *Abraham Cowley: The Muse's Hannibal*. 1931. New York: Russell and Russell, 1967. This reissue includes additional notes.

———. *Sir William D'avenant* [sic]: *Poet Laureate and Playwright-Manager*. 1938. New York: Russell and Russell, 1967. This reissue includes additional notes.

Norbrook, David. *Writing the English Republic: Poetry, Rhetoric and Politics, 1627–1660*. 1999. Cambridge: Cambridge University Press, 2000.

Novak, Maximilian E. "Libertinism and Sexuality." 53–68. Owen.

Owen, Susan J., ed. *A Companion to Restoration Drama*. Oxford: Blackwell, 2001.

Parkin, Jon. "Liberty Transpros'd: Andrew Marvell and Samuel Parker." 269–89. Chernaik and Dzelzainis.

Parry, Graham. "A Troubled Arcadia." 38–55. Healy and Sawday.

Parsons, Philip. "Restoration Tragedy as Total Theatre." 27–68. Love.

Parsons, Robert. *A Sermon Preached at the Funeral of the Rt Honorable John Earl of Rochester.* Oxford: Davis and Bowman, 1680.

Patterson, Annabel. "The Very Name of the Game: Theories of Order and Disorder." 21–37. Healy and Sawday.

Peters, Richard. *Hobbes.* Harmondsworth: Penguin, 1956.

Pinto, Vivian de Sola. *Enthusiast in Wit: A Portrait of John Wilmot, Earl of Rochester, 1647–1680.* Lincoln: University of Nebraska Press, 1962.

Pope, Alexander. *The Poems of Alexander Pope: A One-Volume Edition of the Twickenham Text with Selected Annotations.* Ed. John Butt. New Haven: Yale University Press, 1963.

Pritchard, Allan. Ed. *Abraham Cowley: "The Civil War."* University of Toronto Department of English Studies and Texts 20. Toronto: University of Toronto Press, 1973.

Radzinowicz, Mary Ann. "The Politics of *Paradise Lost.*" 204–29. *Politics of Discourse: The Literature and History of Seventeenth-Century England.* Ed. Kevin Sharpe and Steven N. Zwicker. Berkeley: University of California Press, 1987.

Randall, Dale B. J. *Winter Fruit: English Drama 1642–1660.* Lexington: University of Kentucky Press, 1995.

Reik, Miriam M. *The Golden Lands of Thomas Hobbes.* Detroit: Wayne State University Press, 1977.

Richmond, H. M. *The School of Love: The Evolution of the Stuart Love Lyric.* Princeton: Princeton University Press, 1964.

Rivers, Isabel. *The Poetry of Conservatism 1600–1745: A Study of Poets and Public Affairs from Jonson to Pope.* Cambridge: Rivers, 1973.

Rochester, second Earl of (John Wilmot). *The Works of John Wilmot, Earl of Rochester.* Ed. Harold Love. Oxford: Oxford University Press, 1999.

Rogers, G. A. J. "Introduction." 1–10. Rogers and Ryan.

———. "Hobbes's Hidden Influence." 189–205. Rogers and Ryan.

Rogers, G. A. J. and Alan Ryan, eds. *Perspectives on Thomas Hobbes.* 1988. Oxford: Clarendon, 1990.

Rogers, Malcolm. "The Meaning of Van Dyck's Portrait of Sir John Suckling." *Burlington Magazine* 120 (1978): 741–45.

Rogow, Arnold A. *Thomas Hobbes: Radical in the Service of Reaction.* New York: Norton, 1986.

Ross, Ralph. "Some Puzzles in Hobbes." 42–60. Ross, Schneider, and Waldman.

Ross, Ralph, Herbert W. Schneider, and Theodore Waldman, eds. *Thomas Hobbes in His Time.* Minneapolis: University of Minnesota Press, 1974.

Russell, Conrad. "The First Army Plot of 1641." *Proceedings of the Royal Historical Society* 38 (1988): 85–106.

Rymer, Thomas. *The Critical Works of Thomas Rymer.* Ed. Curt A. Zimansky. New Haven: Yale University Press, 1956.

Saintsbury, George, ed. *The Poems of Sidney Godolphin, Now First Collected.* 227–61. Vol. 2 (1906) of *Minor Poets of the Caroline Period.* Ed. Saintsbury. 3 vols. Oxford: Clarendon, 1905–21.

Salgādo, Gāmini, ed. *Three Restoration Comedies.* 1968. Harmondsworth: Penguin, 1976.

Sawday, Jonathan. " 'Mysteriously Divided': Civil War, Madness and the Divided Self." 127–43. Healy and Sawday.

Shakespeare, William. *The Riverside Shakespeare.* Ed. G. Blakemore Evans et al. 2nd ed. Boston: Houghton Mifflin, 1997.

Shapin, Steven. *The Scientific Revolution.* Chicago: University of Chicago Press, 1996.

Sherman, Stuart, ed. *The Restoration and the 18th Century.* Vol. 1C of *The Longman Anthology of English Literature.* Ed. David Damrosch. 2nd ed. 2 vols. New York: Longman, 2002.

Sidney, Sir Philip. *The Poems of Sir Philip Sidney.* Ed. William A. Ringler, Jr. Oxford: Clarendon, 1962.

Skinner, Quentin. *Reason and Rhetoric in the Philosophy of Hobbes.* Cambridge: Cambridge University Press, 1996.

Smith, David L., Richard Strier, and David Bevington, eds. *The Theatrical City: Culture, Theatre and Politics in London, 1576–1649.* 1995. Cambridge: Cambridge University Press, 2002.

Smith, David L. *The Stuart Parliaments 1603–1689.* London: Arnold, 1999.

Sommerville, Johann P. *Thomas Hobbes: Political Ideas in Historical Context.* New York: St. Martin's, 1992.

Sorell, Tom. *Hobbes.* London: Routledge and Kegan Paul, 1986.

———, ed. *The Cambridge Companion to Hobbes.* Cambridge: Cambridge University Press, 1996.

Spragens, Thomas A., Jr. *The Politics of Motion: The World of Thomas Hobbes.* Lexington: University of Kentucky Press, 1973.

Sprat, Thomas (Bishop of Rochester). *History of the Royal Society.* Ed. Jackson I. Cope and Harold Whitmore Jones. St. Louis: Washington University Press, 1958.

Stephen, Sir Leslie. *Hobbes.* Ann Arbor: University of Michigan Press, 1961.

Strauss, Leo. *The Political Philosophy of Hobbes: Its Basis and Genesis.* Trans. Elsa M. Sinclair. Oxford: Clarendon, 1936. Chicago: University of Chicago Press, 1963.

Strier, Richard. *Resistant Structures: Particularity, Radicalism, and Renaissance Texts.* The New Historicism: Studies in Cultural Poetics 34. Berkeley: University of California Press, 1995.

Suckling, Sir John. *The Works of Sir John Suckling: The Non-Dramatic Works.* Ed. Thomas Clayton. Oxford: Clarendon, 1971.

———. *The Works of Sir John Suckling: The Plays.* Ed. L. A. Beaurline. Oxford: Clarendon, 1971.

Suetonius. Vol. 2 of *Suetonius.* Trans. J. C. Rolfe. 2 vols. 1914. Cambridge, MA: Harvard University Press, 1950.

Tennyson, Alfred, Lord. *The Poetical Works of Tennyson.* Ed. G. Robert Strange. Boston: Houghton Mifflin, 1974.

Thomas, Keith. "The Social Origins of Hobbes's Political Thought." 185–236. Brown.

Thormählen, Marianne. *Rochester: The Poems in Context.* Cambridge: Cambridge University Press, 1993.

Thorpe, Clarence DeWitt. *The Aesthetic Theory of Thomas Hobbes, with Special Reference to His Contribution to the Psychological Approach in English Literary Criticism.* University of Michigan Publications: Language and Literature 18. Ann Arbor: University of Michigan Press, 1940.

Treglown, Jeremy, ed. *The Letters of John Wilmot, Earl of Rochester.* Chicago: University of Chicago Press, 1980.

Trevor-Roper, Hugh. *Catholics, Anglicans and Puritans: Seventeenth Century Essays.* London: Secker and Warburg, 1987. Chicago: University of Chicago Press, 1988.

Tricaud, François. "Hobbes's Conception of the State of Nature from 1640 to 1651: Evolution and Ambiguities." 107–23. Rogers and Ryan.

Trimpi, Wesley. *Ben Jonson's Poems: A Study of the Plain Style.* Stanford: Stanford University Press, 1962.

Trotter, David. *The Poetry of Abraham Cowley.* London: Macmillan, 1979.

Tuck, Richard. *Natural Rights Theories: Their Origin and Development.* 1979. Cambridge: Cambridge University Press, 1998.

———. "Hobbes and Descartes." 11–41. Rogers and Ryan.

———. *Hobbes.* Oxford: Oxford University Press, 1989.

———. "Hobbes's Moral Philosophy." 175–207. Sorell.

Turner, James G. *The Politics of Landscape: Rural Scenery and Society in English Poetry 1630–1660.* Cambridge, MA: Harvard University Press, 1979.

———. "The Properties of Libertinism." 75–87. *Unauthorized Sexual Behavior during the Enlightenment.* Ed. Robert P. Maccubin. *Eighteenth-Century Life* 9 n.s. 3 (1985).

———. *Libertines and Radicals in Early Modern London: Sexuality, Politics, and Literary Culture, 1630–1685.* Cambridge: Cambridge University Press, 2002.

Underdown, David. *A Freeborn People: Politics and the Nation in Seventeenth-Century England.* Oxford: Clarendon, 1996.

Vaughan, Henry. *The Complete Poems.* Ed. Alan Rudrum. Harmondsworth: Penguin, 1976. New Haven: Yale University Press, 1981.

Vieth, David M., ed. *The Complete Poems of John Wilmot, Earl of Rochester.* New Haven: Yale University Press, 1968.

———, ed. *John Wilmot, Earl of Rochester: Critical Essays.* Garland Reference Library of the Humanities 819. New York: Garland, 1988.

Virgil. *The Aeneid.* Trans. Robert Fitzgerald. 1983. New York: Vintage, 1984.

Walker, Keith, ed. *The Poems of John Wilmot, Earl of Rochester.* 1984. Oxford: Blackwell, 1988.

Waller, Edmund. *The Poems of Edmund Waller.* Ed. G. Thorn Drury. 2 vols. 1893. New York: Dutton, 1904.

———. *"Poems 1645," together with Poems from Bodleian MS Don D 55.* Menston: Scolar, 1971.

Wallerstein, Ruth C. "The Development of the Rhetoric and Metre of the Heroic Couplet, Especially in 1625–1645." *PMLA* 50 (1935): 166–209.

———. *Studies in Seventeenth-Century Poetic.* 1950. Madison: University of Wisconsin Press, 1950.

Weber, Kurt. *Lucius Cary, Second Viscount Falkland.* Columbia University Studies in English and Comparative Literature 147. New York: Columbia University Press, 1940.

Wedgwood, C. V. *Seventeenth-Century English Literature.* 2nd ed. Oxford: Oxford University Press, 1970.

Whigham, Frank. *Ambition and Privilege: The Social Tropes of Elizabethan Courtesy Theory.* Berkeley: University of California Press, 1984.

Wikelund, Philip R. " 'Thus I Passe My Time in This Place': An Unpublished Letter of Thomas Hobbes." *ELN* 6.4 (1969): 263–68.

Winn, James Anderson. *John Dryden and His World.* New Haven: Yale University Press, 1987.

Wiseman, Susan J. " 'History Digested': Opera and Colonialism in the 1650s." 189–204. Healy and Sawday.

Wood, Anthony à. *Athenae Oxoniensis*, on Rochester. 170–73. Farley-Hills.

Index

"So Musicall as to all Eares," 22, 48; *The Siege of Rhodes*, 44, 45, 210 n.33; *The Temple of Love*, 22; "To Edward, Earl of Dorset," 24–5, 26, 36, 77; "To Henry Jermin," 23–4; "To the King on New-Yeares Day 1630," 21–3, 38, 135, 209 n.13; "To the Lord Cary of Lepington," 23; "To the Queen," 22; "Whilst by a mixture thus made one," 22
see also under Hobbes
daydreaming, 24, 105–6
definitions, 27–8, 33–4, 40, 41, 93, 101, 123, 155, 169
deliberation, 23, 32–3, 40, 46, 145
democracy, democrats, 10–11, 13, 90, 187
Demosthenes, 23, 87
demystification, 24, 26, 28, 51–3, 70, 71, 72, 73, 74, 75, 76, 77, 130, 151–2, 158, 191–2
Denham, Sir John, 58, 59, 77
"On Mr. Abraham Cowley," 58, 59
Dennis, John, *A Defence of "Sir Fopling Flutter," a Comedy*, 103
Dent, Edward, 44, 45, 210 n.33
Descartes, René, 20, 54–5, 98, 113, 130, 139, 205, 209 n.7
Discours de la Méthode, 130
Devonshire, second earl of (William Cavendish), 176–7, 187
Dewey, John, 43
Dighton, William, 159, 160, 164, 216 n.5
digressions, 28, 37
Donne, John
An Anatomy of the World, 107
Obsequies to the Lord Harrington, 154
The Lamentations of Jeremy, 159
"The Triple Fool," 151
"To Mr. T. W.," 153

see also under Collop, Godolphin, Hobbes, Jonson, Suckling
Doody, Margaret Ann, 211 n.26
Dorset, Edward, Earl of, 24–5, 77
drives (appetites, aversions), 33, 105, 121, 127, 138, 142, 145, 155, 161
Dryden, John, vii, 15, 20, 46–7, 49, 81
adaptation of *The Tempest* (with Davenant) 122, 172
Æneis, 186, 208 n.32
Dedication of the "Æneis," 15, 81
preface to *Fables Ancient and Modern*, 59–60, 204
preface to *Sylvæ*, 203, 204
The Conquest of Granada, 122
The Indian Queen, (with Howard), 122
Dunn, Kevin, 201–2
Durling, Robert, 212 n.5
Dutton, Richard, 200, 202

economic vocabulary, 26, 155, 209 n.18
Edmond, Mary, 209 n.8
egotism, egoism, 95, 137, 172
Elias, Norbert, 140
Eliot, Sir John, 12, 185, 208 n.30
elites, 170, 171, 187–8
eloquence, *see under* rhetoric (uses, abuses)
Engagement, Engagement controversy, 4, 80, 82, 83, 90, 166, 207 n.11, 212 n.24
enjambment, 159
enlightenment, Enlightenment, 26, 53, 56, 122, 130, 166, 191
Epicurus, Epicureanism, 6, 100, 108, 110
epistemology, 2, 111, 112, 113, 202
equality, 123, 125, 129–30, 186
Erasmus, Desiderius, *see under* Hobbes
Etherege, Sir George, 6
The Man of Mode, 103, 213 n.2